Bravo! 365 Yummy Mushroom Recipes

(Bravo! 365 Yummy Mushroom Recipes - Volume 1)

Mavis Olsen

Content

365 Awesome Mushroom Recipes

***

Nutrition Information

- Calories: 470 calories;
- Protein: 18.3
- Total Fat: 25.4
- Sodium: 933
- Total Carbohydrate: 42.2
- Cholesterol: 55

1. Absolutely Fabulous Portobello Mushroom Tortellini

Serving: 4 | Prep: 10mins | Ready in:

Ingredients

- 1 pound cheese tortellini
- 2 large portobello mushrooms
- 1/4 cup white wine
- 1 tablespoon chopped fresh parsley
- 2 cloves garlic, minced
- 8 ounces Alfredo-style pasta sauce
- salt and pepper to taste
- 1/3 cup grated Parmesan cheese

Direction

- Boil lightly salted water in a large pot. Add pasta and cook until al dente, about 8 to 10 minutes then drain.
- In the meantime, prepare mushrooms by washing and slicing the mushroom caps thinly; discard the stems.
- Combine mushrooms, garlic, parsley, and wine in a medium skillet over low heat. Stir it frequently and sauté until mushrooms are cooked thoroughly, approximately 5 minutes.
- Remove the skillet from heat and slowly add the Alfredo sauce. Stir it to blend and season with desired amount of pepper and salt.
- Separate the hot pasta into four equal portions and pour spoonful of sauce over the pasta. Garnish pasta with cheese. Serve immediately.

2. Acorn Squash Tomato Hash

Serving: 4 | Prep: 25mins | Ready in:

Ingredients

- 1 small acorn squash, halved and seeded
- 2 tablespoons olive oil
- 1 small onion, diced
- 2 cloves garlic, minced
- 1 (14.5 ounce) can diced tomatoes, undrained
- 4 ounces fresh mushrooms, chopped
- 3 tablespoons red wine
- 1 tablespoon dried basil
- 1/2 (5 ounce) bag fresh baby spinach, stems removed
- salt and ground black pepper to taste

Direction

- In a glass baking dish, place acorn facing down. With a sharp knife, pierce the skin in several places. Pour 1-inch water.
- Turn the microwave on high and cook the squash for 10 to 15 minutes or until tender. Let the squash cool for about 5 minutes until handled easily. Spoon the flesh of the squash out and transfer to a large bowl. Discard the skin.
- Heat olive oil in a large heavy skillet over medium heat. Add garlic and onion. Cook and stir for 4 to 5 minutes or until onion is translucent. Mix in diced tomatoes along with their juice. Simmer for 3 to 5 minutes until it is

softened. Mix in mushrooms and cook for about 2 minutes or until they softens.

- Gradually stir squash into the skillet. Add red wine and stir to loosen mixture. Add basil and simmer, stirring sometimes, for about 2 minutes. Spread spinach on top. Cover and cook for 3 to 5 minutes until spinach has wilted. Stir spinach into mixture. Season with some pepper and salt.

Nutrition Information

- Calories: 143 calories;
- Total Fat: 7
- Sodium: 218
- Total Carbohydrate: 15.8
- Cholesterol: 0
- Protein: 3.3

3. Alice Chicken

Serving: 4 | Prep: 5mins | Ready in:

Ingredients

- 4 skinless, boneless chicken breast halves
- 5 fluid ounces Worcestershire sauce
- 8 slices bacon
- 2 tablespoons butter
- 8 ounces fresh mushrooms, sliced
- 1 (8 ounce) package Monterey Jack cheese, shredded
- 1 (16 ounce) container honey mustard salad dressing

Direction

- In a glass bowl or dish, put chicken; use a fork to poke a few times, and then add Worcestershire sauce and flip to coat. Put a cover on the bowl or dish and chill for approximately 60 minutes.

- In a big, deep skillet, put bacon. Cook until turning brown evenly over medium-high heat. Strain and put aside.
- In a small skillet, heat butter over medium heat. Add, then sauté mushrooms until tender, about 10 minutes. Put aside.
- Turn on the oven's broil setting to preheat.
- Take the chicken out of the marinade (dispose any leftover liquid), and broil for approximately 5 minutes per side. Once the chicken has nearly done, put 2 slices bacon and then cheese on top of each breast. Keep broiling until the cheese melts, and then take out of the oven. Enjoy with salad dressing and mushrooms for topping.

Nutrition Information

- Calories: 930 calories;
- Protein: 46.8
- Total Fat: 69.5
- Sodium: 1975
- Total Carbohydrate: 31.9
- Cholesterol: 152

4. Allie's Mushroom Pizza

Serving: 8 | Prep: 13mins | Ready in:

Ingredients

- 1 (12 inch) pre-baked pizza crust
- 3 tablespoons olive oil
- 1 teaspoon sesame oil
- 1 cup fresh spinach, rinsed and dried
- 8 ounces shredded mozzarella cheese
- 1 cup sliced fresh mushrooms

Direction

- Begin preheating oven to 175°C (or 350°F). Place pizza crust onto a baking sheet.
- Combine sesame oil and olive oil in a small bowl. Brush all over pre-baked pizza crust,

covering the entire surface. Lay spinach leaves on top of each other and slice lengthwise into 1/2" strips; scatter evenly onto the crust. Top pizza with shredded mozzarella and sliced mushrooms.

- Bake for 8-10 minutes in prepared oven until cheese melts and crisps around the edges.

Nutrition Information

- Calories: 275 calories;
- Sodium: 469
- Total Carbohydrate: 26.2
- Cholesterol: 23
- Protein: 14.3
- Total Fat: 13.2

5. Amazing Italian Lemon Butter Chicken

Serving: 6 | Prep: 10mins | Ready in:

Ingredients

- Lemon Butter Sauce:
- 1/4 cup white wine
- 5 tablespoons fresh lemon juice
- 5 tablespoons heavy cream
- 1 cup butter, chilled
- salt and pepper to taste
- Chicken and Pasta:
- 1/2 pound dry farfalle (bow tie) pasta
- 4 skinless, boneless chicken breast halves - pounded to 1/4 inch thickness
- 1 tablespoon olive oil
- 1 tablespoon butter
- 1/4 cup all-purpose flour
- salt and pepper to taste
- 4 ounces bacon
- 6 ounces mushrooms, sliced
- 6 ounces artichoke hearts, drained and halved
- 2 teaspoons capers, drained
- chopped fresh parsley for garnish

Direction

- To prepare sauce: In a saucepan above medium heat, pour the lemon juice and the wine, then allow to cook at a low boil until mixture has reduced by a third. Stir in the cream and allow it to simmer until thick. Slowly add butter, placing in 1 tablespoon each time, while stirring to fully combine, then season with pepper and salt. Take away from the heat, keep warm.
- Boil a big pot of slightly salted water, then add pasta, cook for 8-10 minutes until they become al dente. Drain and reserve.
- To prepare chicken: In a large skillet, heat 2 tablespoons butter with oil over a medium heat. Stir pepper, salt, and flour together in a bowl. Coat the chicken gently with the flour mixture then place into the hot oil carefully, making sure not to crowd the pan. You can cook all the chicken in batches if you have to. Fry the chicken until both sides are golden brown and thoroughly cooked, then transfer to paper towels. Stir capers, artichokes, mushrooms, and bacon into the oil, then cook until mushrooms are tender.
- Cut chicken breasts into small strips, then return to the skillet, stir in 1/2 of lemon butter sauce.
- Place pasta in a big bowl, then stir in the chicken mixture. Adjust the seasonings to taste. If you want, you can also stir in more lemon butter sauce. Toss the pasta well then garnish with parsley.

Nutrition Information

- Calories: 660 calories;
- Cholesterol: 155
- Protein: 26.8
- Total Fat: 44.9
- Sodium: 660
- Total Carbohydrate: 37.4

6. Andie's Stuffed Mushrooms

Serving: 10 | Prep: 30mins | Ready in:

Ingredients

- 1 pound lean ground beef
- 2 pounds fresh mushrooms-stems removed, chopped and reserved
- 1/4 cup margarine
- 1/2 cup chopped green bell peppers
- 2 teaspoons minced garlic
- 3 teaspoons dried parsley
- 1 teaspoon dried basil leaves, crushed
- 2/3 cup dry bread crumbs
- 1/3 cup soft bread crumbs
- 2 cups shredded sharp Cheddar cheese

Direction

- Set the oven to 400°F (200°C), and start preheating.
- In a large, deep skillet, arrange ground beef; then cook over medium high heat until evenly brown. Drain, crumble and put aside.
- In a medium saucepan, melt the margarine over medium heat; then mix in basil, parsley, garlic, green bell peppers and mushroom stems.
- In a large bowl, mix Cheddar cheese, soft bread crumbs, dry bread crumbs, mushroom stem mixture and ground beef.
- On a large baking pan, arrange the mushroom caps with the hollow sides up. Generously fill each cap with the mixture.
- Bake in the oven for 15-20 minutes, or until the filling turns golden brown.

Nutrition Information

- Calories: 317 calories;
- Cholesterol: 58
- Protein: 18.1
- Total Fat: 22.3
- Sodium: 309
- Total Carbohydrate: 11.7

7. Angela's Alfredo Ham

Serving: 4 | Prep: | Ready in:

Ingredients

- 8 ounces fresh tortellini pasta
- 1 slice ham
- 16 ounces frozen green peas
- 8 ounces fresh mushrooms, sliced
- 1 1/2 (16 ounce) jars Alfredo-style pasta sauce

Direction

- To Cook the Tortellini: Put pasta in a big pot of boiling salted water. Allow to cook until tortellini is al dente, about 8 to 10 minutes. Thoroughly drain then reserve.
- Heat your skillet to medium heat setting. Add mushrooms, peas and ham, and toss them together until heated thoroughly. Add reserved tortellini and sauce, and stir together. Let it simmer for about 3 to 5 minutes then serve.

Nutrition Information

- Calories: 716 calories;
- Total Carbohydrate: 42.9
- Cholesterol: 82
- Protein: 21.5
- Total Fat: 53.6
- Sodium: 1917

8. Artichoke Stuffed Mushrooms

Serving: 12 | Prep: 20mins | Ready in:

Ingredients

- 1 tablespoon olive oil
- 1 onion, chopped
- 24 mushrooms, stems removed and chopped

- salt and ground black pepper to taste
- 1 (12 ounce) jar marinated artichoke hearts, drained and chopped
- 1 (8 ounce) package cream cheese, softened
- 2 tablespoons sour cream
- 1 cup shredded Italian cheese blend
- 2 tablespoons grated Parmesan cheese
- 1/2 teaspoon garlic salt, or to taste

Direction

- Set an oven to 350°F (175°C), and start preheating. Grease a baking sheet with cooking spray.
- In a skillet, heat the olive oil over medium heat; cook the mushroom stems and onions in the hot oil for about 5 minutes until the onion is almost transparent; season with pepper and salt. Place the mixture to a large bowl; add in Parmesan cheese, Italian cheese blend, sour cream, cream cheese and artichoke hearts. Add in salt, garlic salt and pepper for seasoning. Stir until evenly blended. Fill the mixture into mushroom caps. On the baking sheet, arrange the stuffed mushrooms.
- Bake in the oven for about 20 minutes until the filling starts bubbling.

Nutrition Information

- Calories: 156 calories;
- Total Fat: 12.7
- Sodium: 342
- Total Carbohydrate: 6.3
- Cholesterol: 30
- Protein: 6.3

---

9. Asian Style Watercress Soup

Serving: 6 | Prep: 10mins | Ready in:

Ingredients

- 6 cups water

- 1 small onion, diced
- 1/4 cup soy sauce
- 1 1/2 tablespoons soy-based liquid seasoning (such as Maggi®)
- 2 tablespoons chopped garlic
- 1 tablespoon chopped fresh ginger root
- 2 tablespoons cornstarch
- 2 tablespoons boiling water
- 1 1/2 pounds sliced fresh mushrooms
- 1 1/2 tablespoons vegetarian chicken-flavored bouillon
- 1/4 pound tofu, diced
- 1 bunch watercress, coarsely chopped
- 2 eggs, beaten

Direction

- In a saucepan, place in the ginger root, garlic, soy-based liquid seasoning, soy sauce, onion, and water, then set to boil.
- Mix the cornstarch with 2 tablespoons of boiling water. Add to the saucepan. Add in bouillon and mushrooms. Decrease the heat to medium-high and simmer for 7 minutes until the flavors blend. Add in the watercress and tofu. Simmer the soup for another 2 minutes.
- Slowly pour in the eggs, constantly whisking, for 1-2 minutes until cooked.

Nutrition Information

- Calories: 95 calories;
- Protein: 9.6
- Total Fat: 3
- Sodium: 715
- Total Carbohydrate: 10.2
- Cholesterol: 62

---

10. Asparagus And Morel Risotto

Serving: 4 | Prep: 20mins | Ready in:

Ingredients

- 3 1/2 cups chicken stock
- 1/4 cup olive oil, or more to taste, divided
- 1/4 cup unsalted butter, divided
- 1/2 pound asparagus, cut into 1-inch pieces on the bias
- 1/3 pound fresh morel mushrooms, halved
- 1 shallot, minced
- 1 cup Arborio rice
- 1/4 cup dry white wine
- 1 teaspoon fresh thyme leaves
- 1/3 cup freshly grated Parmigiano-Reggiano cheese, or to taste
- 1 tablespoon finely chopped fresh parsley
- salt and ground black pepper to taste
- 1 1/2 tablespoons high-quality balsamic vinegar (optional)

Direction

- In a small saucepan, put the chicken stock on medium heat; simmer.
- In a big saucepan on medium-high heat, heat a tablespoon of the butter and 2 tablespoons of the olive oil till butter begins to bubble. Put in the morel mushrooms and asparagus; sauté for around 4 minutes till soft. Turn out onto a plate including any accumulated juices.
- In the same saucepan, heat a tablespoon of butter and the leftover 2 tablespoons of the olive oil. Put in the shallot; cook and mix for around a minute till softens. Mix in the arborio rice and cook for approximately a minute till it begins to toast. Add wine and cook till it evaporates. Mix in the thyme.
- Add a quarter cup of simmering stock on top of the rice. Cook till stock is absorbed, mixing continuously. Repeat with the rest of the stock for around 12 minutes till rice is soft but firm to the bite. Mix in mushrooms including their juices and asparagus and continue for approximately 3 minutes longer till flavors incorporate.
- Take rice off the heat. Mix in parsley, Parmigiano-Reggiano cheese and the leftover 2 tablespoons of the butter. Add black pepper and salt to season. Jazz up with more olive oil and balsamic vinegar prior to serving.

Nutrition Information

- Calories: 508 calories;
- Sodium: 748
- Total Carbohydrate: 54.3
- Cholesterol: 37
- Protein: 9.5
- Total Fat: 27.6

11. Asparagus And Mushroom Casserole

Serving: 6 | Prep: 20mins | Ready in:

Ingredients

- 1 pound fresh asparagus, trimmed and cut into 1 1/2-inch pieces
- 1 tablespoon olive oil
- 1 (8 ounce) package sliced fresh mushrooms
- 1/4 onion, thinly sliced
- 1 (4 ounce) packet saltine crackers, crushed
- 1 cup shredded sharp Cheddar cheese
- 1/4 teaspoon ground black pepper
- 1 (10.75 ounce) can condensed cream of mushroom soup
- 1/2 cup milk
- 1/2 cup coarsely chopped pecans

Direction

- Preheat oven to 175 degrees C/350 degrees C.
- Grease a 1 1/2-qt. baking dish.
- In a saucepan, put a steamer insert. Fill water to reach below the steamer's bottom. Cover pan. Boil. Add asparagus. Steam for 5-8 minutes, covered, until tender.
- In a big skillet, heat olive oil. Sauté onions and mushrooms for 5-8 minutes until mushrooms release liquid. Mix in asparagus. Toss veggies until hot. Take off heat.
- In a bowl, mix black pepper, sharp cheddar cheese and saltine cracker crumbs. Spread half

- of mixture on the bottom of a prepped baking dish.
- Spoon asparagus mixture on crumb mixture.
- Mix milk and cream of mushroom soup until smooth in a bowl. Pour soup mixture on asparagus mixture.
- Spread remaining crumb-cheese mixture on casserole. Sprinkle pecans on top.
- Bake for about 30 minutes in the preheated oven until casserole bubbles.

Nutrition Information

- Calories: 336 calories;
- Total Fat: 21.2
- Sodium: 700
- Total Carbohydrate: 27
- Cholesterol: 21
- Protein: 12

12. Asparagus And Mushroom Quiche

Serving: 6 | Prep: 25mins | Ready in:

Ingredients

- 5 slices bacon
- 2 tablespoons olive oil
- 1 small onion, cut into 1/2-inch pieces
- 1 cup portobello mushrooms, stem and ribs removed, cut into 1-inch pieces
- 1 cup chopped fresh asparagus
- 1 (8 inch) unbaked pie shell
- 1 egg white, lightly beaten (optional)
- 1 cup shredded sharp Cheddar cheese
- 1/4 cup crumbled feta cheese
- 2 eggs
- 3/4 cup half-and-half cream
- 1/2 teaspoon salt
- Fresh ground pepper

Direction

- Set the oven at 400°F (200°C) and start preheating.
- In a large skillet, cook bacon over medium heat until crispy and evenly brown. Transfer to paper towels to drain then crumble and put aside.
- In a large skillet, heat oil over medium-high heat. Put in onions and cook while stirring until translucent. Lower to medium heat and mix in the portobello mushrooms. Keep on cooking the mushrooms until tender. Put aside.
- In saucepan, bring salted water to boil over high heat. When the water is boiling, cook asparagus for 1-2 minutes, until lightly tender. Drain the water immediately and run under cold water to cool down.
- Beat the egg white then brush onto the pie shell, if using. In the bottom of the pie shell, add bacon, asparagus, the onion and mushroom mixture. Sprinkle feta cheese and Cheddar cheese over the vegetables. Whisk together pepper, salt, cream and eggs in a small bowl until smooth. Transfer the mixture onto the vegetable and the cheese filling.
- Bake without a cover until firm and the top is lightly browned or for about 35-40 minutes. Allow it cool to room temperature before enjoying the meal.

Nutrition Information

- Calories: 368 calories;
- Protein: 15.4
- Total Fat: 28.3
- Sodium: 788
- Total Carbohydrate: 13.5
- Cholesterol: 115

13. Aunty Pasto's Seafood Lasagna

Serving: 8 | Prep: 5mins | Ready in:

Ingredients

- 8 lasagna noodles
- 2 tablespoons butter
- 1 cup chopped onion
- 1 (8 ounce) package cream cheese, softened
- 1 1/2 cups cottage cheese, creamed
- 1 egg, beaten
- 2 teaspoons dried basil
- 1/2 teaspoon salt
- 1/8 teaspoon ground black pepper
- 2 (10.75 ounce) cans condensed cream of mushroom soup
- 1/3 cup milk
- 1/3 cup dry white wine
- 1 (6 ounce) can crabmeat
- 1 pound cooked salad shrimp
- 1/4 cup grated Parmesan cheese
- 1/2 cup shredded sharp Cheddar cheese
- 2 cups fresh sliced mushrooms

Direction

- In a large pot of boiling salted water, cook noodles until done. Rinse; drain noodles. Put aside.
- Over medium heat, in a small saucepan, melt margarine or butter. Add onion; cook while stirring until tender. Add pepper, salt, basil, egg, cottage cheese and cream cheese.
- Mix wine, milk and soup in a medium bowl. Stir in mushrooms, shrimp and crab.
- In the bottom of a well-oiled 9x13 inch pan, place 4 noodles. Top with half cheese mixture and spread; scoop half soup mixture over cheese. Do the same layers again.
- Bake without a cover for 45 minutes at 350°F (175°C). Top with Parmesan cheese and sharp cheese. Brown lasagna under broiler. Take out of the heat; rest 15 minutes; serve.

Nutrition Information

- Calories: 475 calories;
- Total Fat: 25
- Sodium: 1217
- Total Carbohydrate: 28.2
- Cholesterol: 209

- Protein: 33.1

14. Babushka's Slow Cooker Root Vegetable And Chicken Stew

Serving: 10 | Prep: 40mins | Ready in:

Ingredients

- 2 ½ pounds skin-on, bone-in chicken thighs
- 1 yellow onion, coarsely chopped
- 1 red onion, coarsely chopped
- 4 stalks celery with some leaves, coarsely chopped
- 4 mediums red potatoes - peeled, halved, and cubed
- 1 rutabaga - peeled, halved, and cubed
- 2 mediums turnips - peeled, halved, and cubed
- 2 mediums carrots, peeled and sliced
- 1 ½ cups cremini mushrooms, coarsely chopped
- 4 cloves garlic, peeled and crushed
- 2 teaspoons salt
- 1 teaspoon herbes de Provence
- 1 teaspoon onion powder
- 1 teaspoon garlic powder
- freshly ground black pepper
- 1 (32 fluid ounce) container vegetable broth

Direction

- On medium low heat, heat a sauté pan. In batches, cook chicken thighs, 2-3 minutes per side, until skin begins to brown. Do not overcook. Meat should be raw and pink inside. Put chicken in a bowl, keeping juices in the pan.
- In the pan, sauté celery and onion for 5 minutes until edges brown and is translucent. Put in a big bowl.
- Add in garlic, mushrooms, carrots, turnips, rutabaga and potatoes to celery-onion mixture. Sprinkle on pepper, garlic powder, onion

powder, herbes de Provence and salt. Mix and stir veggies until coated.

- In a slow cooker, put 1/2 of veggie mixture. Add 1/2 of chicken. Layer leftover chicken and veggies on top. Put vegetable broth on mixture in the slow cooker.
- Cook for 7 hours on low, stirring gently every several hours if you want.
- Take chicken from stew with tongs. Cool. Separate bones and skin from meat. Shred meat. Put meat back in slow cooker.

Nutrition Information

- Calories: 296 calories;
- Protein: 21.4
- Sodium: 756
- Total Carbohydrate: 26.2
- Cholesterol: 64
- Total Fat: 11.8

15. Baby Bok Choy And Shiitake Stir Fry

Serving: 4 | Prep: 20mins | Ready in:

Ingredients

- 1/2 cup low-sodium chicken or mushroom broth
- 2 tablespoons oyster sauce
- 2 tablespoons rice wine or dry sherry
- 2 teaspoons cornstarch
- 1 1/2 tablespoons peanut or vegetable oil
- 2 medium garlic cloves, minced
- 1 (1 1/2 inch) piece ginger root, peeled and minced
- 1/2 teaspoon kosher salt
- 3 1/2 ounces shiitake mushrooms, stems discarded and caps sliced
- 1 1/4 pounds baby bok choy, chopped

Direction

- In a small bowl, mix in oyster sauce, rice wine, broth, and cornstarch together.
- Using a large skillet or wok over medium-high heat, heat the oil until it starts to shimmer. Cook garlic and ginger and stir-fry with salt for 30 seconds or until fragrant. Stir-fry the shiitake for 1 to 2 minutes or until it softens. Stir-fry the bok choy in for 2 to 3 minutes or until it is crisp and tender.
- Stir the cornstarch mixture again. Create a hole in the vegetables then add in the cornstarch mixture. Once it boils, toss the vegetables to coat. Serve warm.

Nutrition Information

- Calories: 95 calories;
- Total Fat: 5.4
- Sodium: 407
- Total Carbohydrate: 7.2
- Cholesterol: 1
- Protein: 3.3

16. Bacon Stuffed Mushrooms

Serving: 6 | Prep: 20mins | Ready in:

Ingredients

- 4 slices bacon
- 2 (12 ounce) packages fresh white mushrooms
- 3 tablespoons butter, melted
- 6 pitted black olives, finely chopped
- 1/4 cup finely chopped green onion
- 1 teaspoon oil-packed minced garlic
- 1/2 teaspoon salt
- 1/4 teaspoon ground black pepper
- 1 pinch cayenne pepper
- 1 tablespoon all-purpose flour
- 1/4 cup milk
- 4 slices Swiss-flavored American cheese, chopped
- 3 tablespoons grated Parmesan cheese

Direction

- Preheat oven to 375° F (190° C).
- In a large frying pan, add bacon and cook over medium-high heat while sometimes flipping for around 10 minutes, till evenly browned. Move bacon slices to paper towels, keeping the bacon drippings in the pan. Once cooled, crumble bacon.
- Separate stems from the mushrooms and leave the stems aside. On a baking sheet, set mushrooms with hollow sides up; brush the interior with melted butter.
- Slice mushroom stems; cook and whisk the crumbled bacon, green onion, black olives, and chopped stems in the bacon drippings over medium heat for around 5 minutes till the liquid flows out from mushroom stems. Put in cayenne pepper, black pepper, salt, and garlic; stir to coat.
- Slightly tilt the pan; transfer the vegetable-bacon mixture to one side, letting the bacon drippings pool to the other side. Blend flour into the bacon drippings till paste-like and smooth; gradually whisk in milk until the gravy is smooth. Whisk vegetable-bacon mixture into the gravy. Put in Parmesan cheese and American cheese; cook and stir for approximately 5 minutes until cheeses are melted. Mound filling into each mushroom caps.
- In the preheated oven, bake for around 20 minutes till mushrooms become tender and filling turns lightly browned. Take the mushrooms away from baking sheet then let cool on platter for about 2 minutes before use.

Nutrition Information

- Calories: 258 calories;
- Sodium: 770
- Total Carbohydrate: 7.1
- Cholesterol: 48
- Protein: 11.4
- Total Fat: 22.1

17. Bacon And Cheddar Stuffed Mushrooms

Serving: 8 | Prep: 15mins | Ready in:

Ingredients

- 3 slices bacon
- 8 crimini mushrooms
- 1 tablespoon butter
- 1 tablespoon chopped onion
- 3/4 cup shredded Cheddar cheese

Direction

- In a large and deep skillet, cook the bacon over medium-high heat until evenly browned all over. Let it drain and dice; put aside.
- Set the oven to 400°F (200°C) for preheating.
- Remove the mushroom stems and chop them; set the caps aside.
- Melt butter in a large saucepan over medium heat. Stir in chopped stems and onion and cook them slowly, stirring until the onion is tender. Remove from the heat.
- Mix the mushroom stem mixture, a 1/2 cup of Cheddar, and bacon in a medium bowl. Once the mixture is well-combined, scoop it into the mushroom caps.
- Place it inside the preheated oven and bake for 15 minutes or until the cheese has melted completely.
- Remove them from the oven and sprinkle them with the remaining cheese.

Nutrition Information

- Calories: 110 calories;
- Total Carbohydrate: 0.9
- Cholesterol: 22
- Protein: 4.7
- Total Fat: 9.7
- Sodium: 170

18. Bacon, Brussels Sprouts, And Mushroom Linguine

Serving: 6 | Prep: 15mins | Ready in:

Ingredients

- 1 (16 ounce) package linguine
- 2 tablespoons olive oil, or as needed
- 1 pound bacon, cut into bite-size pieces
- 1/2 teaspoon dried rosemary
- 1 1/2 pounds crimini mushrooms, sliced
- salt and ground black pepper to taste
- 1 1/2 pounds Brussels sprouts, trimmed and chopped
- 1/2 cup grated Parmesan cheese

Direction

- Boil a large pot of lightly salted water. Cook linguine for 11 mins at a boil until tender but firm to bite; drain the paste, keeping half cup of pasta water for later use. Take pasta back to the pot and drizzle with olive oil, toss to coat.
- In a large skillet, put bacon; cook while stirring for 10 mins, until bacon starts to crisp. Drain and discard half of bacon fat, leave bacon in skillet and mix in rosemary.
- Mix black pepper, salt, and mushrooms into bacon mixture. Put in Brussels sprouts; cook while stirring for 1-2 mins, until heated through. Pour the reserved pasta water in the bacon mixture, put Parmesan cheese and linguine, mix vegetable with pasta until heated through, about 2 mins. Flavor with pepper and salt.

Nutrition Information

- Calories: 557 calories;
- Sodium: 778
- Total Carbohydrate: 69
- Cholesterol: 33
- Protein: 30.5
- Total Fat: 18.9

19. Baked Brie And Mushroom Sourdough Appetizer

Serving: 8 | Prep: 15mins | Ready in:

Ingredients

- 2 tablespoons butter
- 1 teaspoon minced garlic
- 12 ounces sliced fresh mushrooms
- 1 (8 ounce) wedge Brie cheese, rind removed, cubed
- 1 (1 pound) loaf round sourdough bread
- 2 1/2 tablespoons grated Parmesan cheese

Direction

- Heat the broiler beforehand.
- Melt the butter over low heat in a saucepan. Sauté mushrooms and garlic till soft. Add in the Brie. Cook while stirring until blended well and melted.
- Remove the sourdough bread's top and empty the center. Fill the bread with the brie mixture. Use Parmesan cheese to dredge on top.
- On a baking sheet, place the filled bread; allow to broil in the preheated oven till the top gets browned lightly for 10 minutes. Let cool down slightly; cut into wedges to serve.

Nutrition Information

- Calories: 299 calories;
- Total Fat: 12.3
- Sodium: 589
- Total Carbohydrate: 33.3
- Cholesterol: 37
- Protein: 14.4

20. Baked Potato With Mushrooms

Serving: 1 | Prep: 10mins | Ready in:

Ingredients

- 1 large baking potato
- 1 tablespoon unsalted butter
- 1/4 cup chopped onions
- 1/2 cup chopped mushrooms
- salt to taste
- 2 tablespoons nonfat plain yogurt

Direction

- Preheat the oven to 230 degrees C (450 degrees F).
- Pierce the potato several times using a fork. Add onto the microwave-safe dish, and cook for 10 minutes in the microwave over high heat, till becoming soft yet not mushy. Move the potato into the baking dish, and bake in the preheated oven for 15 minutes.
- Melt the butter on medium heat in the saucepan. Stir in the onion. Cook and stir till becoming soft. Stir in the mushrooms. Use the salt to season. Lower the heat to low, keep covered, and allow it to rest till the mushrooms soften or for 5 minutes. Add the yogurt and mushrooms on top of the potato to serve.

Nutrition Information

- Calories: 427 calories;
- Cholesterol: 31
- Protein: 10.9
- Total Fat: 12.1
- Sodium: 51
- Total Carbohydrate: 71.7

21. Baked Rice And Vegetables In Broth

Serving: 4 | Prep: 15mins | Ready in:

Ingredients

- 3/4 cup uncooked long-grain rice
- 1 tablespoon uncooked wild rice
- 1/4 cup uncooked brown rice
- 1/4 cup sliced fresh mushrooms
- 1/4 chopped fresh broccoli
- 1/4 cup chopped carrots
- 1/4 cup chopped red bell pepper
- 1/4 cup finely chopped onion
- 1 teaspoon salt
- 1 teaspoon dried onion flakes
- 1 teaspoon paprika
- 1/4 teaspoon black pepper
- 2 1/2 cups vegetable broth

Direction

- Set the oven to 425°F (220°C) and start preheating.
- Combine broth, black pepper, paprika, onion flakes, salt, onion, bell pepper, carrots, broccoli, mushrooms, brown rice, wild rice and white rice in a 9 x 13-inch baking dish. Combine well; cover.
- Bake in the prepared oven until cooked through or for half an hour; stir once during baking.

Nutrition Information

- Calories: 210 calories;
- Protein: 5.1
- Total Fat: 1
- Sodium: 877
- Total Carbohydrate: 44.3
- Cholesterol: 0

22. Balsamic Chicken Salad

Serving: 4 | Prep: 20mins | Ready in:

Ingredients

- 1 (16 ounce) bottle light balsamic vinaigrette salad dressing (such as Newman's Own® Lighten Up® Balsamic Vinaigrette Dressing), divided
- 8 chicken tenders
- 1 (6 ounce) package sliced portobello mushroom caps
- 2 hearts of romaine lettuce, chopped
- 2 green onions, sliced diagonally
- 1 pint cherry tomatoes, cut into quarters
- 1 cup shredded mozzarella cheese
- 1/4 cup sliced fresh basil leaves

Direction

- In a bowl, mix 1/3 bottle of balsamic vinaigrette dressing with the chicken tenders. Toss mushroom slices with 1/3 bottle of dressing in another bowl. Set the remaining 1/3 bottle aside. Let mushrooms and chicken tenders to marinate for at least half an hour.
- Preheat the oven's broiler; place the oven rack about 6 inches from the heat source.
- Take the mushrooms and chicken tenders out of the marinade; drain off excess. Broil mushroom and chicken for 5-8 minutes until cooked through and chicken turns brown. Take the mushrooms and chicken out of the heat; slice chicken tenders into bite-sized pieces.
- When serving, distribute chopped romaine lettuce between four plates; place mushrooms and broiled chicken on top of each. Place basil leave slices, mozzarella cheese and cherry tomatoes on top of each plate; serve with the rest of the vinaigrette dressing.

Nutrition Information

- Calories: 240 calories;
- Cholesterol: 81
- Protein: 32.8
- Total Fat: 7.8
- Sodium: 248
- Total Carbohydrate: 10.3

23. Barengate Bay Chicken

Serving: 6 | Prep: 15mins | Ready in:

Ingredients

- 1 (10.75 ounce) can condensed cream of broccoli soup
- 1 (10.75 ounce) can milk
- 6 skinless, boneless chicken breast halves
- 1/4 cup olive oil
- 4 cloves garlic, chopped
- 1 (14.5 ounce) can chicken broth
- 6 fresh button mushrooms
- 2 lemons, quartered and seeded

Direction

- Heat the soup with milk in a small saucepan on low heat; put aside once heated thoroughly. In the meantime, roll the chicken in the bread crumbs and press hard to ensure the chicken is coated thoroughly.
- Set an oven to 175°C (350°F) and start preheating.
- In a 9x13-inch baking dish lightly coated with cooking spray, arrange the coated chicken, sprinkle oil and chopped garlic on top. Mix the chicken broth into the soup mixture and pour the mixture all over the chicken. Scatter with mushrooms and squeeze lemon all over.
- Bake at 175°C (350°F) until the chicken is cooked thoroughly and juices from the chicken run clear, or for 40 minutes.

Nutrition Information

- Calories: 275 calories;
- Cholesterol: 67

- Protein: 26.5
- Total Fat: 14
- Sodium: 376
- Total Carbohydrate: 12.3

24. Barilla® Spicy Sriracha Pasta Bowl

Serving: 8 | Prep: 25mins | Ready in:

Ingredients

- 1 (16 ounce) box Barilla® Spaghetti
- 1/4 cup Sriracha chile sauce
- 1/4 cup honey
- 1 lime, juiced
- 2 tablespoons neutral oil (such as coconut or canola)
- 2 cups thinly sliced mushrooms
- 2 medium carrots, cut into matchstick-size pieces
- 1 cup thinly sliced yellow or green bell pepper
- 1 cup sugar snap peas, halved lengthwise
- 1 (26 ounce) jar Barilla® Spicy Marinara Sauce
- Sesame seeds (optional)
- 3 green onions, thinly sliced

Direction

- In the small-sized bowl, mix lime juice, honey, and Sriracha; put them aside.
- In the big pot, boil to rolling 4-6 qt. of water; put in the salt to taste and the Spaghetti; mix lightly.
- Based on the instruction on package, cook pasta; take out of the heat and drain it well.
- At the same time, in the big skillet, heat oil on medium heat; put in the sugar snap peas, bell pepper, carrots, and mushrooms.
- Cook, mixing often, till becoming soft or for 5 - 7 minutes; put in Spicy Marinara and mix; put in pasta and combine by tossing.
- Serve in bowls and as you want, add a drizzle of the sesame seeds, green onions and a sprinkle of Sriracha-honey mixture on top.

Nutrition Information

- Calories: 345 calories;
- Total Fat: 6
- Sodium: 692
- Total Carbohydrate: 66
- Cholesterol: 0
- Protein: 10.4

25. Barley And Mushrooms With Beans

Serving: 6 | Prep: 15mins | Ready in:

Ingredients

- 1 teaspoon olive oil
- 3 cups sliced fresh mushrooms
- 1 cup chopped onion
- 1/2 cup chopped celery
- 2 cloves garlic, minced
- 1/2 cup uncooked barley
- 3 cups vegetable broth
- 1 (15.5 ounce) can white beans, drained

Direction

- In a medium saucepan, heat oil on medium heat. Sauté garlic, celery, onion and mushrooms until tender.
- Stir vegetable broth and barley in saucepan. Boil, covered, and lower heat. Simmer until barley is tender for 45-50 minutes.
- Mix white beans in barley mixture. Keep cooking until beans are heated for 5 minutes.

Nutrition Information

- Calories: 202 calories;
- Sodium: 245
- Total Carbohydrate: 39
- Cholesterol: 0
- Protein: 9.1

- Total Fat: 2.1

26. Bavarian Chanterelle Mushrooms With Bacon

Serving: 4 | Prep: 10mins | Ready in:

Ingredients

- 1 tablespoon butter
- 2 slices lean bacon, chopped
- 1 small onion, finely chopped
- 1 pound chanterelle mushrooms, cut lengthwise
- salt and freshly ground black pepper to taste
- 2 tablespoons chopped fresh parsley, or to taste

Direction

- Melt the butter on medium heat in a skillet. Cook the onion and bacon for roughly 5 minutes till the bacon turns crispy and the onion softens and translucent.
- Put in the chanterelle mushrooms and let it simmer in skillet for roughly 10 minutes till the liquid is totally boiled off. Drizzle with the parsley and serve right away.

Nutrition Information

- Calories: 101 calories;
- Total Carbohydrate: 8.1
- Cholesterol: 13
- Total Fat: 4.8
- Protein: 4.4
- Sodium: 190

27. Beef Sukiyaki

Serving: 4 | Prep: 30mins | Ready in:

Ingredients

- 1 1/2 cups prepared dashi stock
- 3/4 cup soy sauce
- 3/4 cup mirin
- 1/4 cup white sugar
- 8 ounces shirataki noodles
- 2 tablespoons canola oil
- 1 pound beef top sirloin, thinly sliced
- 1 onion, thinly sliced
- 1 tablespoon canola oil
- 2 stalks celery, thinly sliced
- 2 carrots, thinly sliced
- 5 green onions, cut into 2 inch pieces
- 4 ounces sliced fresh mushrooms (button, shiitake, or enoki)
- 1 (14 ounce) package firm tofu, cut into cubes

Direction

- In a bowl, mix sugar, dashi, mirin, and soy sauce; set aside.
- In boiling water, soak noodles for a minute then drain; rinse under cold water.
- Heat 2 tbsp. canola oil; cook and stir beef for 2-3 mins in hot oil, or until the meat is not pink anymore. Drain the beef then set aside.
- Heat a tablespoon of canola oil in the pan; cook and stir mushrooms, onion, carrot, and celery for 4 mins, or until soft. Mix in tofu, green onions, beef, noodles, and the dashi mixture; simmer. Split the hot sukiyaki between 4 bowls. Serve.

Nutrition Information

- Calories: 576 calories;
- Protein: 34.4
- Total Fat: 25.6
- Sodium: 2941
- Total Carbohydrate: 44.9
- Cholesterol: 61

28. Beef, Mushroom And Guinness® Pie

Serving: 6 | Prep: 25mins | Ready in:

Ingredients

- 3 tablespoons olive oil, divided
- 1 pound cubed beef stew meat
- 2 slices bacon, chopped
- 1 white onion, chopped
- 1 carrot, sliced
- 1/3 pound crimini mushrooms, sliced
- 1 clove garlic, crushed
- 1 teaspoon white sugar
- 1 1/2 tablespoons all-purpose flour
- 1 cup Irish stout beer (such as Guinness®)
- 1 1/4 cups beef stock
- 1/2 teaspoon ground thyme
- 2 bay leaves
- 1/2 teaspoon cornstarch, or as needed
- 1 teaspoon water
- 1 sheet frozen puff pastry, thawed
- 1 egg, beaten

Direction

- In a big pot over medium heat, heat 2 tablespoons olive oil, brown all sides of the beef stew meat for 10 minutes; reserve. Heat the leftover 1 tablespoon olive oil, then cook bacon just till it starts to brown; Mix in the sugar, garlic, mushrooms, carrot and onion. Cook the vegetables for additional of 10 to 15 minutes till browned and soft.
- Mix in the flour till smoothly combined, then slowly add in the beef stock and Irish stout beer. Add in the bay leaves, thyme and the reserved cooked beef. Cover, boil; lower heat to a simmer for an hour and 15 minutes till the meat is tender; mixing from time to time. Uncover, increase heat to medium, and let the stew boil for 15 minutes longer till slightly thickened. Combine water and cornstarch together, then mix into the stew; allow to simmer to incorporate flavors for additional of

30 minutes. Take off heat; Throw bay leaves away.
- Preheat oven to 175°C or 350°F.
- In a 9-inch pie dish, scatter the filling; cut the puff pastry into a 10-inch round, then put over the filling. Using a fork, crimp and pinch pastry edges, securing it to the dish; using a sharp knife, slice 2 steam vents into the pastry. Glaze top of the pie with beaten egg.
- In the preheated oven, bake 30 to 40 minutes till crust is browned.

Nutrition Information

- Calories: 500 calories;
- Total Fat: 31.7
- Sodium: 259
- Total Carbohydrate: 28.6
- Cholesterol: 77
- Protein: 21.8

29. Beef Wrapped Enoki Mushroom

Serving: 10 | Prep: 15mins | Ready in:

Ingredients

- 10 ounces enoki mushrooms, roots removed
- 20 slices thinly sliced deli roast beef
- 1/2 tablespoon butter
- 1 pinch salt and ground black pepper to taste

Direction

- Spread roast beef slices on a work surface. Distribute enoki mushrooms between the middle of every beef slices. Wrap the roast beef around the mushrooms.
- Melt butter over medium-low heat in a skillet. Place beef-wrapped mushrooms into the skillet, sprinkle with pepper and salt to season; cook, about 10 minutes on each side, until browned and thoroughly heated.

Nutrition Information

- Calories: 82 calories;
- Total Fat: 2.4
- Sodium: 595
- Total Carbohydrate: 2.9
- Cholesterol: 29
- Protein: 12.2

30. Beefy Oven Packets

Serving: 5 | Prep: 10mins | Ready in:

Ingredients

- 1 pound ground beef
- 1 (15.25 ounce) can whole kernel corn
- 1 (15 ounce) can green beans
- 2 (4 ounce) jars mushrooms, drained
- 1 (16 ounce) jar processed cheese sauce
- salt and pepper to taste

Direction

- Preheat the oven to 175 degrees C (350 degrees F).
- Chop the square pieces out of the aluminum foil. Shape the beef into small, round flat hamburgers and arrange one (that is seasoned to taste) onto each of the squares. Into each burger, put a bit of mushrooms, beans, corn and one spoonful of cheese sauce. Fold the foil over so that nothing is leaked while baking.
- Bake in preheated oven for 60 minutes.

Nutrition Information

- Calories: 522 calories;
- Total Fat: 32.9
- Sodium: 2191
- Total Carbohydrate: 29.4
- Cholesterol: 122
- Protein: 29

31. Beer Battered Fried Vegetables

Serving: 6 | Prep: | Ready in:

Ingredients

- 2 cups all-purpose flour
- 1 1/2 cups beer
- 2 eggs
- 1 cup milk
- salt and pepper to taste
- 2 cups vegetable oil for frying
- 1 carrot, cut into thick strips
- 1 onion, sliced into rings
- 6 fresh mushrooms, stems removed
- 1 green bell pepper, sliced in rings

Direction

- Combine the beer and 1 1/2 cup flour in a medium bowl using a wooden spoon and allow it to stand at room temperature for a minimum of 3 hours.
- In a small bowl, combine the milk and eggs. Combine the pepper, salt and 1/2 cup flour in another bowl.
- Heat the oil to 190°C (375°F).
- Dip each vegetable in the milk and egg mixture, then dip the vegetable into the seasoning and flour mixture and lastly, dip the vegetable in the flour and beer mixture. Put the vegetables in the oil and let it fry until it turns golden brown.

Nutrition Information

- Calories: 308 calories;
- Total Fat: 10.3
- Sodium: 54
- Total Carbohydrate: 40.4
- Cholesterol: 65
- Protein: 9.1

32. Best Green Beans

Serving: 6 | Prep: | Ready in:

Ingredients

- 1/2 pound sliced bacon, diced
- 4 fresh mushrooms, sliced
- 1 clove garlic, diced
- 2 (15.5 ounce) cans French cut green beans
- 1 1/2 teaspoons soy sauce

Direction

- In a large saucepan, arrange the bacon on medium heat. Cook and occasionally stir until browned. Add in the garlic and mushrooms, turn down the heat to medium-low. To soften the mushrooms, cook for a few minutes. Stir in the soy sauce and green beans; thoroughly heat.

Nutrition Information

- Calories: 96 calories;
- Total Carbohydrate: 5.7
- Cholesterol: 14
- Protein: 6.3
- Total Fat: 5.3
- Sodium: 774

33. Better Slow Cooker Robust Chicken

Serving: 6 | Prep: 5mins | Ready in:

Ingredients

- 1 1/2 pounds skinless, boneless chicken breast halves - cut into 1 inch strips
- 2 tablespoons bacon bits
- 1/4 cup chopped green olives
- 1 (14.5 ounce) can diced tomatoes, drained
- 1 (4.5 ounce) can sliced mushrooms, drained
- 1 (1.25 ounce) envelope dry chicken gravy mix

- 1/2 cup red wine
- 3 tablespoons Dijon mustard
- 1/4 cup balsamic vinegar

Direction

- Mix vinegar, mustard, wine, gravy mix, mushrooms, tomatoes, olives, bacon bits, and chicken in a slow cooker. Combine together.
- Put the lid on the slow cooker and cook for 6-8 hours on Low.

Nutrition Information

- Calories: 198 calories;
- Cholesterol: 62
- Protein: 24.5
- Total Fat: 4.7
- Sodium: 946
- Total Carbohydrate: 10.1

34. Birdman's Marinara Sauce

Serving: 10 | Prep: 15mins | Ready in:

Ingredients

- 1 tablespoon olive oil
- 1 onion, chopped
- 3 cloves garlic, minced
- 2 (15 ounce) cans tomato sauce
- 5 tomatoes, chopped
- 12 mushrooms, sliced
- 1 small bell pepper, chopped
- 2 stalks celery, chopped
- 2 carrots, shredded
- 2 small zucchini, sliced
- 1 (6 ounce) can tomato paste
- 1/4 cup red cooking wine
- 1 tablespoon soy sauce
- 1/2 teaspoon ground black pepper
- 1 teaspoon dried basil
- 1 teaspoon dried oregano
- 1/2 teaspoon dried sage

- 2 bay leaves

Direction

- In a big saucepan, heat olive oil over medium-high heat. Sauté garlic and onion for about 5 minutes until onion becomes translucent. Put in black pepper, soy sauce, cooking wine, tomato paste, zucchini, carrots, celery, bell pepper, mushrooms, tomatoes and tomato sauce. Allow it to simmer for 2 hours.
- Mix bay leaves, sage, oregano and basil into the sauce. Allow it to simmer for 1 to 2 hours until flavors blend. Take the bay leaves out.

Nutrition Information

- Calories: 92 calories;
- Total Fat: 2
- Sodium: 724
- Total Carbohydrate: 17.4
- Cholesterol: 0
- Protein: 4.1

35. Bitkas

Serving: 6 | Prep: 30mins | Ready in:

Ingredients

- 2 pounds round steak, cut into thin strips on the diagonal
- 2 onions, cut into 1/3-inch slices
- 3 teaspoons salt
- ground black pepper to taste
- 2 tablespoons Hungarian sweet paprika
- 4 cups water
- 4 bay leaves
- 4 tablespoons vegetable oil
- 4 dried shiitake mushrooms
- 4 prunes, pitted and chopped
- 1 teaspoon wildflower honey
- 2 cloves garlic, halved

Direction

- Slice beef into pieces approximately 1/3-inch thick. Hammer every piece flat using a meat mallet, till they are one third of their original thickness. Generously scatter paprika, pepper and salt just on 1 side of every piece. On a plate, place 2 or 3 beef pieces, with seasoning side facing up, and top with some slices of onion. Put layers of beef and onion till all the meat is out. With foil or plastic wrap, wrap the plate; put aside at room temperature for an hour, or refrigerate overnight.
- Into a Dutch oven, add the water, and boil. Lower the heat to simmer, and put in bay leaves.
- Preheat an oven to 175 °C or 350 °F.
- In a big heavy skillet, heat oil over medium high heat. Separate onions from bitkas. Set aside 1/2 of onions, and throw away the remainder. Let bitkas fry for 20 seconds on each side, 3 at a time. Into boiling water, put the fried meat. Once all the meat is placed, lower the heat and maintain meat soaked in hot water.
- Coarsely slice reserved onion. In beef drippings, sauté over medium heat. Drain, setting aside drippings, and to the meat, put onions including garlic, honey, prunes and mushrooms. Skim off fat from the drippings, and put into the meat.
- To oven, put the pot. In prepped oven, let it roast for an hour. Switch off the heat, and cool down pot slowly in oven for about 2 hours. Redo the heating cycle thrice. 20 minutes later in the oven, remove the pot, and remove mushrooms; slice to make 1/8-inch-wide stripes, and put back to pot.
- During the period of cooking, remove pot after every 20 minutes and reset bitkas. Check to ensure nothing sticks to the bottom; usually nothing does. Monitor water level. If needed, put in some of boiling water. Normally add approximately half cup of boiling water at the start of every heating cycle. During the final heating cycle, taste sauce for seasoning. Add seasoning to taste.

Nutrition Information

- Calories: 443 calories;
- Total Carbohydrate: 11.4
- Cholesterol: 97
- Protein: 31.8
- Total Fat: 29.9
- Sodium: 1254

36. Blue Cheese Stuffed Mushrooms With Grilled Onions

Serving: 8 | Prep: 30mins | Ready in:

Ingredients

- 1 pound fresh mushrooms, stems removed
- 8 ounces blue cheese
- 3 medium onions, sliced into rings
- 1/4 cup olive oil

Direction

- Preheat an outdoor grill for high heat, then slightly oil grate. Spoon crumbled blue cheese into the mushroom caps.
- On the prepared grill, position mushrooms (cheese side up) and onion slices. Flip onions often until tender. Don't flip mushrooms. Grill till mushrooms become softened and blue cheese has melted. Transfer mushrooms to a serving plate, cover with grilled onions.

Nutrition Information

- Calories: 189 calories;
- Sodium: 400
- Total Carbohydrate: 6.4
- Cholesterol: 21
- Protein: 8.3
- Total Fat: 15.1

37. Bob's Stuffed Mushrooms

Serving: 20 | Prep: 35mins | Ready in:

Ingredients

- 20 mushrooms, stems removed
- 2 (6.5 ounce) cans minced clams, drained
- 1/2 cup melted butter
- 1 small onion, chopped
- 1/2 cup grated Parmesan cheese
- 3/4 cup Italian bread crumbs
- 2 cloves garlic, minced
- 2 tablespoons dried parsley
- 2 tablespoons Italian seasoning
- 1/2 tablespoon ground black pepper
- 1/2 cup shredded mozzarella cheese
- 1 cup melted butter

Direction

- Preheat oven to 350 °F (175 °C). Line a sheet of aluminum foil on a 9x13 inch baking dish, and use nonstick cooking spray to spray lightly. Use a moist paper towel or a soft mushroom brush to cautiously clean the mushrooms, and place, upside down, into the prepared pan.
- In a large mixing bowl, place a half cup of melted butter, clams, Parmesan cheese, onion, garlic, and bread crumbs. Add pepper, Italian seasoning, and parsley to season; mix well. Stuff the clam mixture into the mushroom caps, and mound over the tops. Scatter shredded mozzarella cheese over, and drizzle with the leftover 1 cup of butter.
- In the preheated oven, bake for around 25-30 minutes until the mozzarella cheese has lightly browned and the mushrooms are soften.

Nutrition Information

- Calories: 191 calories;
- Sodium: 206
- Total Carbohydrate: 5.5
- Cholesterol: 53

- Protein: 7.8
- Total Fat: 15.7

38. Bok Choy And Shiitake Stir Fry

Serving: 6 | Prep: 10mins | Ready in:

Ingredients

- 1/2 cup soy sauce
- 1/3 cup mushroom stock
- 1 teaspoon miso paste, or to taste
- 1 teaspoon oyster sauce, or to taste
- 1 1/2 pounds bok choy, chopped
- 10 fresh shiitake mushrooms, sliced

Direction

- Pour mushroom stock and soy sauce in a big skillet on high heat. Mix in the oyster sauce and miso paste until they are dissolved for around 2-3 minutes. Put in the mushrooms and bok choy and let it get to a rolling boil. Bring the heat down to medium, cover it up and allow it to simmer until the veggies get tender for around 15 minutes.

Nutrition Information

- Calories: 39 calories;
- Total Fat: 0.3
- Sodium: 1337
- Total Carbohydrate: 6
- Cholesterol: 0
- Protein: 3.9

39. Bordelaise Sauce With Mushrooms

Serving: 4 | Prep: 25mins | Ready in:

Ingredients

- 1 tablespoon butter
- 2 tablespoons shallot, minced
- 1 teaspoon minced garlic (optional)
- 3 tablespoons butter
- 2 cups sliced fresh mushrooms
- 1 cup beef broth
- 1/3 cup red wine
- 1 tablespoon Worcestershire sauce
- 1 bay leaf
- 1/4 teaspoon chopped fresh thyme, or to taste
- salt and pepper to taste
- 1 tablespoon cornstarch
- 2 tablespoons cold water

Direction

- In a skillet, melt one tablespoon of butter over medium heat. Stir in shallot and garlic. Cook for 3 minutes until shallot has turned translucent and softened. Put in remaining 3 tablespoons of butter, whisk in mushrooms when the butter has melted. Cook while stirring the mushrooms for 5 minutes until they start to soften.
- Add Worcestershire sauce, wine and beef broth; add thyme and bay leaf for seasonings. Bring to a simmer over medium-high heat. While simmering, season with pepper and salt to taste. Lower heat to medium-low, keep cooking, uncovered, for half an hour until the sauce reduces slightly. Dissolve cornstarch in cold water, whisk into simmering sauce until it is thickened. Discard the bay leaf then, serve.

Nutrition Information

- Calories: 146 calories;
- Total Fat: 11.8
- Sodium: 324
- Total Carbohydrate: 5.5
- Cholesterol: 31
- Protein: 2.1

40. Bow Tie Tuna Florentine

Serving: 4 | Prep: 15mins | Ready in:

Ingredients

- 1 (8 ounce) package farfalle (bow tie) pasta
- 1 tablespoon margarine
- 1 1/4 cups milk
- 1 (1.2 ounce) package creamy pesto sauce mix
- 2 cups fresh spinach, rinsed and thinly sliced
- 1/2 cup sliced fresh mushrooms
- 3 (5 ounce) cans tuna, drained
- 3 roma (plum) tomatoes, chopped

Direction

- Boil a big pot of lightly salted water. Put pasta and cook till al dente or for 8 to 10 minutes; let drain.
- Liquefy the margarine in a big saucepan, over medium-high heat. Put in pesto sauce mix and milk; boil, mixing continuously with a wire whisk till well incorporated and boiling. Lower heat, and put mushrooms and spinach. Allow to simmer for 3 to 4 minutes, mixing from time to time.
- Put tomatoes, tuna and cooked pasta, mixing softly to coat. Cook 3 to 5 minutes till heated well.

Nutrition Information

- Calories: 437 calories;
- Total Fat: 7.6
- Sodium: 664
- Total Carbohydrate: 53.4
- Cholesterol: 34
- Protein: 37

41. Braised Beef Cheeks

Serving: 10 | Prep: 20mins | Ready in:

Ingredients

- 2 tablespoons olive oil
- 5 pounds trimmed beef cheeks
- 1 large onion, diced small
- 1 carrot, diced small
- 4 cloves garlic, minced
- 4 cups beef stock
- 1 cup red wine
- 1/3 cup dried porcini mushrooms
- 2 cubes beef bouillon
- 1 teaspoon dried thyme
- 2 bay leaves

Direction

- Set oven to 275°F (135 degrees C) for preheating.
- Over medium-high heat, warm olive oil in a large Dutch oven. Place beef by batch and cook for about 4 minutes each side, until it turns color brown. Put carrot and onion and continue cooking for about 20 minutes, until tender. Add garlic, cook and stir for about 2 minutes, until fragrant.
- Into the Dutch oven, boil the beef stock and wine. Add bouillon cubes, porcini mushrooms, bay leaves, and thyme. On the surface, lay a piece of parchment paper. Tightly cover with a lid.
- In the preheated oven, bake beef for 5 to 6 hours until beef is very tender.
- Move beef to a plate. Throw away bay leaves. Using an immersion blender, blend cooking liquid to make a smooth sauce. Serve sauce along with the beef.

Nutrition Information

- Calories: 685 calories;
- Total Fat: 53.3
- Sodium: 366
- Total Carbohydrate: 6.3
- Cholesterol: 160
- Protein: 39.1

42. Braised Tofu

Serving: 4 | Prep: 10mins | Ready in:

Ingredients

- 1 (14 ounce) package firm tofu
- cooking spray
- 3 teaspoons sesame oil, divided
- 1 (8 ounce) can water chestnuts, drained
- 3 ounces fresh shiitake mushrooms, stems removed
- 1 1/2 cups snow peas, trimmed
- 1/2 teaspoon oyster flavored sauce
- 1 cup water

Direction

- Cut tofu block lengthwise into 3 long slabs. Use paper towels to wrap each slab, and press to remove any excess water.
- In a skillet coated with cooking spray, heat 2 teaspoons sesame oil; add tofu slabs to the skillet when oil is hot. Fry each side for about 5 minutes until nicely browned.
- Take browned tofu out of the skillet, and slice into smaller cubes. Add the rest teaspoon of sesame oil to the skillet and sauté snow peas, mushrooms, and water chestnuts. Combine oyster sauce and water, then pour into the skillet along with the tofu. Cook, covered, for about 10 minutes over low heat.

Nutrition Information

- Calories: 153 calories;
- Sodium: 62
- Total Carbohydrate: 12.7
- Cholesterol: 0
- Protein: 10
- Total Fat: 7.8

43. Braised Venison With Rosemary And Shiitake

Serving: 4 | Prep: 25mins | Ready in:

Ingredients

- 2 tablespoons bacon drippings
- 1 1/2 pounds venison, cut into 2 inch cubes
- 2 cups fresh shiitake mushrooms, stemmed and sliced
- 2 medium onions, chopped
- 4 cloves garlic, minced
- 2 tablespoons cognac or brandy (optional)
- 2 cups dry red wine
- 1 cube beef bouillon
- 1/4 teaspoon black pepper
- 1/2 teaspoon dried thyme leaves
- 1 1/4 teaspoons dried rosemary
- 2 bay leaves
- 1 (8 ounce) package baby carrots (optional)
- 1 tablespoon cornstarch (optional)
- 2 tablespoons water (optional)

Direction

- In a big Dutch oven, melt bacon drippings on medium-high heat. In 2 batches, sear venison till nicely browned; remove. Mix garlic, onions and shiitake in. Cook for 1-2 minutes till soft. Put bouillon cube, wine and cognac in; simmer to remove alcohol flavor and melt bouillon, about 30 seconds.
- Mix bay leaves, rosemary, thyme, pepper and venison in; boil. Lower heat to low. Gently simmer for 2 hours or more till venison is tender; put water as needed.
- Add baby carrots during the last 30 minutes of cooking if using. You can thicken sauce when venison is tender by melting cornstarch in 2 tbsp. water and mixing into sauce.

Nutrition Information

- Calories: 475 calories;
- Sodium: 382
- Total Carbohydrate: 20.4

- Cholesterol: 151
- Protein: 42.2
- Total Fat: 11.3

44. Brazilian Stroganoff

Serving: 10 | Prep: 15mins | Ready in:

Ingredients

- 1 pound stew beef, tenderized and diced
- 1/2 teaspoon vinegar
- salt to taste
- 1 teaspoon oil, or as needed
- 1 onion, diced
- 1 (15 ounce) can corn, drained
- 1 (15 ounce) can sweet peas, drained
- 1 (4.5 ounce) can mushrooms, drained and diced
- 1 (6 ounce) can tomato sauce
- 1/2 quart heavy whipping cream

Direction

- In a bowl, place in beef and cover with salt and vinegar.
- On medium-high heat, heat oil in a big skillet and stir the onion in. Cook until it is soft, about 3-5 minutes. Mix the meat in with the onions, cooking and stirring for 5 minutes until the meat starts to brown and the onions become soft. Add mushrooms, peas and corn in the skillet and stir for 10 minutes until the flavors merge. Stir the cream and tomato sauce in then cook for another 3 minutes. It is ready when the meat is salmon pink. Sprinkle with salt to taste.

Nutrition Information

- Calories: 327 calories;
- Sodium: 387
- Total Carbohydrate: 16.7
- Cholesterol: 90

- Protein: 11.6
- Total Fat: 24.7

45. Brie Soup

Serving: 6 | Prep: 10mins | Ready in:

Ingredients

- 6 cups chicken stock
- 1/4 cup butter
- 8 tablespoons all-purpose flour
- 12 ounces Brie cheese
- 3/8 cup white wine
- 2 ounces julienned carrots
- 1/4 cup chopped celery
- 2 ounces fresh mushrooms, sliced
- 1/4 cup heavy whipping cream
- salt and pepper to taste

Direction

- Over low heat in a saucepan, melt butter. Put in flour and combine well, cooking until just beginning to become golden.
- Pour in stock and vigorously whip, cook to a boil and lower to simmer. Skim the flour and butter and any impurities that rise to the surface and keep simmering until the veloute is cooked to 2/3 of its initial quantity and the sauce becomes the heavy cream consistency.
- Strain through a fine sieve.
- Over low heat, put veloute back to sauce pan and add brie cheese, slowly cook, occasionally stir, until the cheese is melted. Add veggies and wine and lightly simmer until the veggies turn al dente. Over low heat, heat heavy cream and pour into soup. Add salt and pepper to soup to taste. Garnish with scallion or fresh chives.

Nutrition Information

- Calories: 349 calories;

- Total Fat: 27.2
- Sodium: 427
- Total Carbohydrate: 10.2
- Cholesterol: 91
- Protein: 13.5

46. Buckwheat Cereal With Mushrooms And Onions

Serving: 4 | Prep: 15mins | Ready in:

Ingredients

- 1 cup buckwheat groats
- 1 tablespoon olive oil, or to taste
- 1 onion, diced
- 1 carrot, diced
- 1/2 pound mushrooms, diced
- 1 tablespoon butter, or to taste
- 2 cups water
- salt and ground black pepper to taste

Direction

- In a colander, use cold water to rinse buckwheat; strain.
- Put a skillet on medium heat; stir and cook buckwheat for 5-10 minutes until aromatic and toasted. Remove to a bowl.
- In the skillet, heat olive oil over medium heat; stir and cook carrot and onion for 5-10 minutes until the onion is golden. Add mushrooms, then stir and cook for another 5 minutes.
- In a pot, heat butter over medium heat, then add buckwheat and toss to blend. Add pepper, salt, water, and the onion mixture; boil it. Lower the heat, put a cover on and simmer for 20 minutes until the liquid has incorporated.

Nutrition Information

- Calories: 243 calories;
- Sodium: 79

- Total Carbohydrate: 39
- Cholesterol: 8
- Protein: 8.2
- Total Fat: 8

47. Burgundy Mushrooms

Serving: 4 | Prep: 10mins | Ready in:

Ingredients

- 1/2 cup diced onion
- 1 (10.5 ounce) can beef broth
- 2 (8 ounce) cans whole mushrooms, drained, liquid reserved from one can
- 1/3 cup Burgundy wine

Direction

- Simmer the onion in beef broth in a small saucepan for 15 minutes. Put in wine, reserved liquid and mushrooms, then simmer for another 15 minutes, or until the liquid is reduced by half. Serve warm.

Nutrition Information

- Calories: 59 calories;
- Protein: 3.2
- Total Fat: 0.5
- Sodium: 721
- Total Carbohydrate: 8.2
- Cholesterol: 0

48. Busted Up Veggie Omelet

Serving: 2 | Prep: 10mins | Ready in:

Ingredients

- 2 tablespoons extra-virgin olive oil
- 2 egg whites

- 1 egg
- 2 tablespoons milk
- 1/2 tomato, coarsely chopped
- 1/3 cup coarsely chopped red onion
- 1/3 cup sliced mushrooms
- 1/3 cup coarsely chopped spinach
- 1/4 cup shredded mozzarella cheese
- 2 tablespoons grated Parmesan cheese
- salt and ground black pepper to taste

Direction

- In a medium-sized skillet, heat oil over medium heat.
- In a small bowl, whisk together milk, egg and egg whites. In another bowl, toss together spinach, mushrooms, onion and tomato.
- In the hot skillet, pour and cook the egg mixture about 1 minute, until firm on the bottom. Use a spatula to flip the omelette; don't worry as it would be busted up. Add the tomato mixture immediately and top with Parmesan and mozzarella cheeses. Wait about 2 minutes for cheeses to melt slightly.
- Use the spatula to push omelette onto a plate. Add salt and pepper to season.

Nutrition Information

- Calories: 260 calories;
- Total Fat: 20.1
- Sodium: 348
- Total Carbohydrate: 6.4
- Cholesterol: 108
- Protein: 13.9

49. Buttery Herb Wine Sauce

Serving: 8 | Prep: 15mins | Ready in:

Ingredients

- 1/4 cup butter
- 1 (4 ounce) jar mushrooms, drained

- 2 tablespoons all-purpose flour
- 1 teaspoon salt
- 1/2 cup white wine
- 2 teaspoons Italian seasoning
- 1 cup chicken broth
- 1 egg
- 1/2 cup heavy cream

Direction

- In a skillet over medium heat, melt butter. Put in mushrooms and cook until browned. Add salt, Italian seasoning and flour; stir well until smooth. Whisk in chicken broth and wine gradually until no lumps form; bring to a simmer. Combine cream and eggs; mix into the sauce. Heat through but do not boil until the sauce is thickened.

Nutrition Information

- Calories: 136 calories;
- Cholesterol: 59
- Protein: 1.7
- Total Fat: 12
- Sodium: 407
- Total Carbohydrate: 3.3

50. Byrdhouse Spinach Soup

Serving: 6 | Prep: 20mins | Ready in:

Ingredients

- 1/4 cup butter
- 1/4 cup flour
- 1 (8 ounce) package sliced mushrooms
- 1/2 cup dry sherry
- 1 (14.5 ounce) can chicken broth
- 1 quart milk
- 2 bunches fresh spinach, cleaned and chopped
- 4 green onions, chopped
- 1/2 teaspoon ground nutmeg
- salt and pepper to taste

- 8 ounces cooked small shrimp

Direction

- In a large saucepan, melt butter over medium heat. Mix in flour, and cook for about 5 minutes until the mixture turns dark yellow. Mix in mushrooms, cook for 2 minutes. Stir in milk, chicken broth, and sherry, then add pepper, salt, nutmeg, green onion, and spinach, bring to a boil over high heat, stirring constantly; turn heat to medium-low, and simmer for 15 to 20 minutes until the spinach is softened. Top with shrimp, and serve.

Nutrition Information

- Calories: 267 calories;
- Total Fat: 12.2
- Sodium: 708
- Total Carbohydrate: 21.2
- Cholesterol: 108
- Protein: 18.7

51. Cajun Crab Stuffed Mushrooms

Serving: 4 | Prep: 20mins | Ready in:

Ingredients

- 1 (8 ounce) package cream cheese, softened
- 1/2 cup shredded Colby-Monterey Jack cheese
- 1 teaspoon seafood seasoning (such as Old Bay®)
- 1/2 teaspoon Cajun seasoning
- 1/4 teaspoon cayenne hot pepper sauce, or to taste (optional)
- 1/4 teaspoon garlic powder
- 1 (8 ounce) package imitation crabmeat, flaked
- 1/4 cup Italian seasoned bread crumbs
- 1 (8 ounce) package crimini mushrooms, stems removed

Direction

- Preheat an oven to 175°C (350°F). Oil a 9x5-inch baking dish.
- In a mixing bowl, mix garlic powder with hot pepper sauce, Cajun seasoning, seafood seasoning, Colby-Monterey Jack cheese and cream cheese until smooth. Toss in the bread crumbs and crabmeat until uniformly mixed. Pour the cheese blend into the mushroom caps; put them in the prepared baking dish, filling-side up.
- Bake for 7 minutes in the preheated oven; set the oven to broil then broil for about 3 minutes until the tops are crisp and brown.

Nutrition Information

- Calories: 364 calories;
- Total Carbohydrate: 17.9
- Cholesterol: 89
- Protein: 15.9
- Total Fat: 25.7
- Sodium: 1124

52. Cajun Scallop Chowder

Serving: 4 | Prep: 10mins | Ready in:

Ingredients

- 1 (16 ounce) package mixed frozen vegetables (broccoli, corn, red pepper)
- 2 tablespoons butter
- 3/4 cup chopped onion
- 1 clove garlic, minced
- 1 (4 ounce) package sliced fresh mushrooms
- 1 tablespoon Cajun seasoning
- 2 tablespoons all-purpose flour
- 1 1/2 cups milk
- 1 pound scallops - rinsed, drained, and cut in half
- 1 teaspoon salt
- 1/8 teaspoon ground black pepper

Direction

- In a saucepan, cook the mixed vegetables with enough water to cover. Bring it to a boil for about 5 minutes or once the vegetables are tender. Then drain and set aside.
- In a saucepan, melt the butter on medium-low heat. Then stir in the garlic, onion, mushrooms, and Cajun seasoning for about 5 minutes or once the onion is tender but not yet browned. Mix in the flour. Pour in the milk and stir until it is thick and starting to bubble. Add in the scallops, pepper, and salt. Cook for about 5-7 minutes or once the scallops are opaque. Stir in the vegetables into the mixture and cook for 2-3 minutes or until the vegetables are reheated. Serve at once.

Nutrition Information

- Calories: 355 calories;
- Sodium: 1398
- Total Carbohydrate: 32.7
- Cholesterol: 91
- Protein: 37.1
- Total Fat: 9.5

53. California Grilled Pizza

Serving: 6 | Prep: 15mins | Ready in:

Ingredients

- 2 sheets (12x12 inches each) Reynolds Wrap® Aluminum Foil
- 2 (8 inch) pre-baked pizza crusts
- 2 tablespoons olive oil
- 1 teaspoon chopped garlic
- 1/2 medium red onion, sliced thin
- 1 sliced vine ripe tomato
- 1/4 cup marinated artichoke hearts, sliced thin
- 4 baby portabella mushrooms, sliced thin
- 2 tablespoons chopped fresh basil
- 1/2 cup shredded mozzarella cheese

Direction

- Start preheating the grill to medium-high. Put each pizza crust on a sheet of Reynolds Wrap(R) Aluminum Foil; put aside.
- In a small skillet, heat olive oil over medium heat. Put in onion and garlic. Cook until the onion is softened, stirring frequently.
- Brush olive oil mixture over the pizza crust. Place basil, mushrooms, artichoke hearts, tomatoes and onion on the crust. Top with cheese.
- Grill the pizza for 5-7 minutes on the foil sheets in the covered grill, until the cheese is melted.

Nutrition Information

- Calories: 224 calories;
- Total Carbohydrate: 27
- Cholesterol: 11
- Protein: 10
- Total Fat: 9.2
- Sodium: 361

54. Cameroonian Fried Spinach

Serving: 3 | Prep: 10mins | Ready in:

Ingredients

- 1 (10 ounce) package baby spinach, rinsed
- 1 cup fresh shiitake mushrooms, stemmed and quartered
- 1 medium onion, coarsely chopped
- 1 tablespoon olive oil
- garlic powder to taste

Direction

- In a wok or big frying pan, heat olive oil on moderately high heat. Put in onion and mushrooms, then sauté until they are about halfway done. Dump in the spinach and sprinkle generously with garlic powder. Fry about 5-7 minutes, until spinach is wilted.

Nutrition Information

- Calories: 95 calories;
- Protein: 4.2
- Total Fat: 4.9
- Sodium: 86
- Total Carbohydrate: 9.6
- Cholesterol: 0

55. Cauliflower "Risotto" With Porcini Mushrooms And Peas

Serving: 4 | Prep: 20mins | Ready in:

Ingredients

- 1 1/4 cups dried porcini mushrooms
- 3 cups low-sodium chicken broth, or more if needed
- 1 large head cauliflower, chopped
- 3 tablespoons unsalted butter
- 1 shallot, minced
- 2 teaspoons sea salt
- 1 teaspoon freshly ground black pepper
- 1 1/2 cups frozen petite peas, thawed
- 1 tablespoon balsamic vinegar
- 1 teaspoon chopped fresh thyme

Direction

- Add 2 cups of the boiling water to a large bowl. Put in the dried mushrooms; allow to stand for 20 minutes until rehydrated. Use a slotted spoon to take the mushrooms out, then pat them dry; chop the mushrooms into smaller pieces. Save the soaking liquid.
- Add the chicken broth to a saucepan over medium-low heat. Put on a cover and keep it warm.
- Put cauliflower into a food processor with a shredding disc and process into rice-sized grains.

- In a large pot, melt the butter over medium heat. Put in shallot; then cook for 2 minutes until soft. Put pepper, salt, and cauliflower rice. Cook and stir from time to time for 5 minutes until the flavors are blended.
- Mix a cup of the warm chicken broth into the pot; simmer for 5 minutes until absorbed. Pour in the remaining broth, 1 cup at a time, simmering for 10 minutes until the cauliflower rice becomes tender and the broth is absorbed.
- Stir thyme, balsamic vinegar, peas and the chopped mushrooms into the pot. Stir and cook for 5 minutes until peas and mushrooms are heated through.

Nutrition Information

- Calories: 263 calories;
- Total Fat: 10.3
- Sodium: 1043
- Total Carbohydrate: 29.5
- Cholesterol: 26
- Protein: 16.3

56. Cheese Stuffed Mushroom Appetizer

Serving: 6 | Prep: 30mins | Ready in:

Ingredients

- 6 tablespoons butter
- 2 pounds medium fresh mushrooms, stems removed
- 1 (8 ounce) package Neufchatel cheese
- 1 (4 ounce) package goat cheese crumbles
- 2 tablespoons finely chopped onion
- 1/2 cup mushroom stems, chopped
- 1/4 cup butter
- 1 tablespoon finely chopped garlic

Direction

- Start heating two large skillets on medium-high heat; in each skillet, let 3 tablespoons of butter melt and evenly fill each with the mushroom caps. Stir and cook the mushroom caps for around 5 minutes until the edges slightly become soft. To drain and cool the mushrooms, arrange them in a colander.
- Combine goat cheese and cream cheese together until mixed thoroughly. Stir in mushroom stems and the onions. Fill each mushroom cap generously with all the fillings and arrange in a baking pan with filling side up.
- Set the oven broiler and start preheating on high heat.
- In a small saucepan, let the remaining 1/4 cup of butter melt with the garlic on medium heat; when the butter has melted properly, cook the garlic for a minute. Use the garlic butter to lightly sprinkle on the filled mushroom caps.
- Put the pan of mushrooms in the prepared oven to broil for around 5 minutes until they turn golden brown.

Nutrition Information

- Calories: 373 calories;
- Total Fat: 34.1
- Sodium: 391
- Total Carbohydrate: 7.5
- Cholesterol: 94
- Protein: 13

57. Cheese Stuffed Pork Tenderloin

Serving: 3 | Prep: 20mins | Ready in:

Ingredients

- 2 green onions, chopped
- 2 slices cooked bacon, crumbled
- 3 tablespoons shredded Cheddar cheese
- 2 tablespoons cream cheese, softened
- 2 tablespoons frozen chopped spinach

- 2 tablespoons finely chopped white mushrooms
- 1/4 teaspoon chopped garlic
- 1 pinch dried parsley
- salt and ground black pepper to taste
- 1 pork tenderloin, butterflied and pounded flat
- 1 cup dry bread crumbs

Direction

- Start preheating the oven at 350°F (175°C). Oil a baking sheet.
- Mix pepper, salt, parsley, garlic, mushrooms, spinach, cream cheese, Cheddar cheese, bacon, and green onions in a bowl. Pour onto a side of the pounded tenderloin. Roll the tenderloin around the filling following a jelly-roll fashion. Coat the rolled tenderloin with bread crumbs; arrange on the oiled baking sheet.
- Bake in the prepared oven for about 1 1/2 hours until the center of the pork is no longer pink. An instant-read thermometer should show at least 145°F (63°C) when inserted into the center.

Nutrition Information

- Calories: 370 calories;
- Protein: 33.1
- Total Fat: 13.3
- Sodium: 495
- Total Carbohydrate: 27.7
- Cholesterol: 89

58. Cheesy Mashed Potato Stuffed Mushrooms

Serving: 12 | Prep: | Ready in:

Ingredients

- 1 (14.1 ounce) package Idahoan® Buttery Golden Selects Mashed Potatoes
- 1 1/2 cups shredded white Cheddar cheese

- 1/2 cup chives, chopped
- 1 cup chopped, cooked bacon or prepared bacon bits
- 6 tablespoons olive oil
- 4 tablespoons minced garlic
- 24 large mushrooms, or more depending on size

Direction

- Preheat oven to 350 °F.
- Prepare mashed potatoes following the instruction of the package.
- Add bacon, chives, and shredded cheese (reserve enough to top mushrooms).
- Eliminate stems from clean mushrooms and stuff potato mixture into caps.
- On the bottom of baking dish or walled cookie sheet, spread minced garlic and olive oil. Place mushrooms on top.
- Sprinkle top of mushrooms with shredded cheddar.
- Bake for around 20-25 minutes.

Nutrition Information

59. Cheesy Spinach Chicken Rolls

Serving: 6 | Prep: 30mins | Ready in:

Ingredients

- 3 skinless, boneless chicken breasts, halved lengthwise
- salt and ground black pepper to taste
- 1/4 cup olive oil, divided
- 6 mushrooms, chopped
- 2 cloves garlic, minced
- 1 (8 ounce) package cream cheese
- 1/2 (10 ounce) package frozen chopped spinach, thawed
- 2 tablespoons chopped green onions
- 1/2 teaspoon red pepper flakes

- 12 toothpicks

Direction

- On a hard, smooth surface, put chicken breasts between 2 heavy plastic sheets; using the smooth side of a meat mallet, firmly pound on the chicken breasts until the thickness is 1/4-inch. Use pepper and salt to season.
- In a frying pan, heat 1 tablespoon olive oil over medium heat. Add garlic and mushrooms; stir and cook for 5 minutes, or until tender.
- Turn the oven to 400°F (200°C) to preheat.
- In a bowl, mix together red pepper flakes, green onions, spinach, cream cheese, and the garlic-mushroom mixture.
- In the center of each chicken breast, scoop 1 tablespoon of the cream cheese mixture. Roll up the chicken breasts around the filling mixture and hold with toothpicks.
- In an ovenproof frying pan, heat the leftover 3 tablespoons over medium heat. In the frying pan, arrange one layer of the chicken rolls; cook for 5 minutes per side until turning golden.
- Remove the frying pan to the preheated oven; bake for 10-15 minutes longer until the middle of the chicken is not pink anymore.

Nutrition Information

- Calories: 289 calories;
- Sodium: 185
- Total Carbohydrate: 3.2
- Cholesterol: 75
- Protein: 16.6
- Total Fat: 23.7

60. Cheesy Stuffed Mushrooms

Serving: 20 | Prep: 10mins | Ready in:

Ingredients

- 20 crimini mushrooms, stems removed
- 3 tablespoons steak sauce (such as A.1.™)
- 1 (8 ounce) wedge Brie cheese

Direction

- Heat the oven's broiler beforehand and place the oven rack at approximately 6 inches away from the heat source. Use aluminum foil to line a baking sheet.
- Broil the mushrooms, stem-side-down, on the baking sheet for 5 minutes till tender. Remove from the oven, then flip the mushroom caps over. In every cap, lay a dab of the steak sauce, then top with a piece of brie. Put it back in the oven and allow to broil for approximately 5 more minutes till golden brown and the cheese gets bubbly.

Nutrition Information

- Calories: 45 calories;
- Protein: 3.2
- Total Fat: 3.1
- Sodium: 112
- Total Carbohydrate: 1
- Cholesterol: 11

61. Chef John's Chicken And Mushrooms

Serving: 2 | Prep: 10mins | Ready in:

Ingredients

- 2 chicken breast halves, boneless, skin-on
- salt and ground black pepper to taste
- 2 tablespoons olive oil
- 8 ounces fresh mushrooms, sliced 1/4 inch thick
- 1 pinch salt
- 1/2 cup water
- 1 tablespoon butter
- salt and ground black pepper to taste

Direction

- Preheat the oven to 400°F (200°C).
- Put ground black pepper and salt all over the chicken to season.
- Place an ovenproof skillet over medium-high heat and put in olive oil to heat. Cook the chicken, skin-side down, in hot oil for about 5 minutes until brown in color.
- Flip the chicken over and add in the mushrooms with a pinch of salt into the skillet. Increase the heat to high setting and cook the mushrooms for about 5 minutes until the mushrooms reduce in size a little bit. Stir the mushrooms occasionally.
- Place the skillet into the preheated oven and cook for 15-20 minutes until the chicken is no longer pink inside and the juices are clear. Check the temperature of the chicken using an instant-read thermometer inserted in the middle of the chicken, it should be at 165°F (74°C). Take the chicken breasts out of the oven and onto a plate, use a foil to loosely cover the chicken breasts then set aside.
- Put the skillet on a stovetop set on medium-high heat. Cook and stir the mushrooms for about 5 minutes until brown bits are beginning to build up on the bottom of the pan. Put in water and let it boil, scraping off the browned bits on the bottom as it boils. Cook the mushrooms for about 2 minutes until the water is reduced by half. Remove the skillet from heat.
- If there's any extra juices from the chicken, add it in the skillet. Put in the butter into the mushroom mixture and continuously stir until the butter has fully melted and has completely blended with the mixture.
- Put pepper and salt to taste. Top the chicken with mushroom sauce and serve.

Nutrition Information

- Calories: 398 calories;
- Sodium: 355
- Total Carbohydrate: 3.7
- Cholesterol: 91

- Protein: 28.1
- Total Fat: 30.6

62. Chef John's Mushroom Gravy

Serving: 6 | Prep: 10mins | Ready in:

Ingredients

- 1/4 cup butter
- 1 (16 ounce) package sliced mushrooms
- salt to taste
- 1/4 cup all-purpose flour, or as needed
- 1 quart beef stock
- 1 pinch ground black pepper to taste
- fresh thyme leaves, to taste (optional)

Direction

- In a saucepan, heat butter over medium heat till it foams. Mix in mushrooms. Add salt to taste. Allow to simmer for 20 minutes till liquid evaporates.
- Mix in the flour, cooking and mixing for approximately 5 minutes. Put in approximately 1 cup of beef stock, mixing briskly till blended, then add in the leftover stock and mix well. Spice with thyme and black pepper. Lower heat to medium-low, and allow to simmer for half an hour till thickened, mixing frequently.

Nutrition Information

- Calories: 133 calories;
- Sodium: 63
- Total Carbohydrate: 8.9
- Cholesterol: 20
- Protein: 5.7
- Total Fat: 8.7

63. Chicago Style Pan Pizza

Serving: 6 | Prep: 30mins | Ready in:

Ingredients

- 1 (1 pound) loaf frozen bread dough, thawed
- 1 pound bulk Italian sausage
- 2 cups shredded mozzarella cheese
- 8 ounces sliced fresh mushrooms
- 1 small onion, chopped
- 2 teaspoons olive oil
- 1 (28 ounce) can diced tomatoes, drained
- 3/4 teaspoon dried oregano
- 1/2 teaspoon salt
- 1/4 teaspoon fennel seed
- 1/4 teaspoon garlic powder
- 1/2 cup freshly grated Parmesan cheese

Direction

- Heat the oven to 350°F (175°C). Press the dough into up the sides and bottom of a 9x13-inch greased baking dish. Place sausage in a large skillet over medium-high heat and crumble. Stir and cook until brown evenly. Use a slotted spoon to take the sausage, and scatter over the dough crust. Scatter mozzarella cheese evenly over the sausage.
- Add onion and mushrooms to the skillet; stir and cook until the onion soften. Mix in the garlic powder, fennel seeds, salt, oregano, and tomatoes. Scoop over the mozzarella cheese. Scatter Parmesan cheese on top.
- Place in the preheated oven and bake for 25-35 minutes or until the crust turn golden brown.

Nutrition Information

- Calories: 578 calories;
- Total Fat: 27.4
- Sodium: 1816
- Total Carbohydrate: 46.8
- Cholesterol: 61
- Protein: 32.3

64. Chicken And Artichoke Penne With A White Sauce

Serving: 4 | Prep: | Ready in:

Ingredients

- 2 skinless, boneless chicken breast halves - cut into 1 inch cubes
- 1 (8 ounce) can artichoke hearts in water, drained
- 8 fresh mushrooms, sliced
- 3/4 (6 ounce) can black olives, drained and chopped
- 1 pinch paprika
- 1 tablespoon olive oil
- 10 ounces penne pasta
- 2 cups homemade bechamel sauce

Direction

- In a large pot, cook pasta with boiling water. Drain.
- In a pan, heat olive oil over medium heat. Sauté chicken pieces till light-to-golden brown.
- In a pan, put in mushrooms, olives and artichoke hearts; heat in about 1-1/2 seconds. Reduce the heat to low, put in cooked pasta, then heat until warm.
- Pour in the pan with warm bechamel sauce, then toss the ingredients 3 - 4 times. Use fresh Parmesan cheese and freshly grated black pepper to taste, serve. If desired, sprinkle a dash of paprika on top for color.

Nutrition Information

- Calories: 598 calories;
- Total Fat: 22.7
- Sodium: 847
- Total Carbohydrate: 70.5
- Cholesterol: 49
- Protein: 30.6

65. Chicken Breasts Stuffed With Perfection

Serving: 6 | Prep: 1hours | Ready in:

Ingredients

- 6 skinless, boneless chicken breast halves - pounded thin
- 1 (8 ounce) bottle Italian-style salad dressing
- 8 slices of stale wheat bread, torn
- 3/4 cup grated Parmesan cheese
- 1 teaspoon chopped fresh thyme
- 1/8 teaspoon pepper
- 1 1/2 cups feta cheese, crumbled
- 1/2 cup sour cream
- 1 tablespoon vegetable oil
- 3 cloves garlic, minced
- 4 cups chopped fresh spinach
- 1 bunch green onions, chopped
- 1 cup mushrooms, sliced
- 1 (8 ounce) jar oil-packed sun-dried tomatoes, chopped

Direction

- Position chicken breasts into a big resealable plastic bag. Pour in Italian dressing, tightly seal, and let refrigerate for at least 1 hour.
- In a food processor, place the pepper, thyme, Parmesan, and stale bread. Pulse till the bread is processed into crumbs. Leave aside.
- In a big bowl, stir the sour cream and feta together. Leave aside.
- In a large skillet, heat the oil over medium heat. Whisk in the garlic. Then add in the spinach, and cook till it wilts. Mix in green onions, cook for 2 minutes. Transfer spinach into a plate, and reserve leftover liquid in the pan. Mix in mushrooms, then sauté until soft. Transfer mushrooms into a plate along with spinach. Let it cool briefly, then blend mushrooms and spinach with sour cream mixture and feta.

- Whisk into the mixture the sun-dried tomatoes, then pour onto a big cookie sheet. Set in the freezer for around 30 minutes.
- Preheat the oven to 400 °F (200 °C).
- On a cookie sheet, position the chicken breasts then set the middle of each breast with about 3 tablespoons of the filling mixture. Roll the breasts, and use a toothpick to secure. Transfer chicken breasts into a baking dish, then sprinkle the chicken breasts with breadcrumb mixture.
- In a preheated oven, bake while uncovered for 25 minutes.

Nutrition Information

- Calories: 622 calories;
- Total Carbohydrate: 34.7
- Cholesterol: 119
- Protein: 43.4
- Total Fat: 35.2
- Sodium: 1517

66. Chicken Breasts Supreme

Serving: 6 | Prep: 25mins | Ready in:

Ingredients

- 6 skinless, boneless chicken breast halves
- salt and pepper to taste
- 1 pinch paprika, or to taste
- 3 tablespoons butter
- 1 (10.75 ounce) can condensed cream of mushroom soup
- 1/3 cup milk
- 2 tablespoons minced onion
- 1/2 cup processed cheese (such as Velveeta®), diced
- 2 tablespoons Worcestershire sauce
- 1 (4.5 ounce) can sliced mushrooms, drained and chopped
- 2/3 cup sour cream

Direction

- Start preheating the oven to 350°F (175°C). Oil a 2-qt. casserole dish.
- Sprinkle paprika, pepper, and salt over chicken breasts. In a big frying pan, heat butter and brown the chicken breasts for 5 minutes each side until both sides have thoroughly browned. In the bottom of the prepared casserole dish, put the chicken breasts.
- In a saucepan, combine mushrooms, Worcestershire sauce, processed cheese, onion, milk, and mushroom soup over medium-low heat. Let the mixture heat to melt the cheese without boiling. Whisk to blend well, stir in sour cream until smooth. Add the sauce to the dish of the chicken breasts and put on foil to cover.
- Bake for 45 minutes in the preheated oven until the juices run clear and the chicken is soft. Remove the cover, use the sauce to baste, and bake for another 30 minutes, basting sometimes.

Nutrition Information

- Calories: 335 calories;
- Total Fat: 20.6
- Sodium: 769
- Total Carbohydrate: 8.9
- Cholesterol: 100
- Protein: 28.2

67. Chicken Cacciatore

Serving: 6 | Prep: 30mins | Ready in:

Ingredients

- 3 slices bacon, chopped
- 1 (2 to 3 pound) whole chicken, cut into pieces
- salt and pepper to taste
- 1 tablespoon butter
- 1 large onion, sliced

- 2 cloves garlic, chopped
- 1 cup sliced mushrooms
- 1 cup red wine
- 2 teaspoons brown sugar
- 1/2 cup balsamic vinegar
- 1/2 cup baby carrots, sliced
- 1 tablespoon red wine
- 2 teaspoons cornstarch

Direction

- Cook bacon in big deep skillet on medium high heat till browned evenly. In bacon grease, sauté chicken with pepper and salt till browned. Discard the bacon; put aside chicken.
- Add butter to pan, melting. Sauté mushrooms, garlic and onion till onions are transparent. Mix vinegar, brown sugar and 1 cup wine in; cook till bubbly and hot, mixing. Add carrots and chicken.
- Lower heat to medium. Cook till carrots are tender crisp and chicken is well-cooked for 30 minutes.
- Blend cornstarch and 1 tbsp. wine. Mix into chicken; to thicken, mix well.

Nutrition Information

- Calories: 564 calories;
- Total Fat: 36.8
- Sodium: 280
- Total Carbohydrate: 10.6
- Cholesterol: 156
- Protein: 37.7

68. Chicken Cacciatore II

Serving: 8 | Prep: 30mins | Ready in:

Ingredients

- 2 (3 pound) whole chickens, each cut into 8 pieces

- salt and ground black pepper to taste
- 1 cup all-purpose flour
- 2 tablespoons olive oil
- 1 yellow onion, chopped
- 1 large green bell pepper, seeded and chopped
- 6 cloves garlic, minced
- 1 pound white button mushrooms, quartered
- 2 teaspoons chopped fresh oregano
- 1 (28 ounce) can whole peeled tomatoes in juice, coarsely chopped
- 2 tablespoons tomato paste
- 3/4 cup white wine
- 1 1/2 cups chicken stock
- 3 tablespoons capers, drained and rinsed
- 2 tablespoons coarsely chopped fresh basil

Direction

- Season black pepper and salt over the chicken pieces.
- Put flour into a shallow bowl. Press each of the chicken pieces into flour then tap off the excess.
- In a large Dutch oven, heat olive oil over medium-heat until it is almost smoking hot.
- Pan-fry the chicken for 3 minutes per side or until it turns golden brown on both sides. Work in batches to avoid overcrowding the skillet. Put the cooked chicken aside.
- Into the Dutch oven, stir garlic, green bell pepper and onion. Cook until tender, stirring occasionally, about 5 minutes.
- Mix in mushroom. Cook 5-8 minutes longer or until their juice releases.
- Stir in chicken stock, white wine, tomato paste, tomatoes and oregano then bring to a boil.
- Put chicken pieces back to sauce. Cover, lower the heat to medium-low, and simmer for 30-40 minutes or until the juices run clear and inside the chicken is no longer pink.
- Mix in the capers. Top with basil then serve.

Nutrition Information

- Calories: 587 calories;
- Total Fat: 29.7

- Sodium: 543
- Total Carbohydrate: 23.8
- Cholesterol: 145
- Protein: 51

69. Chicken Chili

Serving: 5 | Prep: | Ready in:

Ingredients

- 3 tablespoons vegetable oil
- 2 cloves garlic, minced
- 1 green bell pepper, chopped
- 1 onion, chopped
- 1 stalk celery, sliced
- 1/4 pound mushrooms, chopped
- 1 pound skinless, boneless chicken breast halves - cut into bite size pieces
- 1 tablespoon chili powder
- 1 teaspoon dried oregano
- 1 teaspoon ground cumin
- 1/2 teaspoon paprika
- 1/2 teaspoon cocoa powder
- 1/4 teaspoon salt
- 1 pinch crushed red pepper flakes
- 1 pinch ground black pepper
- 1 (14.5 ounce) can whole peeled tomatoes with juice
- 1 (19 ounce) can kidney beans, drained and rinsed

Direction

- Pour 2 tablespoons of oil into a big skillet and heat it at moderate heat. Add mushrooms, celery, onion, bell pepper and garlic, sautéing for 5 minutes. Put it to one side.
- Insert the leftover 1 tablespoon of oil into the skillet. At high heat, cook the chicken until browned and its exterior turns firm. Transfer the vegetable mixture back into skillet.
- Stir in ground black pepper, hot pepper flakes, salt, cocoa powder, paprika, oregano, cumin and chilli powder. Continue stirring for

several minutes to avoid burning. Pour in the beans and tomatoes and lead the entire mixture to boiling point then adjust the setting to low heat. Place a lid on the skillet and leave it simmering for 15 minutes. Uncover the skillet and leave it simmering for another 15 minutes.

Nutrition Information

- Calories: 308 calories;
- Total Fat: 10.5
- Sodium: 547
- Total Carbohydrate: 25.9
- Cholesterol: 53
- Protein: 29

70. Chicken Lo Mein

Serving: 4 | Prep: 45mins | Ready in:

Ingredients

- 4 skinless, boneless chicken breast halves - cut into thin strips
- 5 teaspoons white sugar, divided
- 3 tablespoons rice wine vinegar
- 1/2 cup soy sauce, divided
- 1 1/4 cups chicken broth
- 1 cup water
- 1 tablespoon sesame oil
- 1/2 teaspoon ground black pepper
- 2 tablespoons cornstarch
- 1 (12 ounce) package uncooked linguine pasta
- 2 tablespoons vegetable oil, divided
- 2 tablespoons minced fresh ginger root
- 1 tablespoon minced garlic
- 1/2 pound fresh shiitake mushrooms, stemmed and sliced
- 6 green onions, sliced diagonally into 1/2 inch pieces

Direction

- Mix 1/4 cup of soy sauce, 1 1/2 tbsp. of vinegar and 2 1/2 tsp. of white sugar with chicken in a medium non-reactive bowl; mix to coat the chicken well. Cover; marinate for 1 hour minimum in the fridge.
- Mix leftover soy sauce, vinegar and sugar with ground black pepper, sesame oil, water and chicken broth in a separate medium bowl. Dissolve cornstarch with some of the mixture in another small bowl; add to the bulk of the mixture slowly, mixing well. Put aside.
- Follow package directions to cook linguine. Drain; put aside. Heat 1 tbsp. of vegetable oil in big saucepan or wok on high heat till it begins to smoke. Add chicken; stir-fry till browned or for 4-5 minutes. Put this and all juices on a warm plate.
- Heat leftover vegetable oil in the pan or wok on high heat. Add green onions, mushrooms, garlic and ginger; stir-fry for half a minute. Add reserved sauce mixture then the chicken; simmer for 2 minutes till sauce starts to thicken. Add reserved noodles; gently toss, coating all well with the sauce.

Nutrition Information

- Calories: 599 calories;
- Protein: 38
- Total Fat: 14.7
- Sodium: 1877
- Total Carbohydrate: 78.6
- Cholesterol: 61

71. Chicken Marsala Meatballs

Serving: 4 | Prep: 15mins | Ready in:

Ingredients

- 3 tablespoons olive oil
- 4 leaves fresh sage
- 1 pound ground chicken
- 1 egg

- 1/4 cup almond flour
- 2 tablespoons grated Parmesan cheese
- 1 teaspoon dried sage
- 1 teaspoon dried parsley
- 1 teaspoon sea salt
- 1/2 teaspoon freshly ground black pepper
- 1 (8 ounce) package sliced fresh mushrooms
- 1 large shallot, minced
- 1 cup low-sodium chicken broth
- 1/3 cup Marsala wine
- 1 tablespoon unsalted butter
- 2 teaspoons arrowroot flour

Direction

- Over moderately-high heat, heat a big skillet. Swirl in the olive oil and heat till extremely hot. Put sage leaves; fry for a minute each side till crisp. With tongs, put sage leaves onto paper towels-lined plate. Take skillet off heat, setting oil aside.
- In a big bowl, combine pepper, salt, parsley, sage, Parmesan cheese, almond flour, egg and ground chicken together. With ice cream scoop, a tablespoon or using hands, shape into balls.
- In a skillet, reheat the oil over moderate heat. Let meatballs cook for 7 minutes till browned on every side. Put the shallot and mushrooms; cook for 5 minutes till soft.
- Into skillet, mix arrowroot flour, butter, Marsala wine and chicken broth. Place a cover and let cook for 5 to 7 minutes, mixing one time, till sauce partially thickens.

Nutrition Information

- Calories: 382 calories;
- Total Fat: 20.6
- Sodium: 605
- Total Carbohydrate: 10.8
- Cholesterol: 123
- Protein: 33.5

72. Chicken Pesto Sandwich

Serving: 8 | Prep: 30mins | Ready in:

Ingredients

- 4 skinless, boneless chicken breast halves, cut into chunks
- 1 tablespoon olive oil
- 1 tablespoon minced garlic
- 1 teaspoon red pepper flakes
- salt and freshly ground black pepper to taste
- 1 yellow bell pepper, sliced
- 1 onion, sliced
- 1 cup diced zucchini
- 1 teaspoon balsamic vinegar
- 1 cup sliced mushrooms
- 1 tablespoon chopped fresh basil
- 1 cup shredded mozzarella cheese
- 1 cup prepared pesto sauce
- 1/2 cup halved cherry tomatoes
- 4 Italian-style hoagie buns, split lengthwise and toasted
- 1 cup crumbled feta cheese, divided
- 2 tablespoons chopped fresh basil, divided

Direction

- In a large bowl, mix black pepper, salt, red pepper flakes, garlic, olive oil, and chicken; toss to coat.
- Set a large Dutch oven or pot over medium-high heat. Put in chicken mixture and cook for about 5 minutes until chicken starts to brown, stirring frequently. Mix in balsamic vinegar, zucchini, onion, and yellow bell pepper and cook for about 5 minutes until the onion starts to soften.
- Mix 1 tablespoon basil and mushrooms into the chicken mixture and cook for about 5 minutes until mushrooms have softened. Put in pesto sauce and mozzarella cheese; toss to coat. Mix in cherry tomatoes and cook for 2-3 minutes until warmed through.
- Scoop chicken mixture into toasted buns and place 1 1/2 teaspoon basil and 1/4 cup feta cheese on top of each sandwich.

Nutrition Information

- Calories: 525 calories;
- Total Fat: 26.9
- Sodium: 960
- Total Carbohydrate: 41.3
- Cholesterol: 65
- Protein: 29.4

73. Chicken Susan

Serving: 4 | Prep: 30mins | Ready in:

Ingredients

- 2 (8 ounce) packages egg noodles, cooked
- 1/2 pound Swiss cheese, cubed
- 2 cups sliced fresh mushrooms
- 4 stalks celery, chopped
- 2 cups chicken stock
- 4 chicken breast halves with skin and bone, steamed

Direction

- Preheat an oven to 200°C/400°F>
- In a 9x13-in. lightly greased baking dish, put cooked egg noodles. Add celery, mushrooms and cheese; stir well. Add chicken stock; add more stock if chicken stock level can't be seen through the noodles, keep adding till it is visible. Put chicken breasts, bone side down, over noodle mixture.
- Bake for 30 minutes at 200°C/400°F or till chicken juices are clear and skin is crisp and brown.

Nutrition Information

- Calories: 589 calories;
- Total Carbohydrate: 34.1
- Cholesterol: 167
- Protein: 52

- Total Fat: 26.5
- Sodium: 558

- Total Carbohydrate: 29
- Cholesterol: 59
- Protein: 20.4

74. Chicken Tava From Turkey

Serving: 8 | Prep: 20mins | Ready in:

Ingredients

- 2 tablespoons olive oil, divided
- 8 boneless chicken thighs, with skin
- 1 (6 ounce) can tomato paste
- 1/4 cup water
- 8 cloves garlic, halved
- salt and pepper to taste
- 4 medium potatoes, sliced
- 4 tomatoes, sliced
- 1 large onion, sliced
- 1 cup fresh mushrooms, sliced
- 8 pepperoncini peppers (optional)

Direction

- Preheat oven to 325 degrees F (165 degrees C).
- Grease a roasting pan using 1 Tbsp. olive oil. Arrange chicken thighs into the roasting pan. Mix together tomato paste and water, then spread it over the chicken thighs. Put in garlic clove halves. Season the chicken thighs using salt and pepper. Then place the potatoes, mushroom, onions and pepperoncini over the chicken. Then pour over the remaining olive oil.
- Bake it in the preheated oven for 1 1/2 hours or until the chicken juices run clear add the vegetables are tender. If the pan starts to get dry out during the baking process gradually pour in some water into the roasting pan.

Nutrition Information

- Calories: 316 calories;
- Total Fat: 13.7
- Sodium: 823

75. Chicken Tetrazzini IV

Serving: 4 | Prep: 15mins | Ready in:

Ingredients

- 1 (8 ounce) package spaghetti, broken into pieces
- 1/4 cup butter
- 1/4 cup all-purpose flour
- 3/4 teaspoon salt
- 1/4 teaspoon ground black pepper
- 1 cup chicken broth
- 1 cup heavy cream
- 2 tablespoons sherry
- 1 (4.5 ounce) can sliced mushrooms, drained
- 2 cups chopped cooked chicken
- 1/2 cup grated Parmesan cheese

Direction

- Turn on the oven to 350°F (175°C) to preheat. Grease a 9x13 inch baking dish lightly.
- Boil lightly salted water in a large pot. Pour in spaghetti; cook until al dente, 8-10 minutes. Drain well.
- At the same time, melt butter in a large saucepan over low heat. Mix in pepper, salt and flour. Cook while stirring until smooth. Take away from the heat; mix in cream and chicken broth gradually.
- Bring it back to heat; bring to a low boil with constant stirs for 1 minute. Pour in sherry; then mix in chicken, mushrooms and cooked spaghetti. Transfer to the baking dish; add Parmesan cheese on top.
- Put into the oven to bake until browned lightly and bubbly, 30 minutes.

Nutrition Information

- Calories: 730 calories;
- Total Fat: 42.6
- Sodium: 919
- Total Carbohydrate: 52.7
- Cholesterol: 173
- Protein: 33.1

76. Chicken Thigh Fricassee With Mushrooms And Rosemary

Serving: 4 | Prep: 15mins | Ready in:

Ingredients

- 4 tablespoons olive oil, divided
- 5 ounces fresh mushrooms, sliced
- 4 cloves garlic, peeled and halved
- 2 tablespoons fresh rosemary, chopped
- 1 pound chicken thighs
- salt and freshly ground black pepper to taste
- 1/4 teaspoon crushed red pepper flakes
- 3/4 cup dry white wine
- 12 cherry tomatoes
- 12 Nicoise olives

Direction

- In a large skillet, heat 2 tablespoons of the olive oil over medium heat. Mix in the mushrooms. Cook until soft. Transfer to a plate.
- Clean the skillet, then heat 2 tablespoons of the olive oil over medium-high heat. Put chicken thighs, rosemary, and garlic into the hot oil. Add pepper and salt for seasonings. Cook, turning the chicken, until the garlic and chicken are well browned.
- Put the mushrooms back into the pan. Add red pepper flakes over the chicken. Add white wine, using a wooden spoon to scrape the bottom of the pan. Cook for 3 minutes.
- Lower the heat to low; gently simmer, covered, for 60 minutes.

- Uncover and add olives and tomatoes over top of the chicken. Cover and cook for 5 minutes longer.

Nutrition Information

- Calories: 402 calories;
- Total Fat: 28.6
- Sodium: 257
- Total Carbohydrate: 7.1
- Cholesterol: 71
- Protein: 21

77. Chicken Thighs With Mushroom Leek Sauce

Serving: 8 | Prep: 10mins | Ready in:

Ingredients

- 1 tablespoon extra-virgin olive oil
- 8 boneless, skinless chicken thighs
- 4 cups baby bella mushrooms, thinly sliced
- 2 leeks, thinly sliced
- 2/3 cup dry white wine
- 1 1/2 cups reduced-sodium chicken broth
- 2 teaspoons cornstarch
- 2/3 cup low-fat sour cream
- 1 1/2 teaspoons Dijon mustard
- salt to taste
- ground black pepper to taste

Direction

- Put oil in a large skillet and heat it over medium-high. Add the chicken and cook each side for 4-5 minutes until evenly browned and the center of the chicken is no longer pink. Place the chicken onto a plate. Cover the chicken and keep it warm.
- Add leeks and mushrooms to the skillet. Cook and stir the mixture frequently over medium heat for 4-6 minutes until the mushrooms start to brown and the moisture has been

evaporated. Pour in the wine. Cook for 1 minute. In a small bowl, mix the cornstarch and broth, and then pour the mixture into the skillet. Cook for 2-3 more minutes until thickened. Mix in the mustard and sour cream. Cook and stir for 1 minute until combined. Season the sauce with salt and pepper.

- Lay the chicken thighs into the sauce and cook for 8-10 more minutes until the inserted instant-read thermometer into the thickest portion of the thigh registers 165°F or 74°C.

Nutrition Information

- Calories: 198 calories;
- Protein: 13.8
- Total Fat: 11.2
- Sodium: 113
- Total Carbohydrate: 7.2
- Cholesterol: 47

78. Chicken With Mushrooms

Serving: 4 | Prep: 15mins | Ready in:

Ingredients

- 3 cups sliced mushrooms
- 4 skinless, boneless chicken breast halves
- 2 eggs, beaten
- 1 cup seasoned bread crumbs
- 2 tablespoons butter
- 6 ounces mozzarella cheese, sliced
- 3/4 cup chicken broth

Direction

- Turn the oven to 350°F (175°C) to preheat.
- In a 9x13-in. pan, put 1/2 of the mushrooms. Dip the chicken in beaten eggs, and then roll in bread crumbs.
- Melt butter in a frying pan over medium heat. In the frying pan, brown the chicken on both sides. Top the mushrooms with the chicken.

On the chicken, put the leftover mushrooms, and put mozzarella cheese on top. Pour chicken broth into the pan.

- Bake for 30-35 minutes in the preheated oven until the juices run clear and the chicken is not pink anymore.

Nutrition Information

- Calories: 454 calories;
- Total Carbohydrate: 23.8
- Cholesterol: 204
- Protein: 44.1
- Total Fat: 19.8
- Sodium: 1108

79. Chicken And Bacon Fajitas

Serving: 4 | Prep: 30mins | Ready in:

Ingredients

- 3 boneless, skinless chicken breast halves
- salt to taste
- 3 slices peppered bacon, diced
- 1/2 cup chopped onion
- 1 chopped green bell pepper
- 1 chopped red bell pepper
- 1 1/2 cups chopped mushrooms
- 1 cup cherry tomatoes, cut in half
- 3/4 cup chopped cilantro
- 8 large flour tortillas (burrito size), warmed to soften

Direction

- Heat a large skillet over medium-high heat. Cook chicken breasts until juices run clear and outside of chicken turns golden brown. Season the breasts to taste with salt. Put aside.
- In the hot skillet, cook bacon until it starts to release some oil. Mix in bell peppers and onion. Cook until onions become translucent and bacon become crispy. Mix in mushrooms

and tomatoes. Keep cooking until mushrooms soften.

- Cut cooked chicken breasts into the bite-sized pieces. Put into skillet along with cilantro. Combine by stirring. Cook to reheat for one minute. Put into the warmed tortillas to enjoy.

Nutrition Information

- Calories: 682 calories;
- Protein: 36.9
- Total Fat: 22.1
- Sodium: 1305
- Total Carbohydrate: 82.1
- Cholesterol: 66

80. Chicken And Mushroom Chowder

Serving: 4 | Prep: 15mins | Ready in:

Ingredients

- 3 cups chicken broth
- 1/2 cup water
- 1 pound cubed cooked chicken breast meat
- 1 1/2 teaspoons dried oregano
- 1/4 teaspoon pepper
- 1/2 cup uncooked long grain rice
- 1 tablespoon olive oil
- 3 cloves garlic, minced
- 1 onion, finely chopped
- 1 carrot, finely chopped
- 3/4 pound mushrooms, sliced
- 3 tablespoons all-purpose flour
- 1 cup milk

Direction

- Bring water and chicken broth to a boil in a large saucepan. Stir in chicken, season with oregano and pepper. Put in rice; reduce the heat.

- In a medium saucepan, heat olive oil over medium heat; sauté mushrooms, carrot, onion, and garlic until softened. Mix in thoroughly the flour. Add to the broth mixture.
- Stir in milk; continue to cook, stirring irregularly, about 30 minutes or until thickened.

Nutrition Information

- Calories: 416 calories;
- Total Fat: 13.6
- Sodium: 113
- Total Carbohydrate: 33.8
- Cholesterol: 90
- Protein: 38.6

81. Chicken And Mushroom Crepes

Serving: 5 | Prep: 25mins | Ready in:

Ingredients

- Filling:
- 5 tablespoons butter, divided
- 2 tablespoons canola oil
- 3 boneless, skinless chicken breasts, cut into chunks
- 1 (8 ounce) package sliced fresh mushrooms
- 1/3 cup finely chopped onion
- 1/4 cup all-purpose flour
- 2 cups milk
- 2 cubes chicken bouillon
- 1/4 teaspoon salt
- 1/8 teaspoon ground black pepper
- 1/2 cup sour cream
- 3 tablespoons dry sherry
- 2 teaspoons dried parsley, divided
- Crepes:
- 1 cup milk
- 3/4 cup all-purpose flour
- 1 egg
- 1 tablespoon butter, melted
- 1 1/2 teaspoons white sugar

- 1/4 teaspoon vanilla extract
- 1/4 teaspoon baking powder

Direction

- In a large skillet over medium heat, put 1 tablespoons butter and oil to heat. Add chicken then stir and cook for about 5 minutes until not pink in the middle. Place to a plate.
- In the same skillet over medium heat, put remaining 1/4 cup butter to dissolve. Place in onion and mushrooms; stir and cook for about 5 minutes until tender. Mix in 1/4 cup flour and cook for 2 minutes. Lower heat. Stir in pepper, salt, chicken bouillon cubes and 2 cups milk; whisk and cook for about 5 minutes until thickened into a sauce. Mix in sherry and sour cream.
- In a bowl, place 1 cup sauce; remain warm. In the skillet with remaining sauce, add 1 teaspoon parsley and chicken. Boil for about 5 minutes until chicken is heated well.
- In a bowl, whisk baking powder, vanilla extract, sugar, 1 tablespoon dissolved butter, egg, 3/4 cup flour and 1 cup milk to create a crepe batter.
- Lightly grease a 7-inch skillet; then heat over medium. Put 2 tablespoons batter into the skillet, whirling to scatter equally. Then cook crepe for about 30 seconds each side, until golden brown. Place crepe to plate. Continue with remaining batter, using waxed paper to separate crepes and covering to remain warm.
- Onto each crepe, place 1/4 cup chicken mixture and turn up. On filled crepes, put reserved 1 cup sauce. Decorate with remaining 1 teaspoon parsley.

Nutrition Information

- Calories: 501 calories;
- Sodium: 872
- Total Carbohydrate: 32.8
- Cholesterol: 131
- Protein: 24.6
- Total Fat: 30

82. Chicken And Portobello Rollups

Serving: 4 | Prep: 30mins | Ready in:

Ingredients

- 1 tablespoon olive oil
- 1 teaspoon minced garlic
- 1 portobello mushroom cap, cut into 1/2-inch slices
- 1 large red bell pepper, cut into strips
- 8 asparagus spears, trimmed
- 1/2 teaspoon seasoned salt
- 1/2 teaspoon dried oregano
- 4 (6 ounce) skinless, boneless chicken breast halves
- 1 (10.5 ounce) can cream of mushroom soup
- 1 cup milk

Direction

- Place a skillet on the stove and turn on to medium heat then put olive oil. Put in the garlic, and cook for about 1 minute until it starts to turn golden brown in color. Stir in the asparagus, red pepper and mushroom; put seasoned salt and oregano to season, then slowly cook until tender. Put the mixture onto a plate, and let it cool.
- Prepare the oven by preheating to 375 degrees F (190 degrees C). Get a small glass baking dish and use cooking spray to coat then reserve.
- Between two sheets of plastic wrap, put each chicken breast, and smash to 1/4-inch thick. Equally split among the flattened chicken breasts the asparagus, red pepper and portobello. Reel up and use toothpicks to secure. Then put into prepared baking dish.
- Place inside the preheated oven and bake for about 30 minutes until pink color fades. In the meantime, in a saucepan over medium-high heat, stir together the milk and cream of mushroom soup. Simmer then lower the heat, and let it stay warm while cooking chicken.

- To present, get toothpicks out the chicken, cut each in half at an angle, and put onto individual plates or serving platter. Scoop cream of mushroom soup all over the top.

Nutrition Information

- Calories: 342 calories;
- Total Fat: 13.3
- Sodium: 709
- Total Carbohydrate: 13.8
- Cholesterol: 102
- Protein: 40.7

83. Chicken And Rice Casserole I

Serving: 6 | Prep: | Ready in:

Ingredients

- 1 cup uncooked white rice
- 1 (1 ounce) package dry onion soup mix
- 2 (10.75 ounce) cans condensed cream of mushroom soup
- 1 (4.5 ounce) can sliced mushrooms
- 1 cup milk
- 6 skinless, boneless chicken breast halves

Direction

- Preheat a 175°C/350°F.
- Mix milk, mushroom pieces, cream of mushroom soup, dry onion soup mix and rice in a big bowl.
- In a 9x13-in. baking dish, put chicken pieces. Put mushroom mixture on chicken. In preheated oven, bake for 1 hour, covered. Bake for another 15 minutes.

Nutrition Information

- Calories: 367 calories;
- Total Fat: 8.6
- Sodium: 1252

- Total Carbohydrate: 37.4
- Cholesterol: 72
- Protein: 33.1

84. Chicken Stuffed Mushrooms

Serving: 6 | Prep: | Ready in:

Ingredients

- 1 pound medium button or mini-bella mushrooms
- 2 tablespoons unsalted butter
- 1 large onion, finely chopped
- 1 large clove garlic, minced
- 1 cooked boneless chicken breast half, finely diced*
- 1 1/2 tablespoons Diamond Crystal® Kosher Salt
- 3/4 teaspoon coarsely ground pepper
- 1 tablespoon all-purpose flour
- 1 cup whipping cream
- 5 tablespoons chopped fresh parsley, divided
- finely shredded mozzarella or Parmesan cheese (optional)

Direction

- Heat oven to 350 °F.
- Eliminate stems from mushrooms, but do not discard. Scoop out insides of mushrooms with a small melon baller, leaving at least half shell to make more room for filling. Chop mushroom stems and centers finely:
- In a large skillet, melt butter over medium heat. Add garlic and onion; cook for about 1 minute. Mix in chopped mushrooms, chicken, pepper, and Diamond Crystal(R) Kosher Salt. Cook and stir for an addition of 3 minutes. Blend in 3 tablespoons parsley, cream and flour. Cook and stir until bubbly and thickened. Take away from heat.
- Spoon mushroom caps evenly with the mixture. Place in lightly oiled, shallow baking dish. Bake for approximately 10 minutes. Put

leftover 2 tablespoons parsley on top and jazz up with mozzarella or Parmesan cheese for garnish, if wished. Bake for about 5 to 10 minutes or until hot and cheese melts. If you want, garnish with additional parsley.

Nutrition Information

- Calories: 228 calories;
- Total Fat: 19.8
- Sodium: 1476
- Total Carbohydrate: 7.6
- Cholesterol: 73
- Protein: 7

85. Chinese Clay Pot Chicken Rice

Serving: 4 | Prep: 15mins | Ready in:

Ingredients

- 1 whole chicken breast, cut into big chunks
- 6 chicken wings, cut into thirds, tips discarded
- 1 cup dark soy sauce
- 1 tablespoon sesame oil
- 8 cloves garlic, smashed
- ground white pepper to taste
- 2 links lop chong (Chinese-style sausage)
- 6 dried shiitake mushrooms
- 2 tablespoons vegetable oil
- 1/2 cup dark soy sauce
- 1 2/3 cups jasmine rice
- 5 tablespoons chile paste
- 2 tablespoons grated fresh ginger root
- 2 tablespoons fresh lime juice
- 1 cup shredded iceberg lettuce

Direction

- In a mixing bowl, combine garlic, a cup of dark soy sauce, chicken wings, chicken breast, and sesame oil. Add white pepper for seasoning. Prepare the Chinese sausages (sliced on an angle) and mix in the chicken

mixture. Cover the container and leave to chill for at least 10 minutes. Pour hot water over well-rinsed shiitake mushrooms. Let the mushrooms be submerged for about 15 minutes or until they are bloated and well-soaked. Drain off the mushrooms and reserve the liquid. Discard the mushroom stalks and slice the tops in half and set aside.

- In a large and deep pan set over medium heat, heat oil and cook the chicken in the hot oil for 7 to 10 minutes or until the chicken juices run clear and they are no longer pink in the center. Top the chicken with a drizzle of half a cup of dark soy sauce.
- Rinse the rice in water until the water runs almost clear and completely drain. In a non-stick skillet, combine 1 and a half of the reserved mushroom liquid and rice. Let the mixture come to a boil. Adjust the heat to low. Cover the pan and allow the mixture to simmer for 10 minutes while keeping the heat on. Mix in the mushrooms and chicken mixture and take off the heat. Let the pot stand while covered for 15 to 20 minutes or until the rice is completely cooked and tender.
- In a small bowl, combine ginger, chili paste, and lime juice. Top chicken rice with a drizzle of the sauce and shredded lettuce before serving.

Nutrition Information

- Calories: 725 calories;
- Total Fat: 29.2
- Sodium: 5990
- Total Carbohydrate: 87.7
- Cholesterol: 46
- Protein: 34.2

86. Chinese Sausage Fried Rice

Serving: 8 | Prep: 15mins | Ready in:

Ingredients

- 2 cups uncooked white rice
- 4 cups water
- 4 dried shiitake mushrooms
- 1 cup hot water
- 1/2 pound ground chicken
- 1 tablespoon soy sauce
- 1 teaspoon sesame oil
- 1 pinch white pepper
- 2 tablespoons vegetable oil
- 3 cloves garlic, sliced
- 2 links lop chong (Chinese-style sausage), thinly sliced
- 1 tablespoon dark soy sauce
- 4 green onions, chopped
- 2 eggs, lightly beaten

Direction

- On high heat, boil four cups of water and rice in a pot; turn to medium-low heat. Cover and let it simmer for 20-25 minutes until rice becomes tender and it has absorbed the liquid. Wash the shitake mushrooms and submerge in a cup of hot water for 10 minutes until soft. Cut the mushrooms and let them stand; keep the liquid. Use white pepper, sesame oil, and soy sauce to season ground chicken.
- On medium heat, heat vegetable oil in a pan; add garlic. Sauté garlic until aromatic. Mix in sausages, mushroom, and ground chicken. Cook until brown, crumbly, and the chicken is not pink; stir continuously. Mix in rice, reserved mushroom liquid, green onions, and dark soy sauce. Keep on stirring and cooking until the sauce coats the rice. Stir in eggs over rice until firm.

Nutrition Information

- Calories: 415 calories;
- Sodium: 562
- Total Carbohydrate: 64.8
- Cholesterol: 46
- Protein: 12.9
- Total Fat: 12.6

87. Chinese Shrimp Wonton

Serving: 12 | Prep: 1hours | Ready in:

Ingredients

- 3 green onions, chopped
- 5 slices fresh ginger
- 3/4 cup water
- 1 pound ground pork
- 3 tablespoons Chinese rice wine, divided
- 2 tablespoons soy sauce
- 3 teaspoons salt, divided
- 1 teaspoon sesame oil
- 1 teaspoon ground white pepper
- 40 shrimps, minced
- 1/2 cup diced mushrooms
- 1 stalk celery, finely chopped
- 100 (3.5 inch square) wonton wrappers
- 1 (14.5 ounce) can chicken stock

Direction

- Fill a bowl with water, and mash ginger and green onion. Add in white pepper, pork, soy sauce, 2 tablespoons of rice wine, 2 teaspoons of salt, and sesame oil.
- In a bowl, mix mushrooms, shrimp, celery, a tablespoon of rice wine, and a teaspoon of salt. Mix the mushroom mixture to the pork mixture until well combined.
- Carefully separate the wonton wrappers and place them on your work surface. Place a tablespoon of the shrimp-pork mixture at the center of each wrapper. Lightly moisten the edges of the wrappers with water with your finger or a pastry brush. Pull a corner of the wrapper over the filling and pull up to form a triangle and press the edges to seal. Boil the chicken stock and cook the wontons for about 5 minutes or until they float to the top.

Nutrition Information

- Calories: 302 calories;

- Total Carbohydrate: 39.9
- Cholesterol: 61
- Protein: 17
- Total Fat: 7.1
- Sodium: 1275

88. Chinese Stir Fried Sticky Rice With Chinese Sausage

Serving: 6 | Prep: 15mins | Ready in:

Ingredients

- 2 cups glutinous rice
- 8 dried shiitake mushrooms
- 1/3 cup dried shrimp
- 2 dried scallops
- 1 teaspoon olive oil
- 3 eggs, beaten
- 3 links Chinese sausage, diced
- 2 cups hot water, or more as needed
- 2 tablespoons light soy sauce, or to taste
- 2 teaspoons dark soy sauce
- 1 teaspoon white sugar
- 1/2 cup chopped cilantro, or to taste

Direction

- In a big bowl with water, submerge rice for approximately 4 hours till mostly clear. Wash and drain well.
- In 3 individual bowls with water, submerge scallops, shrimp and mushrooms for around 15 minutes till softened. Drain, setting aside mushroom liquid and throwing away the other water. Cut scallops, shrimp and mushrooms into small portions.
- In a big skillet, heat the olive oil on medium heat. Into the skillet, add eggs, swirling to spread out into a thin layer. Cook for around a minute till mostly set. Turn over and cook for 3 to 5 minutes till not runny anymore.
- Turn out the egg onto a cutting board and cool slightly. Roll into a long tube and cut into thin ribbons.
- Into the same skillet, mix Chinese sausage on medium heat. Cook and mix for around 3 minutes till aromatic and some of oil is rendered. Put in scallops, shrimp and mushrooms; let it cook for 3 minutes to 5 minutes. Turn out mixture of sausage onto a bowl.
- Into the skillet, mix the drained rice. Cook and mix for 1 to 2 minutes till slightly toasted. Add the reserved mushroom liquid, mixing continuously till water is absorbed. Put in hot water, half a cup at a time, mixing till water is absorbed among every addition. Cook for approximately 25 minutes till rice softens.
- Season the rice with sugar, dark soy sauce and light soy sauce. Mix in the sausage mixture and egg ribbons. Put cilantro on top prior to serving.

Nutrition Information

- Calories: 545 calories;
- Cholesterol: 104
- Protein: 21.8
- Total Fat: 16.4
- Sodium: 831
- Total Carbohydrate: 82.8

89. Chipotle Burgers With Avocado Salsa

Serving: 4 | Prep: 30mins | Ready in:

Ingredients

- 1 bunch fresh cilantro, chopped
- 1 pound ground beef
- 1 (7 ounce) can chipotle peppers in adobo sauce
- 1 cup chopped fresh mushrooms
- 1 tablespoon Worcestershire sauce
- 1 avocado - peeled, pitted, and diced
- 1 onion, diced
- 1 tomato, diced

- 2 jalapeno peppers, seeded and chopped
- 1 lime, juiced
- salt and ground black pepper to taste
- 4 onion rolls, split

Direction

- Preheat the outdoor grill for medium-high heat and grease grate lightly.
- Into a big bowl, put half of the chopped cilantro and combine with Worcestershire sauce, mushrooms, chipotle peppers in adobo sauce and ground beef. Reserve the rest of cilantro. Shape beef mixture into 4 patties.
- In a bowl with black pepper, salt, lime juice, jalapeno peppers, tomato, onion and avocado, gently toss the rest of cilantro.
- On the prepped grill, let the burgers grill for 5 minutes each side till browned and not pink anymore on the inside. Serve burgers on onion rolls with avocado salsa on top.

Nutrition Information

- Calories: 503 calories;
- Total Fat: 24.6
- Sodium: 593
- Total Carbohydrate: 42.3
- Cholesterol: 71
- Protein: 28

90. Citrus Chicken

Serving: 8 | Prep: 15mins | Ready in:

Ingredients

- 8 skinless, boneless chicken breast halves
- 2 tablespoons all-purpose flour
- 2 tablespoons salt
- 2 tablespoons ground black pepper
- 3 tablespoons olive oil
- 1 teaspoon minced garlic

- 1 (6 ounce) can frozen orange juice concentrate, thawed
- 1/2 cup vegetable stock
- 1 teaspoon dried oregano
- 1 teaspoon dried thyme
- 1 green bell pepper, chopped
- 1 red onion, chopped
- 1 cup sliced fresh mushrooms
- 1/2 cup sliced black olives

Direction

- Use the pepper, salt and flour to coat the chicken. Heat the oil on medium-high heat in the big skillet, and sauté the garlic till softened. Put in the chicken and sauté till browned.
- Add the orange juice concentrate on top of the chicken and keep covered; cook for 3-5 minutes, then whisk in the vegetable stock, covered and let simmer for 15 minutes, basting using the skillet juices.
- Put in the onion, pepper, thyme, and oregano; stir them well and let simmer for 5 minutes longer. Whisk in the mushrooms, covered and cook for 5 minutes more. Pour in the olives, cook for 60 seconds longer and serve.

Nutrition Information

- Calories: 249 calories;
- Total Carbohydrate: 17.4
- Cholesterol: 61
- Protein: 24.8
- Total Fat: 8.9
- Sodium: 1978

91. Contadina® Mushroom Chicken Cacciatore

Serving: 4 | Prep: 15mins | Ready in:

Ingredients

- 4 (5 ounce) boneless, skinless chicken breast halves
- Salt and black pepper to taste
- 1/4 cup all-purpose flour
- 3 tablespoons olive oil, divided
- 1 pound mushrooms, quartered
- 1 large onion, thinly sliced
- 3 cloves garlic, minced
- 1 1/2 teaspoons dried thyme
- 1 teaspoon paprika
- 1 cup COLLEGE INN® Fat Free Lower Sodium Chicken Broth
- 2 (14.5 ounce) cans CONTADINA® Diced Tomatoes, undrained
- Cooked wide egg noodles

Direction

- Use pepper and salt to season the chicken. In a bowl, put flour; put in chicken and coat, saving 2 tablespoons of excess flour.
- In a wide, deep frying pan, heat 2 tablespoons oil over medium-high heat. Brown the chicken for 3-5 minutes per side. Take out of the pan and put aside.
- Add the leftover 1 tablespoon oil to the pan. Add paprika, thyme, garlic, onion, and mushrooms. Cook until the mushrooms give off their liquid and the onions are tender, tossing sometimes, about 10-15 minutes. Mix in the saved flour.
- Mix in tomatoes and broth; use a spoon to crumble the whole tomatoes. Boil it, lower the heat and simmer until partially thickened, about 3 minutes.
- Bring chicken back to the pan, simmer until chicken is not pink anymore inside (165 degrees F internal temperature) for 10-12 minutes. For serving, add the mushroom sauce to noodles and chicken.

Nutrition Information

- Calories: 574 calories;
- Sodium: 523
- Total Carbohydrate: 64.6

- Cholesterol: 120
- Protein: 42.3
- Total Fat: 16.1

92. Continental Chicken

Serving: 5 | Prep: 15mins | Ready in:

Ingredients

- 1 (3 pound) whole chicken, cut into pieces
- 1/4 cup all-purpose flour
- 2 tablespoons vegetable oil
- 1 (4.5 ounce) can sliced mushrooms, drained
- 1 (16 ounce) can Italian-style diced tomatoes, drained
- 1/3 cup soy sauce
- 1 clove garlic, crushed
- 1 onion, sliced
- 1/4 cup pitted black olives

Direction

- Dredge the chicken pieces in flour until coated thoroughly. In a large skillet, heat the oil on medium-high, then brown the coated chicken pieces in the heated oil slowly.
- In the meantime, in a large saucepan, mix garlic, soy sauce, and tomatoes with the retained mushroom liquid and stir them together. Add onion and the browned chicken, stir them together; put a cover on the saucepan and let it simmer on low heat until the chicken is tender and cooked thoroughly, or for 45 minutes.
- Stir in olives and mushrooms, boil; serve while hot, if desired, coat them with extra soy sauce.

Nutrition Information

- Calories: 709 calories;
- Total Fat: 47.4
- Sodium: 1464
- Total Carbohydrate: 13

- Cholesterol: 204
- Protein: 53.9

93. Coq Au Vin, My Way

Serving: 6 | Prep: 30mins | Ready in:

Ingredients

- 3 tablespoons olive oil
- 6 skinless chicken thighs
- 2 cloves garlic, crushed
- 1 tablespoon Italian seasoning
- 3 medium tomatoes, sliced
- 4 portobello mushrooms, sliced
- 1 pinch salt (optional)
- 1 teaspoon freshly ground black pepper
- 1 sweet onion, chopped
- 1/3 cup Burgundy wine
- 1 cup heavy cream
- 1/4 cup shredded Gruyere cheese
- 2 tablespoons cornstarch (optional)

Direction

- Pour the oil in a big skillet and heat over medium heat. Drop the chicken thighs, Italian seasoning and crushed garlic. Cook the chicken thighs on both sides until browned, then put in portobello mushrooms and tomatoes. Spice it up with pepper and salt. Adjust the heat to low, and make it to a simmer for roughly half an hour while covered.
- Drain off about half of the liquid from the skillet, and add in the Burgundy wine. Make it to a simmer while covered for 30 minutes more. Take away the chicken, mushrooms and tomatoes to an 8 or 9 inch square baking dish. Cover it off with the onion slices, and put aside.
- Set the oven for preheating to 350°F (175°C). Bring the remaining liquid in the skillet to the boiling point over medium-low heat. Whisk in the heavy cream gently and the Gruyere

cheese. Take them off from the heat, and stir until the consistency turns smooth. If the sauce ended up thin, whisk in the cornstarch, and make it to a simmer over very low heat until it turns thick. Pour the sauce over the chicken in the baking dish.
- Let it bake inside the oven for half an hour until the onions are softened. Let it sit for 5 minutes before you serve it in.

Nutrition Information

- Calories: 373 calories;
- Total Fat: 28.1
- Sodium: 78
- Total Carbohydrate: 12.9
- Cholesterol: 102
- Protein: 16.8

94. Country Fried Onion And Mushroom Steak

Serving: 4 | Prep: 20mins | Ready in:

Ingredients

- 3/4 cup dry bread crumbs
- 1/4 cup grated Parmesan cheese
- 1 green onion, chopped
- 4 3-ounce steaks
- 1 egg
- 1/2 cup milk
- 2 tablespoons butter
- 2 tablespoons olive oil
- 1/4 cup chopped onion
- 1/4 cup sliced fresh mushrooms
- 1/2 cup beef broth
- 2 tablespoons all-purpose flour
- 1 tablespoon cornstarch
- salt and pepper to taste
-

Direction

- Mix green onion, Parmesan cheese and breadcrumbs in container. In a bowl, beat egg till fluffy. Put milk in; whisk. Dip steaks in egg batter then into breadcrumb mixture till coated. Put on a plate.
- Heat olive oil and butter in saucepan on medium heat. Turn heat to medium-high; put steaks in saucepan. Cook for 2 minutes, avoid moving steaks. Keep on cooking for 2 more minutes till golden brown. Put steaks on serving place; lower heat to medium.
- Add mushrooms and onion in saucepan; cook for 3-5 minutes till soft. Add cornstarch, flour and broth slowly, mixing gravy while adding these ingredients. Lower heat to low; cook for 1 minute without mixing. Mix again; take off heat. Let sit for 1-2 more minutes; it will thicken while cooling. Use gravy to cover steaks.

Nutrition Information

- Calories: 711 calories;
- Protein: 73.7
- Sodium: 566
- Total Carbohydrate: 22.5
- Cholesterol: 195
- Total Fat: 34.3

95. Crab And Mushroom Enchiladas

Serving: 8 | Prep: 15mins | Ready in:

Ingredients

- 1 pound imitation crabmeat, chopped
- 1 (10 ounce) can red enchilada sauce
- 1 (10.75 ounce) can condensed cream of mushroom soup
- 1/2 pound fresh mushrooms, sliced
- 1 (8 ounce) package shredded Mexican-style cheese blend
- 8 (10 inch) flour tortillas

Direction

- Preheat an oven to 190°C/375°F. Grease medium baking dish lightly.
- Mix 1/2 of the cheese, mushrooms, cream of mushroom soup, red enchilada sauce and imitation crabmeat in big bowl. Roll even amount of mixture in every tortilla. Put filled tortillas in the prepared baking dish; cover using enchilada sauce. Put leftover cheese on top.
- In preheated oven, bake till cheese is bubbly for 20 minutes. Before serving, let sit for 5 minutes.

Nutrition Information

- Calories: 465 calories;
- Total Fat: 21.1
- Sodium: 1361
- Total Carbohydrate: 50.4
- Cholesterol: 51
- Protein: 18.5

96. Crab Stuffed Mushrooms

Serving: 10 | Prep: | Ready in:

Ingredients

- 1 pound large fresh mushrooms
- 4 tablespoons butter, divided
- 1/4 cup Kikkoman Panko Bread Crumbs
- 1/2 cup imitation crabmeat, flaked
- 1/4 teaspoon onion powder
- 1/8 teaspoon salt
- 2 tablespoons Kikkoman Panko Bread Crumbs
- 1/8 teaspoon black pepper

Direction

- Heat oven to 375 °F. Use a damp paper towel to wipe mushrooms gently. Take and finely chop stems. In a large skillet, melt 3 tablespoons of the butter over medium heat.

Add mushroom stems and cook for 5 minutes or until tender. Take away from heat and stir in the shredded crab, 1/4 cup of the panko, onion powder, pepper and salt.

- Fill crab mixture into mushrooms caps and arrange them on unoiled baking sheet with rim, stuffing side facing up. Mix panko and remaining butter in a small bowl. Sprinkle the mixture evenly over the mushroom tops and bake for approximately 15 minutes.

Nutrition Information

- Calories: 770 calories;
- Total Carbohydrate: 158.3
- Cholesterol: 14
- Protein: 20.9
- Total Fat: 8.1
- Sodium: 392

97. Crazy Good Stuffing And Baked Chops

Serving: 6 | Prep: 20mins | Ready in:

Ingredients

- 1/2 pound sliced fresh mushrooms, or more to taste
- 1 onion, chopped
- 1/4 cup dry sherry, or to taste
- 2 tablespoons all-purpose flour, or as needed
- 2/3 cup milk, or as needed
- 1 (10.75 ounce) can condensed cream of mushroom soup
- 1 (14 ounce) package dry bread stuffing mix
- 1/4 cup butter
- 6 boneless pork chops
- 1/2 cup water
- 1 (10.75 ounce) can condensed cream of mushroom soup
- 1/2 (10.75 ounce) can milk

Direction

- Start preheating the oven to 375°F (190°C). Spray cooking spray over a 9x13 inches baking dish.
- In a large saucepan, cook while stirring onion and mushrooms over medium-low heat for 5 mins or until mushrooms have given up the liquid and turn soft. Mix in sherry, boil and simmer for 2-3 more mins until onions become tender. Sprinkle the mixture with flour. Cook until thick while stirring constantly. Mix in 2/3 cup of milk gradually to create the creamy gravy, stirring constantly to prevent it from burning. Mix in dry stuffing and one can of cream of mushroom soup. Simmer, then cook for 5 mins until stuffing mix becomes moist.
- Melt butter in a large pan over medium heat until no longer foamy. Pan-fry chops for 5 mins on each side until browned but not cooked through. In the prepared baking dish, place chops. Stir the water into skillet, boil, then scrape and dissolve all the remaining flavor bits in skillet. Allow mixture to boil for 10 mins until reduced by half. Put skillet drippings into stuffing mix. Then mix thoroughly.
- Scoop up the generous amounts of the stuffing then mound on each chop. Whisk one can of the cream of the mushroom soup with half of soup can of the milk together. Cover each chop with soup mixture.
- Bake in prepared oven for 20 mins until the chops are cooked through and tender. An instant-read thermometer should register at least 165°F (74°C) when inserted into middle of chop.

Nutrition Information

- Calories: 633 calories;
- Sodium: 1878
- Total Carbohydrate: 66.1
- Cholesterol: 84
- Protein: 35.9
- Total Fat: 24.1

98. Cream Cheese Alfredo Sauce

Serving: 6 | Prep: 10mins | Ready in:

Ingredients

- 2 tablespoons butter
- 2 portobello mushroom caps, thinly sliced
- 1 (8 ounce) package cream cheese
- 1/2 cup butter
- 1 1/2 cups milk
- 6 ounces grated Parmesan cheese, or to taste
- 1 clove garlic, crushed
- 1 tablespoon minced fresh basil leaves
- ground white pepper, to taste

Direction

- In a skillet over medium heat, heat 2 tablespoons of butter. Mix in the mushrooms; cook while stirring for around 5 minutes or till softened. Set aside.
- Meanwhile, in a saucepan over medium heat, melt 1/2 cup of butter and the cream cheese while stirring sometimes. Mix in the Parmesan cheese and milk; mix till smooth. Put in white pepper, basil and garlic. Simmer for 5 minutes; discard the garlic. Mix the cooked mushrooms. Serve.

Nutrition Information

- Calories: 464 calories;
- Protein: 16.9
- Total Fat: 41.6
- Sodium: 708
- Total Carbohydrate: 7.2
- Cholesterol: 122

99. Cream Of Mushroom Chicken

Serving: 7 | Prep: | Ready in:

Ingredients

- 2 tablespoons butter
- 1 (10.75 ounce) can condensed cream of mushroom soup
- 1 1/4 cups water, or as needed
- 1 (12 fluid ounce) can evaporated milk
- 1 onion, chopped
- salt and pepper to taste
- 2 pounds skinless, boneless chicken breast halves - cubed
- 1 (6 ounce) can sliced mushrooms, drained

Direction

- Melt butter or margarine in a large saucepan. Add milk, water, and soup. Mix together over medium heat. Add pepper, salt, and onion; bring to a boil.
- When mixture begins to boil, put in chicken meat; let simmer altogether until chicken is thoroughly cooked. Add sliced mushrooms; boil over medium heat, stirring constantly, for about 5 minutes. Serve.

Nutrition Information

- Calories: 294 calories;
- Total Fat: 11.6
- Sodium: 549
- Total Carbohydrate: 11
- Cholesterol: 100
- Protein: 35

100. Cream Of Mushroom Soup II

Serving: 4 | Prep: 15mins | Ready in:

Ingredients

- 1 pound fresh mushrooms
- 1/4 cup margarine
- 4 green onions, thinly sliced

- 3 cloves garlic, chopped
- 1 teaspoon chopped fresh thyme
- 2 tablespoons all-purpose flour
- 4 cups vegetable broth
- 1 cup light cream
- salt and pepper to taste
- 1 sprig fresh thyme leaves
- 1 tablespoon chopped fresh chives

Direction

- Slice mushroom caps thinly and discard the stalks.
- In a heavy-based pan, melt butter; sauté lemon thyme, garlic, and spring onion in melted butter, stirring, until the garlic turns golden, about 1 minute. Add white pepper, salt, and mushroom. Cook until the mushroom just softens, 3 to 4 minutes. Put in flour; cook and stir for 1 minute.
- Take away from the heat and add the stock, stirring constantly. Bring back to heat and bring the mixture to a boil, stirring well. Lower the heat and gently simmer, stirring often, for 2 minutes.
- Stir cream into the soup, then reheat lightly, stirring well. Do not bring the soup to a boil. Add pepper and salt to taste, and top with thyme and chopped chives to garnish.

Nutrition Information

- Calories: 295 calories;
- Total Carbohydrate: 16
- Cholesterol: 40
- Protein: 7.1
- Total Fat: 23.8
- Sodium: 624

101.   Creamy Beef Mushroom Barley Soup In A Slow Cooker

Serving: 14 | Prep: 15mins | Ready in:

Ingredients

- 1 pound ground beef
- 1 cup dried shiitake mushrooms
- 5 cups beef broth
- 16 ounces barley
- 1 sweet onion, diced
- 4 cloves garlic, chopped
- 1 teaspoon ground black pepper
- 1 teaspoon salt
- 1/2 teaspoon celery seed
- 1 teaspoon dried parsley
- 1 cup heavy cream (optional)
- 1 cup frozen green beans (optional)

Direction

- In a large skillet, cook and mix ground beef over medium heat for 7 to 10 minutes until evenly browned, crumbly, and no longer pink. Drain excess grease and place beef in a slow cooker.
- Process shiitake mushrooms in a food processor for several times until the mushrooms are cut into small pieces.
- Stir parsley, celery seed, salt, black pepper, garlic, sweet onion, barley, beef broth, and shiitake mushrooms with the ground beef in the slow cooker.
- Cook for 5 hours on Low setting.
- Stir green beans and heavy cream into the soup and cook for 60 minutes more.

Nutrition Information

- Calories: 278 calories;
- Total Fat: 11.3
- Sodium: 479
- Total Carbohydrate: 34.1
- Cholesterol: 44
- Protein: 12.2

102. Creamy Chicken And Mushroom Tart With Nabisco® Chicken In A Biscuit Cracker Crust

Serving: 8 | Prep: 30mins | Ready in:

Ingredients

- Crust:
- 1 3/4 cups crushed chicken-flavored crackers (such as Nabisco® Chicken in a Biscuit)
- 6 tablespoons melted butter
- 1 egg white, beaten
- Filling:
- 3/4 pound boneless chicken breast, cut into small pieces
- salt and ground black pepper to taste
- 1 tablespoon olive oil
- 2 tablespoons butter
- 1/2 cup chopped shallot
- 6 ounces cremini mushrooms, thinly sliced
- 1 tablespoon minced garlic
- 2 teaspoons finely chopped fresh rosemary
- 1 cup heavy whipping cream
- 2 eggs
- 6 tablespoons grated Parmesan cheese, divided
- 1/4 cup finely chopped Italian parsley, divided
- 1/2 teaspoon salt
- 1/2 teaspoon ground black pepper

Direction

- Set the oven at 1750C (3500F) and preheat.
- In a bowl, combine melted butter and cruched cracker together. Press down the mixture and up the sides of a 9 inch springform pan.
- Bake in the prepared oven for 10 minutes. Move out the crust, brush in egg white to seal. Bake for 4 additional minutes. Move out and let it cool at room temperature.
- Flavor chicken with pepper and salt.
- In a large skillet, heat the olive oil over medium heat, cook while stirring chicken for 2 minutes per sides or just until it looks brown. Put it into a plate.
- Decrease the heat to medium low, put in 2 tablespoons butter. In hot butter, cook while stirring shallot for 2 minutes, until it start to soften. Add 1 pinch salt, rosemary, garlic and mushroom, cook and stir for 8 minutes or until mushrooms look tender and juices evaporate.
- In a bowl, whisk together 1/2 teaspoon pepper, 1/2 teaspoon salt, 2 tablespoons parsley, 1/4 cup grated Parmesan cheese, eggs and cream.
- Put the baked crust on a baking tray, place chicken and mushrooms on the top. Top with the egg mixture then the remaining 2 tablespoons Parmesan cheese.
- Bake in the prepared oven for 30 to 35 minutes until it is set in the center and lightly golden on the top. Allow to rest for 10 minutes. Take away the outer ring. Sprinkle 2 tablespoons remaining parsley on the top.

Nutrition Information

- Calories: 454 calories;
- Total Fat: 35.1
- Sodium: 598
- Total Carbohydrate: 18.3
- Cholesterol: 145
- Protein: 16

103. Creamy Coconut Carbonara (Without Milk!)

Serving: 2 | Prep: 20mins | Ready in:

Ingredients

- 4 ounces fettuccine pasta
- 1 tablespoon vegetable oil
- 2 onions, coarsely chopped, or to taste
- 1 tablespoon minced garlic
- 1 cup coconut milk, divided
- 1/2 cup fresh oyster mushrooms, diced small

- 1/3 cup thinly sliced red bell pepper
- 1/3 cup thinly sliced green bell pepper
- salt and ground black pepper to taste
- 2 spring onions, sliced, or more to taste
- 1 tablespoon chopped fresh basil

Direction

- Put big pot of lightly salted water on rolling boil. Mix fettuccine in and boil again. Cook on medium heat for 8 minutest till tender yet firm to bite; drain.
- Heat oil in big saucepan on high heat. Add garlic and onion; cook for 2-4 minutes till slightly browned, constantly mixing. Add green and red bell pepper, oyster mushrooms and 1/2 cup coconut milk. Mix and cook for 3-5 minutes till just tender.
- Mix leftover 1/2 cup coconut milk and fettuccine into saucepan; season with pepper and salt. Mix basil and spring onions in. Cook for 2-3 minutes longer till sauce coats fettuccine and is creamy, uncovered.

Nutrition Information

- Calories: 601 calories;
- Total Fat: 32.6
- Sodium: 112
- Total Carbohydrate: 70.4
- Cholesterol: 0
- Protein: 13.7

---

104. Creamy Keto Cauliflower Risotto

Serving: 4 | Prep: 15mins | Ready in:

Ingredients

- 1/4 cup ghee
- 1/2 onion, finely chopped
- 1 clove garlic, minced
- 1 head cauliflower, grated

- 1 cup sliced fresh mushrooms
- 1/2 cup heavy whipping cream
- 1 cup grated Parmesan cheese
- 1/2 teaspoon salt
- 1/4 teaspoon ground black pepper
- 1/4 teaspoon ground nutmeg

Direction

- In a skillet, melt the ghee on medium heat. Add in garlic and onion and let it cook for about 3 minutes until it becomes soft. Stir in grated cauliflower and let it cook for an additional 3 minutes. Add the mushrooms and let it cook for about 3 minutes until it becomes soft.
- Mix nutmeg, pepper, salt, Parmesan cheese and heavy cream into the skillet. Let it cook for 5-7 minutes on medium heat until it becomes creamy.

Nutrition Information

- Calories: 350 calories;
- Sodium: 653
- Total Carbohydrate: 11.8
- Cholesterol: 91
- Protein: 12.1
- Total Fat: 29.8

---

105. Creamy Mushroom Soup

Serving: 4 | Prep: 10mins | Ready in:

Ingredients

- 1/4 cup butter
- 1 cup chopped shiitake mushrooms
- 1 cup chopped portobello mushrooms
- 2 shallots, chopped
- 2 tablespoons all-purpose flour
- 1 (14.5 ounce) can chicken broth
- 1 cup half-and-half
- salt and pepper to taste

- 1 pinch ground cinnamon (optional)

Direction

- In a large saucepan, melt butter over medium high heat. Sauté for about 5 minutes or until tender the Portobello mushrooms, shallots and shiitake mushrooms. Add the flour until smooth. Stir in chicken broth little by little. Stir while cooking for 5 minutes, until soup is thick and bubbly.
- Mix in the half-and-half; add salt, pepper and cinnamon to taste. Simmer the soup but do not bring to a boil.

Nutrition Information

- Calories: 234 calories;
- Total Carbohydrate: 13.3
- Cholesterol: 53
- Protein: 4.4
- Total Fat: 18.6
- Sodium: 119

---

106. Creamy Pork With Sour Cream Sauce

Serving: 8 | Prep: 15mins | Ready in:

Ingredients

- 1 egg, lightly beaten
- 1 tablespoon water
- 1/2 teaspoon crushed dried rosemary
- 1/4 teaspoon black pepper
- 1 pinch garlic powder
- 3 tablespoons vegetable oil
- 3 pounds pork cube steaks
- 1 cup seasoned bread crumbs
- 2 tablespoons butter
- 3/4 pound fresh mushrooms, coarsley chopped
- 1 (10.5 ounce) can condensed cream of chicken soup

- 1 cup sour cream
- 1/2 cup chicken broth

Direction

- Preheat an oven to 165°C/325°F.
- Mix garlic powder, black pepper, rosemary, water and egg in a shallow dish.
- Heat vegetable oil in a big skillet on medium heat. In egg mixture, dip pork steaks; coat in breadcrumbs. Brown pork for 5 minutes per side; remove. Put in a 9x13-in. baking dish.
- Heat butter in the same skillet on medium heat and mix mushrooms in; cook till tender. Mix chicken broth, sour cream and soup in; warm through. Put over pork; use aluminum foil to cover the dish.
- In the preheated oven, bake for 1 hour.

Nutrition Information

- Calories: 685 calories;
- Total Carbohydrate: 15.8
- Cholesterol: 163
- Protein: 35.7
- Total Fat: 52.9
- Sodium: 652

---

107. Creamy Seafood Noodles

Serving: 5 | Prep: 20mins | Ready in:

Ingredients

- 1 large onion, diced
- 3 cloves garlic, minced
- 1 cup fresh sliced mushrooms
- 1/2 pound uncooked scallops
- 3 cups water
- 2 (3 ounce) packages Oriental flavored ramen noodles
- 2 (3 ounce) packages shrimp flavored ramen noodles
- 2 tablespoons sour cream

- salt and pepper to taste
- 1/2 pound cooked medium shrimp
- 1/2 pound imitation crabmeat

Direction

- In a butter/lightly oiled skillet, sauté garlic and onions on medium heat till tender for 5 minutes. Add scallops and mushrooms. Sauté for 2 minutes more. Take off heat. Put aside. Don't overcook scallops.
- Boil water in a big saucepan on high heat. Add ramen noodles. Boil, lower heat if needed, for 3 minutes. Mix reserved scallop mixture, sour cream and soup flavor packets in. Season to taste with pepper and salt. Lower heat to low. Simmer it for 5 minutes.
- Add crab and cooked shrimp. Let it heat through; serve.

Nutrition Information

- Calories: 447 calories;
- Total Carbohydrate: 56.1
- Cholesterol: 96
- Protein: 26.4
- Total Fat: 12.7
- Sodium: 1804

108.   Creamy Spinach Mushroom Risotto

Serving: 4 | Prep: 10mins | Ready in:

Ingredients

- 2 tablespoons butter
- 1/2 cup sliced mushrooms
- 1/2 cup chopped onion
- 2 1/2 cups water
- 1 (8 ounce) package ZATARAIN'S® Yellow Rice
- 1/2 cup heavy cream
- 1/2 cup shredded Monterey Jack cheese

- 1 cup baby spinach leaves

Direction

- In medium saucepan, melt butter on medium high heat. Add onion and mushrooms; mix and cook till onion starts to soften for 2 minutes.
- Mix in Rice Mix and water. Boil, occasionally mixing. Lower heat to low; cover and simmer for 20 minutes. Mix in cheese and cream; cover and cook till rice is tender for 5 minutes more. Mix in spinach. Take it off the heat. Let stand for 5 minutes. Before serving, fluff using a fork.

Nutrition Information

- Calories: 420 calories;
- Sodium: 1101
- Total Carbohydrate: 46.9
- Cholesterol: 69
- Protein: 4.8
- Total Fat: 21.6

109.   Creamy Spinach Tortellini

Serving: 4 | Prep: 15mins | Ready in:

Ingredients

- 1 (9 ounce) package refrigerated cheese tortellini
- 2 tablespoons Butter
- 1 small onion, chopped
- 1 (8 ounce) package cream cheese
- 1/2 cup grated Parmesan cheese
- 1/2 cup milk
- fresh mushrooms, sliced
- 1 (10 ounce) package frozen chopped spinach, thawed and drained
- cherry tomatoes, halved

Direction

- Cook the tortellini following the package instructions.
- Grab a large skillet and heat butter on medium heat. Stir in the onion; cook until translucent and soft. Mix in spinach, mushrooms, milk, parmesan and cream cheese.
- Slowly mix in cherry tomatoes and tortellini with the skillet contents. Warm thoroughly and serve.

Nutrition Information

- Calories: 546 calories;
- Total Fat: 35
- Sodium: 671
- Total Carbohydrate: 40.2
- Cholesterol: 116
- Protein: 21.8

---

110. Creamy Spinach And Zucchini Soup

Serving: 4 | Prep: 20mins | Ready in:

Ingredients

- 1 large onion, chopped
- 6 cups water, divided
- 3 potatoes, chopped
- 3 zucchini, sliced
- 1 tablespoon low-sodium soy sauce
- 2 cups tightly packed spinach leaves
- ground black pepper to taste
- 1/3 cup sliced fresh enoki mushrooms

Direction

- In a big saucepan, mix together 1/2 cup of water and onion over medium-high heat, stir and cook for 3 minutes until the onion is tender.

- Add the leftover water to the saucepan; add soy sauce, zucchini, and potatoes. Boil the water, lower the heat to low, put a cover on the saucepan, and cook for 35 minutes.
- Mix spinach into the soup, use black pepper to season. Keep cooking for another 2 minutes; take the saucepan away from heat.
- Put the soup in a blender to blend in batches until totally pureed. Put the pureed soup back to the saucepan and put on medium-low heat.
- Mix mushrooms into the pureed soup, cook for 5 minutes until the mushrooms are thoroughly warmed.

Nutrition Information

- Calories: 162 calories;
- Sodium: 176
- Total Carbohydrate: 36
- Cholesterol: 0
- Protein: 5.6
- Total Fat: 0.4

---

111. Creolized Stuffed Chicken Breasts

Serving: 3 | Prep: 5mins | Ready in:

Ingredients

- 1/2 pound smoked sausage, sliced thinly
- 1/2 pound fresh button mushrooms
- 3 tablespoons chopped green onion
- 1 teaspoon minced garlic
- 4 tablespoons blue cheese salad dressing, divided
- 3 skinless, boneless chicken breasts
- 1 tablespoon Cajun-style seasoning

Direction

- For the stuffing: In a big frying pan, brown sausage over medium-high heat. When the sausage begins to turn brown, put in

mushrooms and sauté for 5 minutes, and then add garlic and green onion and sauté for 2 minutes more. Take the stuffing mixture away from heat, add to a food processor and add 1 tablespoon salad dressing. Gradually blend in the processor until roughly chopped.
- Turn the oven to 375°F (190°C) to preheat.
- On each side of the chicken breasts, slice 2-in. slits and fill with as much stuffing as the breast can contain. Use Cajun-style seasoning to generously season the breasts on both sides and sear in a hot frying pan for 1-2 minutes each side, and then put in a lightly oil-coated 9x13-in. baking dish. Put the leftover 3 tablespoons salad dressing and the remaining stuffing on top.
- Bake at 375°F (175°C) until the juices run clear and the chicken has thoroughly cooked, about 30 minutes.

Nutrition Information

- Calories: 553 calories;
- Total Fat: 36.5
- Sodium: 1914
- Total Carbohydrate: 7.5
- Cholesterol: 123
- Protein: 47.7

---

112. Crepes With Spinach, Bacon And Mushroom Filling

Serving: 4 | Prep: 35mins | Ready in:

Ingredients

- 1 recipe Basic Crepes
- 6 slices bacon
- 1 tablespoon unsalted butter
- 1/2 pound fresh mushrooms, sliced
- 3 tablespoons unsalted butter
- 1/4 cup all-purpose flour
- 1 cup milk
- 1 (10 ounce) package frozen chopped spinach, thawed and drained
- 1 tablespoon chopped fresh parsley
- 2 tablespoons grated Parmesan cheese
- salt and pepper to taste
- 2/3 cup chicken broth
- 2 eggs
- 1/2 cup lemon juice
- salt and pepper to taste

Direction

- Prepare the basic crepes recipe based on the directions. Use wax paper to separate each crepe and keep it warm until ready to serve.
- In a big, deep skillet, put the bacon in. Over medium high heat, cook the bacon until brown evenly. Strain, break into pieces and reserve. Keep about 1 tablespoon drippings on the skillet then add in sautéed mushrooms and 1 tablespoon butter.
- Melt 3 tablespoons butter over medium heat in a separate saucepan. Add in 1/4 cup flour, mixing regularly until it forms a smooth paste. Slowly mix in 1 cup milk, mixing regularly until it forms a smooth thick gravy. Stir in pepper, salt, Parmesan cheese, parsley, spinach, mushroom and bacon. Let it cook for about 10 minutes until somewhat thick.
- Place broth in a saucepan and make it boil. Whisk together in a small bowl the lemon juice and eggs. Temper together the broth and eggs mixing regularly to cook the eggs but not to scramble it. (Cook the eggs to 170°F). Then again, add pepper and salt to taste.
- Stuff each crepe with meat filling and spinach, roll up and put warm egg sauce on top.

Nutrition Information

- Calories: 445 calories;
- Total Fat: 35.6
- Sodium: 785
- Total Carbohydrate: 17.9
- Cholesterol: 160
- Protein: 15.9

113. Crispy Tofu And Bacon Wraps

Serving: 10 | Prep: 30mins | Ready in:

Ingredients

- 1 (16 ounce) package tofu, drained and cubed
- 1 yellow onion, roughly chopped
- 6 large green onions, chopped
- 1 medium red bell pepper, coarsely chopped
- 8 cloves garlic
- 20 mushrooms
- 1 tomato, coarsely chopped
- 3/4 cup crumbled cooked bacon
- 1 tablespoon fish sauce
- 2 tablespoons red wine
- 1/4 cup chopped fresh Italian parsley
- 1/4 teaspoon salt
- 1/2 teaspoon black pepper
- 1/4 teaspoon curry powder
- 1/4 teaspoon mustard powder
- 1/4 teaspoon dill weed
- 1/2 teaspoon ground ginger
- 1 (12 ounce) package egg roll wrappers
- canola oil for frying

Direction

- In the bowl of a processor, combine bacon, tomato, mushrooms, garlic, red pepper, green onion, yellow onion, and tofu. Season with ginger, dill, mustard powder, curry powder, pepper, salt, parsley, red wine, and fish sauce; process the mixture until smooth.
- In a work surface, place an egg roll wrapper with a corner pointing towards you. Ladle 1-2 tablespoons of tofu puree between the center and bottom corner of the wrapper. Fold the closest corner over the filling, then fold the two sides. Moisten the furthest corner with some water and roll up carefully.
- In a large pot, heat a few inches of canola oil to 350°F (175°C). Fry a few tofu wraps at a time until center is cooked and outside turns golden brown. Transfer to paper towels to drain and serve hot.

Nutrition Information

- Calories: 296 calories;
- Sodium: 634
- Total Carbohydrate: 26.7
- Cholesterol: 9
- Protein: 12.7
- Total Fat: 16

114. Crustless Spinach, Mushroom, And Tomato Quiche (Keto)

Serving: 8 | Prep: 15mins | Ready in:

Ingredients

- cooking spray
- 1 tablespoon butter
- 1 onion, sliced
- 1/2 cup halved cherry tomatoes
- 1 cup sliced mushrooms
- 2 cups fresh spinach
- 1 cup heavy cream
- 3 eggs
- 1/2 teaspoon salt
- 1/4 teaspoon ground black pepper
- 1/4 teaspoon ground nutmeg
- 1 cup shredded Gouda cheese

Direction

- Set an oven to preheat to 190°C (375°F). Use cooking spray to grease a 9-inch pie plate.
- In a medium cast-iron frying pan, melt the butter on medium heat. Add onion, then cook and stir for about 5 minutes, until it becomes translucent and tender. Stir in cherry tomatoes for about 3 minutes, until it becomes a bit tender. Add mushrooms and let it cook for

about 3 minutes, until soft. Stir in spinach, then cook for a minute more.

- In a bowl, whisk together the nutmeg, pepper, salt, eggs and cream.
- In the prepped pie plate, spread 1/2 of the Gouda cheese, then put spinach mixture on top. Cover it with egg mixture then sprinkle the remaining Gouda cheese on top.
- Let it bake in the preheated oven for about 25 minutes, until the top turns golden and the eggs are set.

Nutrition Information

- Calories: 208 calories;
- Total Fat: 18.6
- Sodium: 324
- Total Carbohydrate: 3.7
- Cholesterol: 131
- Protein: 7.5

115. Decadent Omelette

Serving: 2 | Prep: 10mins | Ready in:

Ingredients

- 2 tablespoons truffle oil or olive oil
- 3 eggs
- 1 truffle*
- Grated Parmesan cheese (optional)

Direction

- In a nonstick 8 inches pan, heat olive (or truffle) oil.
- In a bowl, beat the eggs until fluffy; pour into prepared pan and cook until the edges set.
- Slightly push the edges toward the center and allow raw egg to fill edges. Repeat until omelet is set.
- Add cheese over one half of the omelet. Flip the other half to cover the filling. Slide onto a plate.

- Serve with shaved truffle on top.

Nutrition Information

- Calories: 257 calories;
- Sodium: 182
- Total Carbohydrate: 1.1
- Cholesterol: 283
- Protein: 11.5
- Total Fat: 22.9

116. Diane's Chicken Dish

Serving: 6 | Prep: 20mins | Ready in:

Ingredients

- 1/4 cup vinegar
- 1/4 cup olive oil
- 1/4 cup water
- 1 (.7 ounce) package dry Italian salad dressing mix (such as Good Seasons®)
- 1 pound boneless chicken pieces, cut into bite-size chunks
- 1 tablespoon butter
- 1 large onion, chopped
- 1 large green bell pepper, chopped
- 1 (10 ounce) package sliced crimini mushrooms
- 1 large tomato, chopped
- 2 cups shredded sharp Cheddar cheese

Direction

- In a bowl, stir Italian dressing mix, water, olive oil and vinegar together. Whisk in chicken; let the chicken marinate when preparing the rest of ingredients.
- Heat butter on medium high heat in a skillet. Whisk in bell pepper and onion; cook and whisk for roughly 5 minutes till onion softens and becomes translucent. Take chicken out of marinade with a slotted spoon, and move into the skillet; save rest of the marinade. Cook and

whisk chicken for 3-5 minutes till not pink in middle anymore

- Whisk in mushrooms; cook and whisk for roughly 2 minutes till they start to become tender. Put in the reserved marinade and tomato, and then drizzle the cheese over the top. Don't whisk. Keep covered and let it simmer over low heat for roughly 20 minutes till the chicken softens and the cheese melts. Let the dish stand for several minutes prior to serving.

Nutrition Information

- Calories: 370 calories;
- Protein: 26.9
- Total Fat: 25.1
- Sodium: 832
- Total Carbohydrate: 8.5
- Cholesterol: 84

---

117. Dynamite Halibut

Serving: 6 | Prep: 15mins | Ready in:

Ingredients

- 2 pounds halibut, cut into bite size pieces
- 1 cup mayonnaise
- 1 teaspoon fresh lemon juice
- 3/4 teaspoon chile-garlic sauce
- 1/2 teaspoon white sugar
- 1/2 teaspoon soy sauce
- 1/8 teaspoon sesame oil
- 4 cups thinly sliced mushrooms
- 2 cups thinly sliced onions
- 1 lemon, cut in half
- Kosher salt, to taste
- 1 tablespoon sesame seeds
- 3/4 cup sliced green onions

Direction

- Preheat an oven to 190°C/375°F.

- In middle of oven, put an oven rack.
- Line aluminum foil on baking sheet. Put a layer of cooking spray.
- On prepped baking sheet, put halibut pieces so all pieces are touching.
- In a bowl, mix sesame oil, soy sauce, sugar, chili garlic sauce, lemon juice and mayonnaise. Fold onion and mushrooms into mayonnaise mixture.
- Spread mushroom mixture on halibut pieces.
- Over mushroom mixture, squeeze 1/2 lemon. Sprinkle kosher salt on top.
- In preheated oven, bake for 15-20 minutes till nearly opaque. Take baking sheet out of oven.
- Raise oven rack with baking sheet to the following highest level switch of the oven to broil.
- Keep cooking fish under the broiler for 10 minutes till top is browned.
- Evenly squeeze leftover 1/2 lemon on fish.
- Sprinkle green onions and sesame seeds on top.

Nutrition Information

- Calories: 477 calories;
- Total Fat: 33
- Sodium: 420
- Total Carbohydrate: 8.7
- Cholesterol: 70
- Protein: 35.6

---

118. Easier Chicken Marsala

Serving: 4 | Prep: 10mins | Ready in:

Ingredients

- 1/4 cup all-purpose flour
- 1/2 teaspoon garlic salt
- 1/4 teaspoon ground black pepper
- 1/2 teaspoon dried oregano
- 4 boneless, skinless chicken breast halves
- 1 tablespoon olive oil

- 1 tablespoon butter
- 1 cup sliced fresh mushrooms
- 1/2 cup Marsala wine

Direction

- Stir oregano, pepper, garlic salt and flour together in a medium bowl. Coat the chicken lightly with the mixture.
- In a large skillet over medium heat, heat butter and olive oil. In the skillet, fry the chicken until it turns light brown on one side or for 2 minutes. Turn the chicken over; add mushrooms. Cook until the second side of chicken turns light brown, about 2 minutes. Stir mushrooms to cook them evenly.
- Pour Marsala wine over the chicken. Cover the skillet, lower the heat to low; simmer until chicken is no longer pink and juices run clear or for 10 minutes.

Nutrition Information

- Calories: 286 calories;
- Total Fat: 10.1
- Sodium: 313
- Total Carbohydrate: 11.4
- Cholesterol: 80
- Protein: 27.9

119. Eastern Market Ramen Noodles

Serving: 1 | Prep: 20mins | Ready in:

Ingredients

- 5 green beans, trimmed, or more to taste
- 1 teaspoon olive oil
- 1 tablespoon chopped garlic
- 2 cups chicken broth
- 2 cups water
- 1 red finger chile pepper, sliced
- 2 cloves garlic, sliced

- 1 tablespoon soy sauce
- 1 tablespoon fish sauce
- 1 tablespoon ground black pepper
- 1 teaspoon rice wine vinegar
- 1 (3 ounce) package Korean ramen noodles (such as Nature is Delicious®)
- 1 (3 ounce) package enoki mushrooms, halved
- 3 scallions, cut into 1-inch pieces, or more to taste
- 1/3 cup whole Thai basil leaves
- 1/4 cup whole cilantro leaves

Direction

- Boil a big pot of lightly-salted water. Put in the green beans and cook, while uncovering, for roughly 2 minutes till becoming soft. Drain in a colander and wash in the cold water to stop cooking process. Drain.
- Heat the olive oil on medium heat in a small-sized skillet. Put in the chopped garlic; fry, whisk frequently, for 2-3 minutes till golden-brown. Take out of the heat.
- In a pot, mix sliced garlic, red chile pepper, water and chicken broth. Boil; let it simmer for roughly 3 minutes or till the flavors are combined. Whisk in the rice wine vinegar, black pepper, fish sauce and soy sauce; let it simmer for 2 minutes.
- Whisk the seasoning packet included in package, ramen noodles and green beans to the pot. Cook for roughly 3 minutes till the noodles become soft. Whisk in the enoki mushrooms; let it simmer for roughly 2 minutes till becoming soft. Put in the scallions; cook for roughly 60 seconds till wilted.
- Ladle the broth, mushrooms, green beans and noodles to a bowl. Add the cilantro leaves and basil on top. Drizzle the fried garlic over the top.

Nutrition Information

- Calories: 495 calories;
- Total Carbohydrate: 85
- Cholesterol: 10
- Protein: 23.4

- Total Fat: 7.8
- Sodium: 4865

---

120. Easy Baked Cheese And Vegetable Twist

Serving: 16 | Prep: 20mins | Ready in:

Ingredients

- 2 eggs
- 4 ounces PHILADELPHIA Cream Cheese, softened
- 1/2 cup KRAFT 2% Milk Shredded Italian* Three Cheese Blend
- 3 cups frozen broccoli cuts, thawed, drained
- 1/2 cup fresh mushrooms, cut into quarters
- 1/2 cup cherry tomatoes, cut in half
- 4 green onions, sliced
- 2 (8 ounce) cans refrigerated crescent dinner rolls

Direction

- Heat oven to 375°F.
- In large bowl, mix the first three ingredients until blended well. Mix in next four ingredients.
- Unroll the dough; then divide into 16 triangles. Place on foil-covered baking sheet in 11-in. circle, the short sides of triangles overlapping in the middle and the triangles points toward outside. (In middle of circle should have a 5-in. diameter opening). Put the cheese mixture onto the dough near middle of the circle. Bring the outside points of triangles up over the filling and cover the filling by tucking under the dough in middle of the ring.
- Bake until filling is heated through and crust turns golden brown, about 35-40 mins.

Nutrition Information

121. Easy Beef Stroganoff In The Slow Cooker

Serving: 5 | Prep: 10mins | Ready in:

Ingredients

- 1 1/3 pounds cubed beef stew meat
- 2 cups fresh mushrooms, thickly sliced
- 1 (10.75 ounce) can condensed cream of mushroom soup
- 1 cup milk
- 2 onions, chopped
- 2 tablespoons Worcestershire sauce
- 6 ounces herb and garlic-flavored cream cheese
- 1 cup fusilli pasta
- 1/4 cup sour cream (optional)

Direction

- In a slow cooker, mix Worcestershire sauce, onions, milk, mushrooms, beef and cream of mushroom soup together.
- Cook for 3 to 4 hours on a high setting and for 5 to 7 hours on low. Whisk in the cream cheese until it is thoroughly dissolved then cook for another hour.
- Boil a big pot filled with lightly salted water and put the fusilli. Cook for about 12 minutes until it's firm to the bite yet tender, stirring every now and then. Drain the noodles and Place the stroganoff over fusilli and garnish with sour cream. Serve.

Nutrition Information

- Calories: 450 calories;
- Sodium: 738
- Total Carbohydrate: 23.9
- Cholesterol: 106
- Protein: 29.4
- Total Fat: 25.3

122. Easy Chanterelle Mushrooms In Cream Sauce

Serving: 4 | Prep: 20mins | Ready in:

Ingredients

- 2 tablespoons butter
- 3 shallots, minced
- 3 cups chanterelle mushrooms, finely chopped
- 1/2 cup heavy whipping cream
- 1 1/2 teaspoons all-purpose flour
- 1/2 teaspoon cold water, or as needed
- 1/2 teaspoon salt
- 1/2 teaspoon herbes de Provence, or to taste
- fresh ground black pepper, to taste

Direction

- Melt the butter on medium heat in a pan and cook the shallots for roughly 5 minutes till becoming tender and translucent. Put in the chanterelle mushrooms and cook for 2 more minutes. Put in the cream and cook for 5-10 minutes till the mushrooms soften.
- Whisk together the water and flour and put to the mushrooms. Boil. Use the pepper, herbes de Provence and salt to season.

Nutrition Information

- Calories: 227 calories;
- Total Fat: 16.8
- Sodium: 372
- Total Carbohydrate: 14
- Cholesterol: 56
- Protein: 4.2

123. Easy Cheesy Cream Of Broccoli Soup

Serving: 3 | Prep: | Ready in:

Ingredients

- 1 (10 ounce) package frozen chopped broccoli
- 1 (10.75 ounce) can condensed cream of mushroom soup
- 1 1/4 cups milk
- 8 ounces processed cheese food (eg. Velveeta)
- salt and pepper to taste

Direction

- Prepare broccoli as directed on package. Drain off any excess liquid.
- Add 1 can of milk and cream of mushroom soup to broccoli. Stir over low heat until thoroughly heated. Stir in cheese until melted. Season with pepper and salt. Serve the soup right away.

Nutrition Information

- Calories: 331 calories;
- Sodium: 1910
- Total Carbohydrate: 24.9
- Cholesterol: 39
- Protein: 21.9
- Total Fat: 15.9

124. Easy Chicken With Mushrooms And Zucchini In Cream Sauce

Serving: 2 | Prep: 10mins | Ready in:

Ingredients

- 1 tablespoon butter
- 2 (5 ounce) boneless, skinless chicken breasts, cubed
- salt and freshly ground pepper to taste
- 1 tablespoon olive oil
- 4 green onions, chopped
- 2 green zucchini, cut in half lengthwise and into 1/4-inch slices

- 8 large fresh mushrooms, sliced
- 1 tablespoon all-purpose flour
- 3/4 cup heavy whipping cream
- 1 tablespoon chopped fresh parsley

Direction

- Take a skillet and melt butter on medium heat then cook chicken for 5-7 minutes until it becomes brown while frequently stirring. Use salt and pepper to season; then transfer chicken onto a plate. Keep it warm by covering it with foil or a bowl.
- Use the same skillet to heat olive oil on medium heat; then cook green onions for 2 minutes until they become soft. Add in the zucchini slices and cook for 5 minutes until they softened. Mix in mushrooms. Put chicken back in skillet and drizzle on flour. Mix in cream and cook for 3-5 minutes until the sauce starts to thicken. Top with chopped parsley.

Nutrition Information

- Calories: 671 calories;
- Total Carbohydrate: 17.9
- Cholesterol: 224
- Protein: 39.7
- Total Fat: 50.8
- Sodium: 257

125.   Easy Mushroom Spread

Serving: 5 | Prep: 5mins | Ready in:

Ingredients

- 2 tablespoons butter
- 1/2 teaspoon fresh rosemary
- 4 cloves garlic, minced
- 3 cups chopped fresh mushrooms
- 1/4 cup fresh parsley
- 3 tablespoons vegetable stock
- 1 teaspoon cornstarch

- 1 tablespoon Scotch whiskey

Direction

- Melt the butter in a big skillet on medium heat and sauté the garlic and rosemary until it becomes tender. Mix in the mushrooms and sauté until the juices run. Add the parsley and mix from time to time to avoid sticking. Once the mushrooms become tender, mix in the stock and stir well prior to adding the cornstarch. Let it cook for 1-2 minutes, then add the whiskey and let it cook for another minute.

Nutrition Information

- Calories: 65 calories;
- Sodium: 46
- Total Carbohydrate: 3.3
- Cholesterol: 12
- Protein: 1.1
- Total Fat: 4.8

126.   Easy Portobello Mushroom Saute

Serving: 2 | Prep: 10mins | Ready in:

Ingredients

- 3 tablespoons olive oil, divided
- 1 1/2 tablespoons garlic flavored olive oil
- 1/4 onion, cut into chunks
- 2 portobello mushroom caps, sliced
- salt and black pepper to taste
- freshly grated Parmesan
- freshly grated Asiago cheese

Direction

- In a skillet, warm up 1 1/2 tablespoons garlic-flavored olive oil and 1 1/2 tablespoons olive oil over medium heat. Stir in mushrooms and onions; reduce the heat to low; cook until the onions are black around the edges and the mushrooms are tender and blackened. (Add more olive oil if needed.) Turn the heat off, then scatter with 1 1/2 tablespoons olive oil, and season with pepper and salt. Generously sprinkle with Asiago and Parmesan cheeses.

Nutrition Information

- Calories: 349 calories;
- Sodium: 166
- Total Carbohydrate: 7.2
- Cholesterol: 10
- Protein: 6.6
- Total Fat: 34

127.   Eggs Over Toast

Serving: 8 | Prep: 15mins | Ready in:

Ingredients

- 2 (10.75 ounce) cans condensed cream of mushroom soup, undiluted
- 6 hard-cooked eggs, sliced
- 1 (16 ounce) package frozen mixed vegetables, thawed
- 2 cups milk
- salt and pepper to taste
- 8 slices white bread, toasted

Direction

- Mix together the pepper, salt, milk, mixed vegetables, sliced eggs and cream of mushroom soup in a big saucepan. Let the mixture simmer over medium heat and continue to cook until vegetables are heated completely. To serve, arrange the toast on the plates, and scoop the sauce on top.

Nutrition Information

- Calories: 256 calories;

- Total Fat: 10.8
- Sodium: 760
- Total Carbohydrate: 28.7
- Cholesterol: 164
- Protein: 11.8

128.   Empty Wallet Casserole

Serving: 5 | Prep: 20mins | Ready in:

Ingredients

- 1 pound ground beef
- salt and pepper to taste
- 1 1/2 teaspoons ground cumin
- 2 teaspoons poultry seasoning
- 2 teaspoons minced garlic
- 2 teaspoons dried thyme
- 2 tablespoons butter
- 1 small onion, sliced into thin rings
- 2 cups sliced fresh mushrooms
- 3 large potatoes, thinly sliced
- 1 (10.75 ounce) can condensed cream of chicken soup
- 20 saltine crackers, crushed
- 1 pinch paprika, for garnish

Direction

- Set the oven to 350°F (175°C) and start preheating.
- Break ground beef into crumbles into a large skillet over medium heat. Season with thyme, poultry seasoning, garlic, cumin, pepper and salt. Cook while stirring to crumble until browned evenly. Drain; place on a 9x13 inch baking dish, or large casserole dish.
- Place 2 layers of potato slices over ground beef, season each with pepper and salt. Over medium heat, in the skillet, melt butter; sauté mushrooms and onions until tender. Spread over the top of potatoes.
- Stir just enough water into the soup so that you can pour it; scoop over the top of casserole, be sure that you spread it out

evenly. Scatter cracker crumbs over top; top with paprika. Use aluminum foil to cover the dish.

- Bake in the prepared oven for about an hour until potatoes become soft. Get rid of aluminum foil; place back to the oven for about 10 minutes until top turns brown.

Nutrition Information

- Calories: 500 calories;
- Total Fat: 20.7
- Sodium: 631
- Total Carbohydrate: 55.6
- Cholesterol: 72
- Protein: 23.9

---

129.   Farro With Wild Mushrooms

Serving: 6 | Prep: 15mins | Ready in:

Ingredients

- 1/2 ounce dried porcini mushrooms
- 2 tablespoons olive oil
- 10 brown mushroom caps, diced
- salt to taste
- 1/2 onion, diced small
- 2 cloves garlic, minced
- 1 cup pearled farro, rinsed, or more to taste
- 3 cups chicken stock, divided
- 2 tablespoons creme fraiche
- 2 tablespoons chopped fresh flat-leaf parsley
- freshly ground black pepper to taste
- 2 tablespoons freshly grated Parmigiano-Reggiano cheese, or to taste

Direction

- Arrange porcini mushrooms in a bowl and pour in warm water to cover; submerge for 20 to 30 minutes until mushrooms are reconstituted. Drain and chop mushrooms.

- Heat olive oil over medium-high heat in a pot. Sauté brown mushrooms with a dash of salt in hot oil, for 5 to 10 minutes until moisture evaporates and mushrooms turn golden slightly for 2-4 minutes.
- Stir onion into mushrooms. Sauté for 5 to 7 minutes until golden and transparent. Add garlic; sauté for another minute until aromatic.
- Pour in farro into the mushroom mixture; mix until coated with olive oil. Raise heat to high; pour in 1 cup chicken broth and sprinkle with a pinch of salt to mushroom mixture; bring to a boil. Turn the heat to medium low; simmer, covered for about 10 minutes, stirring once, until liquid is absorbed.
- Raise the heat to high and mix the remaining chicken broth into farro mixture; bring to a boil; turn the heat to medium low; simmer, covered for about 15 minutes, stir sometimes, until farro is just softened. Uncover the pan; keep simmering for about 15 minutes more until a desired doneness of farro is reached.
- Turn the heat to low; mix in parsley and creme fraiche into the farro mixture. Sprinkle with black pepper and salt to season. Mix in Parmigiano-Reggiano cheese into farro and pour into bowls.

Nutrition Information

- Calories: 193 calories;
- Total Fat: 8.2
- Sodium: 401
- Total Carbohydrate: 27.8
- Cholesterol: 9
- Protein: 6.5

---

130.   Fettuccine Pasta With Portobello Mushrooms

Serving: 3 | Prep: 10mins | Ready in:

Ingredients

- 1 (12 ounce) box dry fettuccine pasta
- 2 tablespoons olive oil
- 1/2 onion, minced
- 1 clove garlic, minced
- 1 (8 ounce) package portobello mushrooms, thickly sliced
- 1/4 cup butter
- 3 tablespoons vegetable stock
- 1/2 bunch fresh spinach, finely chopped
- 1 sprig fresh rosemary, chopped, or to taste
- salt and freshly ground black pepper to taste
- 3 tablespoons grated Parmesan cheese

Direction

- Prepare a large pot and pour in mildly salted water; bring it to a rolling boil. Cook fettuccine at a boil for 8 minutes until soft but firm to the bite. Drain.
- In the meantime, on medium heat, heat olive oil in a skillet and cook garlic and onion for 4 minutes until tender. Put in butter and mushrooms; cook while stirring for 3 minutes until tender. Pour in vegetable stock and cook on high heat for 2 minutes until stock has reduced. Put in rosemary and spinach. Sprinkle with pepper and salt to season. Stir to blend. Put in cooked linguine and toss everything to blend well. Cook for another 2 to 3 minutes.
- Top pasta with Parmesan cheese and mix properly. Take out from heat and serve in warmed bowls.

Nutrition Information

- Calories: 686 calories;
- Total Fat: 28.8
- Sodium: 309
- Total Carbohydrate: 90.8
- Cholesterol: 45
- Protein: 21

131.   Fettuccini Al Fungi

Serving: 6 | Prep: | Ready in:

Ingredients

- 1 pound crimini mushrooms, sliced
- 2 fresh shiitake mushrooms, stemmed and sliced
- 1 large portobello mushrooms, sliced
- 2 cloves crushed garlic
- 1/4 cup olive oil
- 2 tablespoons pesto
- 1 cup milk
- 2 tablespoons cream cheese
- 12 ounces dry fettuccine pasta

Direction

- Cook the pasta following the package directions.
- While waiting for the pasta, cook and sauté garlic and mushrooms in olive oil over low heat until tender. Stir in milk, cream cheese, and pesto mix. Adjust the heat to medium and bring the mixture to boil. Reduce the heat and let it simmer, stirring constantly until the mixture is thick and the cream cheese melts completely.
- Drain the cooked pasta. Coat the pasta with the prepared sauce, and then serve.

Nutrition Information

- Calories: 377 calories;
- Total Fat: 15.2
- Sodium: 105
- Total Carbohydrate: 47.2
- Cholesterol: 10
- Protein: 14.1

132.　Flaky Crescent Mushroom Turnovers

Serving: 8 | Prep: 20mins | Ready in:

Ingredients

- 1/4 pound fresh mushrooms, coarsely chopped
- 2 tablespoons minced fresh parsley
- 2 tablespoons minced onion
- 3 tablespoons butter, divided
- 1 (8 ounce) can refrigerated crescent roll dough
- 2 1/2 tablespoons grated Parmesan cheese
- 2 tablespoons sesame seeds

Direction

- Preheat an oven to 190 °C or 375 °F.
- In a medium saucepan, gently cook and mix onion, parsley and mushrooms in 2 tablespoons of butter over medium heat till soft. Let drain and reserve.
- Split dough into 4 rectangles. Halve each rectangle, creating 8 squares, and set on a big baking sheet. On every square, put 1 tablespoon mushroom mixture. Put 1 teaspoon Parmesan cheese on top of every square. Fold squares forming triangles.
- Melt the rest of butter in a small saucepan. With butter, glaze triangles and scatter sesame seeds on top.
- In the prepped oven, bake till golden brown for 10 to 15 minutes. Serve while warm.

Nutrition Information

- Calories: 172 calories;
- Total Carbohydrate: 12.5
- Cholesterol: 13
- Protein: 3.4
- Total Fat: 11.9
- Sodium: 276

133.　Foil Pack Mushrooms

Serving: 4 | Prep: 15mins | Ready in:

Ingredients

- 24 fresh crimini mushrooms, stems removed
- 4 green onions, chopped
- 2 tablespoons pine nuts
- 1/4 cup olive oil
- salt and freshly ground black pepper to taste

Direction

- Preheat a grill to high heat. Grease 4 big heavy-duty aluminum foil sheets lightly.
- Stuff even amounts of pine nuts and green onions in every mushroom. On each aluminum foil piece, put 6 mushrooms. Drizzle olive oil on. Season with pepper and salt. Seal foil around mushrooms, making 4 packets.
- On preheated grill, put foil packets. Cook till mushrooms are tender for about 20 minutes.

Nutrition Information

- Calories: 184 calories;
- Total Fat: 15.7
- Sodium: 45
- Total Carbohydrate: 5.3
- Cholesterol: 0
- Protein: 6.1

134.　Four Cheese Mashed Potato Stuffed Portobello Mushrooms

Serving: 4 | Prep: 15mins | Ready in:

Ingredients

- 1 (4 ounce) package Idahoan® Four Cheese Flavored Mashed Potatoes

- 2 large portobello mushrooms, or more depending on size
- Oil
- Salt and pepper
- 1/2 cup Cheddar cheese, shredded
- 2 tablespoons bell pepper, diced and lightly sauteed
- 2 tablespoons scallions, chopped

Direction

- Set oven to 350°F or grill to 400°F to preheat.
- Clean and rub oil over mushrooms.
- Add pepper and salt on top and arrange on a foil-lined baking tray.
- Bake until tender, about 5 minutes. Or if grilling, flip mushrooms one or two times while cooking on the grill until soft.
- While cooking the mushrooms, follow the package's instructions to make Idahoan Four Cheese Mashed Potatoes.
- Mix in the peppers and the cheddar cheese.
- When mushrooms are cooked, sprinkle a bit more pepper and salt on top and stuff the mashed potatoes into mushrooms.
- Add the scallions on top and serve hot.

Nutrition Information

- Calories: 88 calories;
- Total Carbohydrate: 5.6
- Cholesterol: 15
- Protein: 4.1
- Total Fat: 5.5
- Sodium: 236

---

135.   French Onion Chicken

Serving: 8 | Prep: 10mins | Ready in:

Ingredients

- cooking spray (optional)
- 4 frozen whole chicken breasts
- 1 (8 ounce) package sliced fresh mushrooms
- 1 (10.75 ounce) can condensed cream of mushroom soup
- 8 ounces sour cream
- 1 (1 ounce) package dry onion soup mix

Direction

- Set the oven to 190°C or 375°F to preheat. Coat the bottom of a 3-qt casserole dish with cooking spray.
- In the prepped baking dish, arrange the chicken breasts and put mushrooms on top. In a bowl, combine together onion soup mix, sour cream and cream of mushroom soup, then drizzle this mixture over mushrooms as well as chicken. Use aluminum foil to cover the dish.
- In the preheated oven, bake for an hour, until juices run clear and is not pink in the middle anymore. An instant-read thermometer should reach at least 74°C or 165°F after being inserted in the center.

Nutrition Information

- Calories: 239 calories;
- Total Fat: 11.2
- Sodium: 630
- Total Carbohydrate: 6.9
- Cholesterol: 80
- Protein: 27.1

---

136.   Fried Tilapia With Oyster Mushrooms

Serving: 4 | Prep: 10mins | Ready in:

Ingredients

- 2 tablespoons butter
- 3 cups fresh oyster mushrooms, stemmed and sliced
- 1 cup heavy whipping cream

- salt and freshly ground black pepper to taste
- 4 (8 ounce) fillets tilapia
- 2 tablespoons all-purpose flour
- 2 tablespoons vegetable oil

Direction

- In a frying pan, melt butter over medium heat and cook mushroom for 5 minutes until browned. Add in pepper, salt and cream and let them simmer for about 5 minutes to get desired thickness.
- Divide tilapia into large chunks and use pepper and salt for seasoning. Sprinkle flour over the top.
- In a frying pan over medium heat, heat oil and cook tilapia for 3 minutes each side until heated through and browned. Set on a plate and pour mushroom-cream sauce on top.

Nutrition Information

- Calories: 580 calories;
- Sodium: 213
- Total Carbohydrate: 8
- Cholesterol: 180
- Protein: 50
- Total Fat: 37.9

137.   Garage Noodles

Serving: 4 | Prep: 10mins | Ready in:

Ingredients

- 4 (3 ounce) packages ramen noodles (without flavor packet)
- 1 tablespoon vegetable oil
- 2 medium onions, cut into thin wedges
- 1 (6 ounce) package sliced fresh mushrooms
- 1 small bunch Tuscan kale, stemmed and chopped
- kosher salt
- 1/2 cup rice vinegar

- 1/3 cup soy sauce
- 1 teaspoon sesame oil

Direction

- Boil a pot of water. Add ramen; cook, occasionally mixing, for 3 minutes till soft. Drain; put 1/2 cup cooking liquid aside.
- Heat oil on medium heat in a big skillet; cook onions for 3-5 minutes till soft. Add salt, kale, mushrooms and drained ramen. Add sesame oil, soy sauce, rice vinegar and some cooking liquid; cook for 5 minutes till mushrooms are soft and kale is wilted.

Nutrition Information

- Calories: 490 calories;
- Sodium: 1727
- Total Carbohydrate: 67.5
- Cholesterol: 0
- Protein: 14.4
- Total Fat: 19.5

138.   Garlic Mushroom Pasta

Serving: 4 | Prep: 10mins | Ready in:

Ingredients

- 2 tablespoons olive oil
- 1/2 large onion, diced
- 5 large mushrooms, sliced
- 8 cloves garlic, crushed
- 1 teaspoon olive oil, or as needed
- 1 (12 ounce) package spaghetti
- 2 eggs, beaten
- 1/4 cup grated Parmesan cheese, plus more for garnish

Direction

- In a frying pan, heat 2 tablespoons olive oil over medium heat. In the hot oil, stir and cook garlic, mushrooms, and onion for 5-7 minutes until the onion turns translucent.

- Boil lightly salted water in a big pot; add approximately 1 teaspoon olive oil to prevent the spaghetti from sticking. In the boiling water, cook spaghetti for 12 minutes until fully cooked but remain firm to bite, tossing from time to time. Strain and return the hot spaghetti to the pot.
- Mix the spaghetti with eggs, cooking the eggs with the heat from the spaghetti. Mix 1/4 cup Parmesan cheese and mushroom and onion mixture into the spaghetti over low heat until the cheese melts and the eggs have fully cooked. Use more Parmesan cheese to garnish.

Nutrition Information

- Calories: 467 calories;
- Protein: 17.7
- Total Fat: 13.3
- Sodium: 120
- Total Carbohydrate: 68.8
- Cholesterol: 97

139.   Giant Stuffed Mushrooms

Serving: 4 | Prep: | Ready in:

Ingredients

- 4 large portobello mushrooms
- 2 tablespoons olive oil, divided
- salt to taste
- ground black pepper to taste
- 1 clove garlic, minced
- 1 cup chopped fresh cilantro
- 1 large carrot, finely chopped
- 1 stalk celery, finely chopped
- 2/3 cup kasha (toasted buckwheat groats)
- 1 1/4 cups water
- 3 tablespoons chopped fresh parsley

Direction

- Set oven to 400°F (200°C) to preheat. Cut off mushroom stems from the caps, and put the stems to one side. Arrange the mushroom caps on a baking sheet, gill-side up. Sprinkle 1 tablespoon olive oil over the caps, and add pepper and salt to season. Roast mushroom caps for 25 minutes in the preheated oven.
- In the meantime, make the pilaf stuffing. Cut mushroom stems into small pieces. In a skillet, heat the remaining olive oil over medium heat. Sauté garlic and chopped mushroom stems in oil until tender. Mix in kasha, celery, carrot, and cilantro; sauté for 2 minutes longer. Add in water. Bring to a boil. Turn heat to low; simmer, with cover until kasha is tender, for 20 minutes. Put off the heat, and mix in parsley. Season mixture with pepper and salt.
- Fill pilaf into the warm mushroom caps, and enjoy.

Nutrition Information

- Calories: 198 calories;
- Sodium: 328
- Total Carbohydrate: 29.2
- Cholesterol: 0
- Protein: 6.6
- Total Fat: 7.9

140.   Gina's Creamy Mushroom Lasagna

Serving: 8 | Prep: 30mins | Ready in:

Ingredients

- 12 uncooked lasagna noodles
- cooking spray
- 1 tablespoon olive oil
- 1 cup chopped shallots
- 2 garlic cloves, minced
- 1 cup diced red bell pepper
- 1 teaspoon crushed red pepper flakes
- 4 cups sliced fresh mushrooms

- salt and ground black pepper to taste
- 1 1/2 cups ricotta cheese
- 1/4 cup butter
- 2 tablespoons all-purpose flour
- 4 cups milk
- 1 cup grated Parmesan cheese
- 1 cup shredded mozzarella cheese
- 1/4 cup chopped fresh flat-leaf parsley

Direction

- Boil the lightly salted water in a large pot. Stir in the lasagna noodles. Bring back to a boil. Cook pasta with no cover, for 8 minutes or until noodles are cooked through yet firm to bite, stirring occasionally. Drain. Put aside.
- Start preheating the oven to 350°F (175°C).
- Spray cooking spray over a baking dish of 9x13-inch.
- In a large skillet, heat olive oil over medium-high heat. In hot oil, cook garlic and shallots while stirring for 5 minutes or until shallots are translucent and tender.
- Stir red pepper flakes and red bell pepper into shallot mixture for 1-2 minutes or until the bell pepper soften slightly.
- Mix the mushrooms into skillet; add black pepper and salt to season. Cook while stirring for 10 more minutes or until mushrooms turn brown and have given up the liquid.
- Stir the ricotta cheese into mushroom mixture. Take skillet off the heat. Put aside.
- In another skillet, melt butter over medium heat. Whisk in the flour for 2-3 minutes or until they become smooth.
- Whisk the milk into the flour mixture until they become smooth. Simmer for 5 minutes until thicken, whisk constantly. Season with black pepper and salt.
- Use a small amount of white sauce to coat the bottom of prepared baking dish.
- Place four lasagna noodles over white sauce, in a single layer.
- Spread noodles with about 1/3 mushroom mixture.
- Pour about one-third white sauce over mushroom mixture. Repeat these layers twice

more, beginning with four extra lasagna noodles.
- Sprinkle lasagna with parsley, mozzarella cheese and Parmesan cheese.
- Bake in prepared oven for 30-40 minutes or until sauce is bubbly and cheese melts. Let lasagna rest 10 minutes. Then slice and serve.

Nutrition Information

- Calories: 371 calories;
- Total Fat: 16
- Sodium: 356
- Total Carbohydrate: 40.3
- Cholesterol: 41
- Protein: 18.2

141. Gluten Free Elbows With Mixed Mushrooms And Italian Sausage Soup

Serving: 6 | Prep: 15mins | Ready in:

Ingredients

- 1 (12 ounce) box Barilla® Gluten Free Elbows
- 3 quarts chicken stock
- 3 cloves garlic, minced
- 4 tablespoons extra-virgin olive oil
- 1 sprig rosemary
- 4 (6 ounce) packages mixed mushrooms
- 1 pound Italian sausage, boiled for 10 minutes and cut into 1/3 inch slices
- 1 (15 ounce) can cannellini beans, drained
- 1 pint cherry tomatoes, halved
- Salt and black pepper to taste
- 1 tablespoon parsley, chopped

Direction

- Bring chicken stock to a simmer in a big soup pot.
- In the meantime, sauté garlic with rosemary and olive oil in a saucepan until turning light

yellow, about 1 minute. Add mushrooms and sauté until turning light brown. Add sausage and sauté for 2 minutes.

- Add sausage and mushrooms to the broth, mix in Barilla® Gluten Free Elbows, tomatoes, and beans. Cook for 1/2 of the time the box recommends.
- Allow the soup to sit for 10 minutes before eating. Use pepper and salt to season. Use parsley to garnish and use olive oil to drizzle on top.

Nutrition Information

- Calories: 818 calories;
- Sodium: 2094
- Total Carbohydrate: 99.2
- Cholesterol: 59
- Protein: 24
- Total Fat: 36.6

---

142. Gluten Free Penne With Chicken And Vodka Sauce

Serving: 6 | Prep: | Ready in:

Ingredients

- 1 (12 ounce) box Barilla Gluten Free Penne
- 4 tablespoons extra-virgin olive oil
- 1/2 cup diced yellow onion
- 1 boneless, skinless chicken breast, cut into strips
- 10 white button mushrooms, quartered
- 1/2 cup vodka
- 1 cup heavy cream
- 1 (14 ounce) can tomato puree
- 1 tablespoon chopped fresh parsley
- 1/2 cup grated Parmesan cheese
- Salt and black pepper to taste

Direction

- In a large pot, boil water.

- In the meantime, in a large skillet, add olive oil sauté onions for around 5 minutes over medium heat. Raise to high heat, then put in mushrooms and chicken; brown for an addition of 5 minutes.
- Pour in vodka and reduce completely. Put in tomato sauce and cream, then set to a simmer. Add salt and pepper for seasoning.
- Cook pasta following the instruction of the package. Drain and toss with sauce, then mix in cheese and parsley just before serving.

Nutrition Information

- Calories: 551 calories;
- Sodium: 417
- Total Carbohydrate: 54.1
- Cholesterol: 70
- Protein: 13.3
- Total Fat: 27.2

---

143. Gnocchi And Peppers In Balsamic Sauce

Serving: 4 | Prep: 30mins | Ready in:

Ingredients

- 2 tablespoons olive oil
- 3 cloves garlic, chopped
- 1/2 cup diced red onion
- salt to taste
- 6 crimini mushrooms, chopped
- 4 small mixed sweet peppers, julienned
- 1/2 cup cherry tomatoes, halved
- 4 leaves fresh basil, chopped
- 1/2 cup balsamic vinegar
- 1 (16 ounce) package potato gnocchi
- 1 cup Additional butter or margarine

Direction

- Following the package instructions, cook the gnocchi; then drain the gnocchi.

- In a skillet, heat olive oil over medium heat. Put the garlic into the skillet, cook for 2 minutes. Stir in the chopped onions, then flavor with salt; cook for 5 minutes until the onions start to soften. Stir in basil, tomatoes, peppers, and mushrooms; cook for 5 more minutes. Add the butter, stirring to melt. Pour the balsamic vinegar into the skillet, stir it, then turn down the heat and simmer the sauce for 15-20 minutes. Toss the sauce and the cooked gnocchi together.

Nutrition Information

- Calories: 693 calories;
- Sodium: 435
- Total Carbohydrate: 33.8
- Cholesterol: 143
- Protein: 5.9
- Total Fat: 61

144.   Golden Lasagna

Serving: 5 | Prep: 15mins | Ready in:

Ingredients

- 6 lasagna noodles
- 1/4 cup chopped onion
- 1 (4.5 ounce) can sliced mushrooms, drained
- 3 tablespoons chicken broth
- 1 (10.75 ounce) can condensed cream of chicken soup
- 1/3 cup milk
- 1/2 teaspoon dried basil
- 2 cups diced chicken breast meat
- 1 pound ricotta cheese
- 1 1/2 cups shredded Cheddar cheese
- 1/8 cup grated Parmesan cheese

Direction

- Turn the oven to 350°F (175°) to preheat. Boil lightly salted water in a big pot. Put in noodles and cook until al dente, about 8-10 minutes; strain.
- Sauté mushrooms and onion in chicken broth in a small saucepan. Take away from heat. Mix in basil, milk, and soup. Stir thoroughly. Put aside.
- Arrange 3 cooked lasagna noodles in a lightly oiled 9x13-in. baking dish. Make the layers as follows: half of the chicken, half of the ricotta cheese, half of the Cheddar cheese, half of the Parmesan cheese, and half of the soup/mushroom mixture. Put on 3 more lasagna noodles and duplicate layers. Bake without a cover for about 50 minutes in the preheated oven.

Nutrition Information

- Calories: 545 calories;
- Total Carbohydrate: 33.4
- Cholesterol: 124
- Protein: 46.6
- Total Fat: 24.7
- Sodium: 928

145.   Gourmet Bacon, Onion, And Mushroom Burgers

Serving: 8 | Prep: 20mins | Ready in:

Ingredients

- 7 strips thick-cut bacon
- 1 onion, chopped
- 1 (8 ounce) package baby bella mushrooms, sliced
- 3 tablespoons red wine
- 8 bakery-style hamburger buns, split
- 2 pounds ground beef
- 1 tablespoon sea salt
- 1 tablespoon garlic powder
- 1 tablespoon ground black pepper
- 8 slices pepper jack cheese

Direction

- On medium-high heat, cook bacon for 10mins in a big pan until evenly browned, flip from time to time; place on paper towels to drain. Keep a tablespoon of grease in the pan. Slice the bacon into big chunks.
- On medium-high heat, sauté mushrooms and onion in the same pan for 8mins until golden brown; pour in wine. Turn to medium heat, stir regularly for 5mins until the wine reduces by 1/2. Take off heat.
- Preheat the outdoor grill to medium heat; grease the grate lightly. Grill hamburger buns for 2-3mins until lightly toasted.
- Form the ground beef into eight patties; season with ground black pepper, garlic powder, and salt.
- Grill patties for 6mins until one side is brown; flip then place a slice of cheese on each patty. Grill for another 6mind until the center is not pink. An inserted thermometer in the middle should register at least 71°C or 160°Fahrenheit.
- Place burgers on the toasted buns then top with onion mixture using a slotted spoon. Place bacon chunks on top.

Nutrition Information

- Calories: 528 calories;
- Total Fat: 30.9
- Sodium: 1276
- Total Carbohydrate: 27.4
- Cholesterol: 107
- Protein: 32.6

---

146.   Gourmet Cream Of Wild Mushroom Soup

Serving: 4 | Prep: 25mins | Ready in:

Ingredients

- 3 tablespoons extra-virgin olive oil
- 1 pound assorted wild mushrooms, thinly sliced
- 1 large yellow onion, finely chopped
- 2 portobello mushrooms, thinly sliced
- 1 tablespoon chopped fresh thyme
- 1 teaspoon chopped fresh rosemary
- 1/2 teaspoon sea salt
- 1/4 cup dry white wine
- 3 cups gluten-free chicken broth
- 1 cup heavy whipping cream
- 1/2 cup chopped fresh parsley, divided
- 1 tablespoon gluten-free all-purpose flour
- sea salt and ground white pepper to taste

Direction

- In a large saucepan over low heat, put olive oil. Add sea salt, rosemary, thyme, Portobello mushrooms, yellow onion, and wild mushrooms; cook for about 3 minutes, covered, until mushrooms soften.
- Remove the cover of the saucepan and add white wine; stir and cook for about 5 minutes until most of the wine vaporizes. Add chicken broth; simmer the soup for about 15 minutes until flavors blend.
- In a small bowl, mix flour, 1/4 cup parsley, and heavy cream. Add into the soup; cook for about 5 minutes, whisking occasionally, until heated through. Add pepper and salt to the soup to taste; put the rest 1/4 cup parsley on top.

Nutrition Information

- Calories: 375 calories;
- Sodium: 1056
- Total Carbohydrate: 13
- Cholesterol: 85
- Protein: 6.7
- Total Fat: 33.1

147. Gourmet Mushroom Risotto

Serving: 6 | Prep: 20mins | Ready in:

Ingredients

- 6 cups chicken broth, divided
- 3 tablespoons olive oil, divided
- 1 pound portobello mushrooms, thinly sliced
- 1 pound white mushrooms, thinly sliced
- 2 shallots, diced
- 1 1/2 cups Arborio rice
- 1/2 cup dry white wine
- sea salt to taste
- freshly ground black pepper to taste
- 3 tablespoons finely chopped chives
- 4 tablespoons butter
- 1/3 cup freshly grated Parmesan cheese

Direction

- Warm broth in a saucepan on low heat.
- In a big saucepan, warm 2 tablespoons of the olive oil on medium-high heat. Mix in mushrooms, and cook for around 3 minutes till tender. Take out the mushrooms including their liquid, and put aside.
- To skillet, put a tablespoon of olive oil, and mix in shallots. Cook for a minute. Put in the rice, mixing for approximately 2 minutes to coat in oil. Once rice has taken on a pale, golden color, add the wine, mixing continuously till wine is completely absorbed. Put half a cup of the broth into the rice, and mix till broth is absorbed. Keep putting in broth, half a cup at a time for approximately 15 to 20 minutes, mixing constantly, till liquid is absorbed and the rice turns al dente.
- Take off the heat, and mix in parmesan, chives, butter and mushrooms including their liquid. Season to taste with pepper and salt.

Nutrition Information

- Calories: 431 calories;
- Total Carbohydrate: 56.6
- Cholesterol: 29
- Protein: 11.3
- Total Fat: 16.6
- Sodium: 1131

148. Greek Pasta

Serving: 4 | Prep: 15mins | Ready in:

Ingredients

- 1 pound linguine pasta
- 3 tomatoes
- 1/3 cup olive oil
- 3 cloves garlic, minced
- 1 pound mushrooms, sliced
- 1 teaspoon dried oregano
- 3/4 cup crumbled feta cheese
- 1 (2 ounce) can sliced black olives, drained

Direction

- Boil a big pot of lightly salted water; briefly plunge whole tomatoes in water till skin begins to peel. Use a slotted spoon to remove; put in cold water. Put pasta in boiling water; cook till al dente or for 8-10 minutes. Drain.
- Peel then chop blanched tomatoes as pasta cooks.
- Heat olive oil in a big skillet on medium heat. Mix in mushrooms and garlic; sauté till mushrooms start to give up their juices. Mix in oregano and tomatoes; cook till tomatoes are tender.
- Serving: Plate pasta then put hot tomato sauce on top; sprinkle olives and feta.

Nutrition Information

- Calories: 759 calories;
- Protein: 23.3
- Total Fat: 31
- Sodium: 866
- Total Carbohydrate: 102.4

- Cholesterol: 25

149. Greek Pita Pockets

Serving: 4 | Prep: 15mins | Ready in:

Ingredients

- 1/2 cup Greek-style (thick) unflavored yogurt
- 1 lemon, juiced
- 4 ounces bulk pork sausage
- 1 small onion, diced
- 1/3 cup Greek olives, diced
- 3/4 cup wild mushrooms, chopped
- 1 cup fresh baby spinach leaves, packed
- 6 eggs, beaten
- 2/3 cup Nikos® feta cheese crumbles
- 2 pitas, halved crosswise

Direction

- Combine lemon juice and yogurt in a small bowl; put aside.
- Cook sausage, stirring often and crumbling, on medium-high heat for 2 minutes in a non-stick skillet. Put in mushrooms, olives and onion, then cook for another 4 minutes.
- Put in spinach leaves and cook for about 1-3 minutes until vegetables give up all liquid and the sausage is cooked through. Crack in eggs and cook while stirring constantly until almost dry. Take off the heat and whisk in feta.
- Pack feta-egg mixture into each pita half. Serve at once with lemon yogurt.

Nutrition Information

- Calories: 382 calories;
- Cholesterol: 317
- Protein: 21
- Total Fat: 23.4
- Sodium: 896
- Total Carbohydrate: 23.4

150. Greek Vegetables

Serving: 6 | Prep: 20mins | Ready in:

Ingredients

- 1 clove garlic, minced
- 1 teaspoon dried oregano
- salt and ground black pepper to taste
- 6 tablespoons extra-virgin olive oil
- 8 red potatoes, cut into quarters
- 10 crimini mushrooms, quartered
- 1 large zucchini cut in half lengthwise, then cut into 1-inch moons

Direction

- In a big skillet, cook and stir together olive oil, pepper, salt, oregano and garlic on moderate heat for a minute, until tangy. Put in zucchini, mushrooms and potatoes, then cover the skillet and cook the vegetables on high heat for 5 minutes. Stir, replace the lid and lower heat to moderate. Cook for 15 minutes while stirring sometimes, until the potatoes are softened.

Nutrition Information

- Calories: 340 calories;
- Total Carbohydrate: 48.3
- Cholesterol: 0
- Protein: 7.4
- Total Fat: 14
- Sodium: 34

151. Green Bean Casserole My Way

Serving: 6 | Prep: 15mins | Ready in:

Ingredients

- 2 tablespoons vegetable oil
- 1 small onion, chopped
- 2 cups chopped mushrooms
- 1/2 cup whiskey
- 2/3 cup sour cream
- 1/2 cup vegetable broth
- 2 tablespoons all-purpose flour
- 1 whole roasted chicken, dark meat removed from bones and shredded
- 4 cups frozen cut green beans
- salt and ground black pepper to taste
- 1 1/2 cups French-fried onion rings
- 1/2 (12 ounce) jar pork gravy (optional)

Direction

- Pre heat the oven to 200 degrees C (400 degrees F).
- Heat the oil on medium high heat in the big ovenproof skillet. Put in the onion; cook and whisk for roughly 5 minutes till becoming tender and translucent. Put in the mushrooms and cook for 1-2 minutes. Add whiskey carefully to the hot skillet. Lower the heat to medium and allow the whiskey to cook down, roughly 5 minutes.
- Stir together flour, vegetable broth and sour cream in a bowl. Whisk into skillet. Boil; lower the heat and let it simmer for roughly 5 minutes till the sauce becomes thickened.
- Mix the green beans and chicken in a big bowl; add the sauce and toss till well-coated. Use pepper and salt to season. Add the mixture back to skillet and cover using the tight-fitting lid or aluminum foil.
- Bake in preheated oven for roughly half an hour till thoroughly heated. Remove the cover and scatter the onion rings over the top. Keep baking for roughly 15 minutes longer till the rings become crispy and golden brown. Whisk the gravy into hot casserole.

Nutrition Information

- Calories: 715 calories;
- Total Fat: 45.2
- Sodium: 772

- Total Carbohydrate: 36.2
- Cholesterol: 78
- Protein: 24.9

---

152.   Green Bean And Mushroom Medley

Serving: 6 | Prep: 20mins | Ready in:

Ingredients

- 1/2 pound fresh green beans, cut into 1-inch lengths
- 2 carrots, cut into thick strips
- 1/4 cup butter
- 1 onion, sliced
- 1/2 pound fresh mushrooms, sliced
- 1 teaspoon salt
- 1/2 teaspoon seasoned salt
- 1/4 teaspoon garlic salt
- 1/4 teaspoon white pepper

Direction

- In 1" of boiling water, add carrots and green beans. Cover and cook until softened but still firm, then drain.
- In a big skillet, melt butter on moderate heat. Sauté mushrooms and onions until nearly softened. Lower heat, then cover and simmer about 3 minutes. Stir in white pepper, garlic salt, seasoned salt, salt, carrots and green beans. Cover and cook on moderate heat, about 5 minutes.

Nutrition Information

- Calories: 103 calories;
- Sodium: 610
- Total Carbohydrate: 7.7
- Cholesterol: 20
- Protein: 1.9
- Total Fat: 7.9

153.   Grilled Mushroom Swiss Burgers

Serving: 6 | Prep: 15mins | Ready in:

Ingredients

- 1 1/2 pounds lean ground beef
- 1/2 teaspoon seasoned meat tenderizer
- salt and pepper to taste
- 2 teaspoons butter
- 2 (4 ounce) cans sliced mushrooms, drained
- 2 tablespoons soy sauce
- 4 slices Swiss cheese
- 6 hamburger buns

Direction

- Prepare the grill for medium heat. Grease grate lightly with oil.
- Split the ground beef into 6 patties. Put meat tenderizer, pepper and salt to taste. Reserve.
- In a skillet, liquefy butter over medium heat. Put in the soy sauce and mushrooms; cook and mix till browned. Reserve and retain warmth.
- Grill patties till cooked through, about 6 minutes each side. Distribute the mushroom mixture equally between the burgers and put atop each one with 1 slice of Swiss cheese. To let the cheese melt, cover the grill for a minute. Take away from the grill and put on hamburger buns, serve.

Nutrition Information

- Calories: 520 calories;
- Total Fat: 32.4
- Sodium: 868
- Total Carbohydrate: 25
- Cholesterol: 106
- Protein: 30

154.   Grilled Oyster Mushrooms

Serving: 4 | Prep: 5mins | Ready in:

Ingredients

- 16 ounces oyster mushroom caps
- 1/8 pound grated Parmesan cheese

Direction

- Prep grill to medium heat.
- Oil the grate. On grill, put mushroom caps. They'll cook fast on the grill and dry out. For better heat control to avoid burning, move them around the fire. You can blacken edges a bit for more flavor. When edges start toast, sprinkle each mushroom with parmesan cheese. Let it melt. Immediately serve.

Nutrition Information

- Calories: 99 calories;
- Protein: 10.5
- Total Fat: 4.1
- Sodium: 255
- Total Carbohydrate: 4.3
- Cholesterol: 12

155.   Grilled Portobello Mushrooms

Serving: 3 | Prep: 10mins | Ready in:

Ingredients

- 3 portobello mushrooms
- 1/4 cup canola oil
- 3 tablespoons chopped onion
- 4 cloves garlic, minced
- 4 tablespoons balsamic vinegar

Direction

- Clean mushrooms. Remove stems. Put aside for other use. On a plate, put caps, gill side up.
- Mix vinegar, garlic, onion and oil in a small bowl. Evenly pour mixture on mushroom caps. Let it stand for an hour.
- Grill for 10 minutes over hot grill. Immediately serve.

Nutrition Information

- Calories: 217 calories;
- Total Fat: 19
- Sodium: 13
- Total Carbohydrate: 11
- Cholesterol: 0
- Protein: 3.2

156. Grilled Steak And Vegetable Salad From Publix®

Serving: 4 | Prep: 30mins | Ready in:

Ingredients

- 1 1/2 pounds grilling steaks (strip, rib eye, tenderloin)
- 1 teaspoon kosher salt, divided
- 1/2 teaspoon ground black pepper
- 1 medium zucchini, halved lengthwise
- 3 plum (Roma) tomatoes, halved
- 1 (6 ounce) package fresh sliced portobello mushrooms, stems and gills removed
- 2 tablespoons olive oil
- 8 tablespoons balsamic glaze (reduced balsamic vinegar), divided
- 1 (5 ounce) bag mixed salad greens with arugula
- 4 tablespoons Caesar salad dressing, divided

Direction

- Preheat grill pan (or grill).
- Use pepper and a half teaspoon of salt to season steaks. Put steaks on grill pan (or grill).

Grill each side for 3-4 minutes or till the internal temperature of the steak reaches 145°F. Take the steaks out of the grill and allow them to sit about 5 minutes then slice.
- Put portobellos, tomatoes, zucchini, oil and the remaining a half teaspoon of salt together. Transfer the vegetables to the grill, grill each side of the vegetables for 2-3 minutes or until they becomes tender and you can see grill marks on the vegetables.
- Take vegetables out of the grill; chop them into bite-size pieces. Cut steaks into slices.
- Distribute salad greens among four serving plates. Put vegetables and steak on top of the salad. Pour drizzles of balsamic glaze, salad dressing on each salad. The dish is ready to serve.

Nutrition Information

- Calories: 385 calories;
- Total Fat: 25.1
- Sodium: 683
- Total Carbohydrate: 15.3
- Cholesterol: 99
- Protein: 22.9

157. Ground Beef Stroganoff Casserole

Serving: 8 | Prep: 15mins | Ready in:

Ingredients

- cooking spray
- 1 pound extra-lean (94%) ground beef
- 1 teaspoon salt
- 1/2 teaspoon ground black pepper
- 1 (8 ounce) package sliced fresh mushrooms
- 1 large onion, chopped
- 3 cloves garlic, minced
- 1/2 cup dry white wine
- 1 (10.75 ounce) can fat-free condensed cream of mushroom soup (such as Campbell's®)

- 1/2 cup fat-free sour cream
- 1 tablespoon Dijon mustard
- 4 cups cooked egg noodles

Direction

- Preheat an oven to 175 degrees C (350 degrees F). Use cooking spray to coat a 9x13-inch baking dish.
- Use cooking spray to spritz a large nonstick skillet; set on medium-high heat. Place in ground beef and cook for 10 minutes while breaking up until browned. Add pepper and salt to taste.
- Mix garlic, onion and mushrooms into the skillet. Cook while stirring for about 2 minutes until the onion becomes tender. Pour in wine, then decrease the heat to low and let to simmer for three minutes. Add mustard, sour cream, and cream of mushroom soup.
- Place cooked noodles in a large bowl and add the beef mixture on top. Coat by tossing. Transfer to the greased baking dish; cover with aluminum foil.
- In the preheated oven, bake for about 25 minutes until bubbling.

Nutrition Information

- Calories: 298 calories;
- Total Carbohydrate: 28.8
- Cholesterol: 66
- Protein: 18.1
- Total Fat: 10.6
- Sodium: 681

158. Grzybki Marynowane (Pickled Wild Mushrooms)

Serving: 16 | Prep: 30mins | Ready in:

Ingredients

- 4 pounds fresh porcini mushrooms
- 5 1-pint canning jars with lids and rings
- 3 1/2 cups water
- 1 cup white vinegar
- 1 onion, roughly chopped
- 1 tablespoon superfine sugar
- 1 teaspoon salt
- 6 whole black peppercorns, or to taste
- 2 whole allspice berries
- 1 bay leaf

Direction

- Trim the mushrooms and rinse. Put in a big saucepan, cover in water, and boil. Take saucepan off the heat and drain. Put mushrooms back to saucepan, put in fresh water to cover, and boil once more. Take off the heat and drain. Slice bigger mushrooms into bite-sized portions.
- In boiling water, sterilize lids and jars for a minimum of 5 minutes. Into sterilized, hot jars, pack the mushrooms.
- In a big pot, boil bay leaf, allspice, peppercorns, salt, sugar, onion, vinegar and water for 5 minutes. Take off the heat and put aside for approximately 20 minutes to cool. On top of mushrooms, evenly transfer the liquid, filling to within a quarter-inch of surface.
- Around the insides of jars, trace a thin spatula or clean knife after having filled to get rid of any air bubbles. Using a damp paper towel, wipe jar rims to get rid of any food residue. Put on lids and screw on the rings.
- In the big stockpot bottom, put a rack and fill with water midway. Boil and into the boiling water, lower jars with a holder. Retain a 2-inch gap among the jars. Put in additional boiling water if needed to let water level come to at least an-inch over the jar tops. Let water come to a rolling boil, place cover on the pot, and process for 7 minutes.
- Take jars out of stockpot and put onto a wood or cloth-covered surface, a few-inch apart, till cool. Press the surface of every lid using a finger, making sure that seal is tight, lid must not move down or up at all. Keep in a dark, cool place.

Nutrition Information

- Calories: 38 calories;
- Total Fat: 0.1
- Sodium: 154
- Total Carbohydrate: 6.4
- Cholesterol: 0
- Protein: 3

---

159. Gumbo Style Chicken Creole

Serving: 5 | Prep: 15mins | Ready in:

Ingredients

- 1/4 cup oil for frying
- 1/4 cup all-purpose flour
- 1 green bell pepper, chopped
- 1 onion, chopped
- 2 cups cooked, chopped chicken breast meat
- 1 (14.5 ounce) can diced tomatoes with green chile peppers, with liquid
- 1 (4.5 ounce) can sliced mushrooms, drained
- 2 tablespoons chopped fresh parsley
- 2 teaspoons Worcestershire sauce
- 3 cloves garlic, minced
- 1 teaspoon soy sauce
- 1 teaspoon white sugar
- 1/2 teaspoon salt
- 1/2 teaspoon ground black pepper
- 3 dashes hot sauce

Direction

- In a large skillet over high heat, heat oil. Stir in flour and cook for 5 minutes or until mixture has the same color as a cooper penny, remember to stir constantly while cooking. Lower the heat to low and stir in onion and bell pepper. Cook, stirring sometimes, for 10 to 15 minutes until softened.

- Add hot sauce, pepper, salt, sugar, soy sauce, garlic, Worcestershire sauce, parsley, mushrooms, green chile peppers, tomatoes and chicken. Stir together until well combined and simmer, covered, for 20 minutes.

Nutrition Information

- Calories: 167 calories;
- Total Fat: 3.3
- Sodium: 807
- Total Carbohydrate: 14.7
- Cholesterol: 48
- Protein: 19.8

---

160. Ham Mushroom Barley Soup

Serving: 4 | Prep: 10mins | Ready in:

Ingredients

- 2 tablespoons butter
- 1 cup chopped onion
- 1 (8 ounce) pre-cooked ham steak, diced
- 2 tablespoons curry powder, or to taste
- 3 1/2 cups chicken broth
- 1 (14.5 ounce) can stewed tomatoes
- 1/2 cup pearl barley
- 1 pound quartered mushrooms
- 1 cup thickly sliced carrots

Direction

- In a big saucepan, melt butter over medium heat. Add onions; cook for 5 minutes until clear. Mix in curry and ham for 30-60 seconds until the curry is aromatic. Add barley, tomatoes, and chicken broth. Boil it, lower the heat and bring to a simmer with a cover for 30-35 minutes until the barley is soft. Add carrots and mushrooms and cook for 10-15 minutes until soft.

Nutrition Information

- Calories: 361 calories;
- Cholesterol: 51
- Protein: 20.6
- Total Fat: 15
- Sodium: 2103
- Total Carbohydrate: 39.3

161.   Healthy Mince Pies

Serving: 4 | Prep: 25mins | Ready in:

Ingredients

- 1 tablespoon vegetable oil
- 8 ounces lean ground beef
- 1/2 onion, finely chopped
- 1/2 cup spaghetti sauce
- 1 small zucchini, peeled and grated
- 4 button mushrooms, finely chopped
- 1 small carrot, peeled and grated
- salt and ground black pepper to taste
- olive oil cooking spray
- 4 sheets phyllo pastry
- 4 teaspoons grated Parmesan cheese

Direction

- Preheat the oven to 400°F (200°C).
- In a large skillet, heat oil over medium heat. Cook and stir onion and beef in the hot oil for about 5 minutes, until browned. Mix in carrot, mushrooms, zucchini and spaghetti sauce; season with pepper and salt. Allow to simmer for about 5 minutes, until flavors combine.
- Spray cooking spray on half of each phyllo dough sheet and fold lengthwise in half. On one edge of each phyllo sheet, add a half cup of the beef mixture; add 1 teaspoon of Parmesan cheese on top. Fold up into rectangular parcels.
- Place parcels on a baking sheet. Coat the parcels with cooking spray.

- Bake in the prepped oven in about 15 minutes, until golden brown.

Nutrition Information

- Calories: 299 calories;
- Protein: 14.1
- Total Fat: 17.9
- Sodium: 344
- Total Carbohydrate: 19.8
- Cholesterol: 45

162.   Hearty Meat Sauce

Serving: 4 | Prep: 15mins | Ready in:

Ingredients

- 1/2 pound ground beef
- 2 (16 ounce) jars spaghetti sauce
- 1 diced yellow pepper
- 1 diced red bell pepper
- 1 (14.5 ounce) can peeled and diced tomatoes, drained
- 6 fresh mushrooms, coarsely chopped

Direction

- Place a skillet over medium heat and brown the ground beef till no pink shows; drain.
- In a large pot over medium heat, mix spaghetti sauce and browned beef together, about 5-10 minutes. Put in mushrooms, canned tomatoes, red peppers and yellow peppers. Turn the heat down; simmer with a cover while stirring every once in a while, about 30 minutes.

Nutrition Information

- Calories: 351 calories;
- Total Fat: 14
- Sodium: 1111
- Total Carbohydrate: 39.3
- Cholesterol: 39

- Protein: 15.8

163.   Hearty Vegetable Lasagna

Serving: 12 | Prep: 25mins | Ready in:

Ingredients

- 1 (16 ounce) package lasagna noodles
- 1 pound fresh mushrooms, sliced
- 3/4 cup chopped green bell pepper
- 3/4 cup chopped onion
- 3 cloves garlic, minced
- 2 tablespoons vegetable oil
- 2 (26 ounce) jars pasta sauce
- 1 teaspoon dried basil
- 1 (15 ounce) container part-skim ricotta cheese
- 4 cups shredded mozzarella cheese
- 2 eggs
- 1/2 cup grated Parmesan cheese

Direction

- Cook lasagna noodles for about 10 minutes in a large pot containing boiling water or until al dente. Then rinse under cold water and drain them.
- Cook while stirring garlic, onion, green peppers and mushrooms in oil in a large saucepan. Mix in basil and pasta sauce. Heat to boil. Decrease the heat and let to simmer for 15 minutes.
- Combine eggs, 2 cups mozzarella cheese, and ricotta.
- Preheat an oven to 175 degrees C (350 degrees F). Scatter one cup of tomato sauce on the bottom of a 9x13 inch baking dish that is greased. Then layer 1/2 each, Parmesan cheese, sauce, ricotta mix and lasagna noodles. Repeat layering and add the remaining two cups of mozzarella cheese on top.
- Bake without covering for 40 minutes. Leave to sit for 15 minutes prior to serving.

Nutrition Information

- Calories: 462 calories;
- Total Fat: 19.5
- Sodium: 843
- Total Carbohydrate: 49.6
- Cholesterol: 77
- Protein: 23.2

164.   Hearty Vegetable Salad

Serving: 6 | Prep: 20mins | Ready in:

Ingredients

- 1 (8 ounce) package DOLE® Field Greens
- 1 large large tomato, cut in thin wedges
- 1/2 cucumber, sliced
- 1 cup Parmesan cheese-flavored croutons
- 1/2 cup enoki mushrooms
- 1/2 cup walnut halves, toasted
- 8 pitted kalamata olives, cut in half
- Bacon, Onion and Mustard Salad Dressing (recipe below)

Direction

- In a big bowl, mix the olives, walnuts, mushrooms, croutons, cucumber, tomato and salad. Toss along with the Mustard Salad Dressing, Onion and Bacon to taste. Keep in the refrigerator any of the leftover dressing.

Nutrition Information

165.   Holiday Vegan Gravy

Serving: 8 | Prep: 20mins | Ready in:

Ingredients

- 2 teaspoons vegetable oil

- 2 onions, sliced
- 2 large carrots, cut into chunks
- 4 ounces fresh mushrooms, halved
- 3 cloves garlic, crushed
- 1 teaspoon salt
- 1/2 teaspoon ground black pepper
- 1/2 cup white wine
- 4 sun-dried tomatoes, quartered
- 2 sprigs fresh marjoram
- 1 sprig fresh thyme
- 2 1/2 cups water
- 1 tablespoon vegetable oil
- 2 tablespoons all-purpose flour

Direction

- In a big skillet over medium-low heat, heat 2 teaspoon vegetable oil. In hot oil, cook and mix black pepper, salt, garlic, mushrooms, carrots and onions for a minute till coated. Cover and cook for half an hour till vegetables are tender. Remove cover and raise heat to medium; cook and mix for 7 to 10 minutes longer till vegetables are caramelized and brown.
- Add white wine to the vegetables and let simmer for 2 to 3 minutes till wine is decreased by 2/3. Mix in water, thyme, marjoram and sun-dried tomatoes. Simmer, put cover, and cook for half an hour till vegetables are so soft. Filter liquid into a big measuring cup, with a spoon, force as much liquid as you can into the cup.
- In a saucepan over medium heat, heat 1 tablespoon vegetable oil; mix in flour and cook for 5 minutes, mixing continuously, till flour mixture is golden brown. Mix in leftover vegetable liquid and allow to simmer for 3 to 5 minutes till thickened.

Nutrition Information

- Calories: 83 calories;
- Cholesterol: 0
- Protein: 1.7
- Total Fat: 3.1

- Sodium: 330
- Total Carbohydrate: 10.4

---

166.   Hot Chicken Salad Casserole

Serving: 6 | Prep: 15mins | Ready in:

Ingredients

- 4 boneless chicken breast halves, cooked and diced
- 1 cup chopped celery
- 1 (8 ounce) can sliced water chestnuts
- 1 (4.5 ounce) can sliced mushrooms
- 3/4 cup mayonnaise
- 1 teaspoon lemon juice
- 1/2 teaspoon salt
- 3 teaspoons grated onion
- 1/2 cup sliced almonds
- 1/2 cup shredded Cheddar cheese
- 1 1/2 cups crushed potato chips

Direction

- Set oven to 175°C (350°F) and start preheating. Prepare a 9x13" baking dish greased with a thin layer of cooking spray.
- Combine almonds, onion, salt, lemon juice, mayonnaise, mushrooms, water chestnuts, celery and chicken in a big bowl. Move to the baking dish, then place on top with crushed potato chips and Cheddar cheese.
- Bake for half an hour in prepared oven until browned slightly.

Nutrition Information

- Calories: 548 calories;
- Sodium: 661
- Total Carbohydrate: 18.3
- Cholesterol: 75
- Protein: 26.4
- Total Fat: 41.5

167.   Hummus Stuffed Portobello Caps

Serving: 6 | Prep: 15mins | Ready in:

Ingredients

- 2 tablespoons olive oil
- 6 small portobello mushroom caps, stems and ribs removed
- 1/2 cup cream cheese, softened
- 1/2 green bell pepper, diced
- 3/4 cup roasted red pepper hummus
- salt and pepper to taste
- 1 teaspoon lemon pepper seasoning

Direction

- Preheat oven to 375° F (190° C).
- In a big frying pan, heat olive oil over medium-high heat. Sear each side of the portobello mushrooms for about 3 minutes until browned.
- Mix hummus, green pepper, and cream cheese together till thoroughly blended. Spice each side of the mushroom caps with pepper and salt. On a baking sheet set the mushrooms with the stem-side upward. Dust with lemon pepper, then fill with hummus mixture.
- In the preheated oven, bake for 15 minutes till the filling becomes hot.

Nutrition Information

- Calories: 198 calories;
- Total Fat: 15
- Sodium: 425
- Total Carbohydrate: 12.6
- Cholesterol: 21
- Protein: 5.5

168.   Hunt's® Beef And Mushroom Bolognese

Serving: 4 | Prep: 15mins | Ready in:

Ingredients

- 1/2 (12 ounce) box dry fettuccine pasta, uncooked
- PAM® Olive Oil No-Stick Cooking Spray
- 1 pound ground sirloin beef (90% lean)
- 3/4 cup chopped yellow onion
- 3/4 teaspoon salt
- 1/2 teaspoon ground red pepper
- 2 teaspoons finely chopped garlic
- 1 1/2 cups chopped fresh fennel
- 1 (8 ounce) package sliced fresh button mushrooms
- 3 tablespoons Hunt's® Tomato Paste
- 2 (14.5 ounce) cans Hunt's® Petite Diced Tomatoes, undrained

Direction

- Follow package directions to cook pasta.
- Meanwhile, spray cooking spray on big skillet; heat on medium high heat. Add pepper, salt, onion and beef. Cook till beef isn't pink anymore but crumbled for 5-6 minutes, occasionally mixing. Add garlic and cook till fragrant for 1 minute longer.
- Add mushrooms and fennel; cook till veggies are tender for 3-5 minutes. Mix tomato paste in then add undrained tomatoes; lower heat. Simmer for 5 minutes. Mix cooked pasta in then simmer till hot for 2 minutes.

Nutrition Information

- Calories: 429 calories;
- Total Carbohydrate: 49.4
- Cholesterol: 69
- Protein: 31.1
- Total Fat: 13.2
- Sodium: 1114

169. Hunter Style Chicken

Serving: 4 | Prep: | Ready in:

Ingredients

- 4 tablespoons olive oil
- 1 (3 pound) whole chicken, cut into pieces
- 6 slices bacon, diced
- 2 onions, chopped
- 1 cup fresh sliced mushrooms
- 1 tablespoon chopped fresh parsley
- 1 tablespoon chopped fresh basil
- 1 teaspoon salt
- freshly ground black pepper
- 1 cup white wine
- 1 pound tomatoes, diced

Direction

- In a large skillet, heat oil; brown the chicken; remove. Add bacon; sauté for about 2 minutes over medium heat.
- Add onions and mushrooms and keep sautéing until onions become translucent. Transfer chicken back to the skillet; scatter with pepper, salt, basil and parsley. Add tomatoes and wine. Simmer, covered, for 25-30 minutes; during cooking, turning the chicken once. Take the chicken out of the skillet; pour the sauce over the chicken.

Nutrition Information

- Calories: 1142 calories;
- Sodium: 1182
- Total Carbohydrate: 12.1
- Cholesterol: 284
- Protein: 70.4
- Total Fat: 84

170. Instant Pot® Butternut Squash Risotto With Mushrooms

Serving: 6 | Prep: 10mins | Ready in:

Ingredients

- 2 tablespoons olive oil
- 1 medium white onion, chopped
- 4 cups peeled and cubed butternut squash (1/2-inch pieces), divided
- 3 cloves garlic
- 2 cups Arborio rice
- 1/4 cup dry white wine
- 2 cups vegetable broth
- 1 (8 ounce) package sliced portobello mushrooms
- 1/2 cup chopped red bell pepper
- 1/2 teaspoon kosher salt
- 1/4 teaspoon freshly grated nutmeg
- 2 tablespoons chopped fresh flat-leaf parsley, or to taste
- 1/4 cup grated Parmesan cheese

Direction

- Turn on Instant Pot® or any multi-functional pressure cooker you're using and put on Sauté. Once the pot is hot, pour in olive oil then toss in onion. Stir-fry for 5 minutes, occasionally stirring, until onion is translucent. Stir in garlic and half of the butternut squash. Continue cooking for 5-10 minutes, stirring from time to time, until all sides of the squash has browned.
- Move the squash mixture to side of the pot then add rice. Mix to blend well. Continue cooking for 3-4 minutes, stirring often, until rice starts to stick on the bottom of the pot. Pour in wine and boil. Use a wooden spoon to scrape the bottom of the pot to get the browned bits off.
- Add in the rest of the squash, red bell pepper, mushrooms, salt, nutmeg and vegetable broth. Mix well then seal the lid of the pressure cooker. Choose high pressure following the

manufacturer's manual and set timer to 5 minutes. Let the pressure build for 10-15 minutes.

- Using a towel, cover the vent and rotate it to release the pressure with the quick-release method for 5 minutes. Open the pot and mix in parsley. Serve with Parmesan cheese on top.

Nutrition Information

- Calories: 409 calories;
- Cholesterol: 3
- Protein: 9
- Total Fat: 5.9
- Sodium: 373
- Total Carbohydrate: 78.8

---

171.   Instant Pot® Shredded Flank Steak

Serving: 4 | Prep: 10mins | Ready in:

Ingredients

- 1 (1 1/4 pound) flank steak, cut into 8 pieces
- 2 tablespoons avocado oil
- 1 (8 ounce) package cremini mushrooms, roughly chopped
- 1 onion, finely chopped
- 2 large cloves garlic, grated
- 1 teaspoon dried thyme
- 1/4 cup dry red wine
- 1 1/2 cups beef broth
- 1 tablespoon Worcestershire sauce
- 3/4 teaspoon salt, or to taste
- freshly ground black pepper to taste
- 1/4 cup water
- 3 tablespoons all-purpose flour

Direction

- Set a multi-functional cooker like Instant Pot® on and select sauté mode. Cook the steak, working in batches for 3-5 minutes on each side until brown. Transfer in a plate and set aside.

- In a pot, heat avocado oil; sauté onion and mushrooms for 5 minutes until the onion is translucent. Cook in thyme and garlic for a minute until aromatic. Add wine and cook for about 2 minutes until almost evaporated; stir. Put pepper, salt, Worcestershire sauce, and broth; simmer.

- Place the beef with broth mixture; flip to coat. Secure lid; set the cooker on Meat mode following the cooker's manual. Secure lid and set the timer on 20 minutes. Let the pressure build up for 10-15 minutes.

- Relieve pressure for at least 20 minutes in accordance with the cooker's manual using the natural release method. Take the beef out of the pot and let it rest. Make a slurry by combining flour and water. Set the cooker on Sauté mode then gradually pour in the slurry. Cook and stir for 3-5 minutes until thick. Use two forks to shred the beef. Put the beef back in the liquid.

- Release pressure using the natural-release method according to manufacturer's instructions, at least 20 minutes. Remove the beef and set aside. Stir water and flour together to make a slurry. Select the Sauté option and add the slurry slowly. Cook until liquid thickens, 3 to 5 minutes. Pull the beef apart using 2 forks. Stir beef back into the liquid.

Nutrition Information

- Calories: 264 calories;
- Sodium: 831
- Total Carbohydrate: 11.3
- Cholesterol: 31
- Protein: 21.5
- Total Fat: 13

172. Italian Sausage Delight!

Serving: 6 | Prep: 30mins | Ready in:

Ingredients

- 6 (3.5 ounce) links hot Italian sausage
- 1 large onion, chopped
- 1 red bell peppers, seeded and diced
- 1 green bell pepper, seeded and diced
- 1 (4 ounce) can mushrooms, drained
- 1 (16 ounce) package penne pasta
- 1/2 cup Italian salad dressing
- 1/4 cup grated Parmesan cheese for topping

Direction

- Bring water in a large pot to a boil. Cook penne pasta for about 10 minutes until tender. Drain.
- In a small skillet over medium heat, arrange Italian sausage links. Cook until firm and thoroughly cooked, turning sometimes.
- Sauté Italian dressing, mushrooms, green and red bell peppers in a separate large skillet for about 5 minutes until vegetables are tender. Cut Italian sausages into round slices, and mix into the vegetables. Continue to cook and stir for 5 more minutes.
- Arrange servings of pasta on plates to serve. Spoon sausage and vegetable mixture over the top. Scatter generously with Parmesan cheese.

Nutrition Information

- Calories: 680 calories;
- Total Fat: 36.9
- Sodium: 1126
- Total Carbohydrate: 62.8
- Cholesterol: 72
- Protein: 25.3

173. Jap Chae Korean Glass Noodles

Serving: 2 | Prep: 20mins | Ready in:

Ingredients

- 1/2 pound Korean dang myun noodles
- 1 teaspoon sesame oil
- 2 tablespoons soy sauce
- 2 teaspoons white sugar
- 1 tablespoon vegetable oil
- 2 cloves garlic, minced
- 3/4 cup thinly sliced onions
- 2 carrots, cut into match-stick size pieces
- 1/2 pound asparagus, thinly sliced
- 3 green onions cut into 1-inch pieces
- 1/2 cup dried shiitake mushrooms, soaked until soft, then sliced into strips
- 1 tablespoon sesame seeds
- 1 1/2 teaspoons sesame oil

Direction

- Add lightly salted water into a large pot until filled and then heat rolling to a boil on high heat. When water is boiling, mix in dang myun noodles and heat to boil. Cook noodles while uncovered and stirring often for 4 to 5 minutes until noodles are cooked through and still firm to bite. Then rinse under cold water and drain thoroughly in a colander that is set in a sink. Toss the noodles with one teaspoon sesame oil and reserve. In a small bowl, whisk sugar and soy sauce and reserve.
- Over medium-high heat, heat vegetable oil in a skillet and then mix in the asparagus, carrots, onion and garlic. Cook while stirring for about 5 minutes until veggies have softened. Mix in shiitake mushrooms and green onions and continue to cook while stirring for 30 seconds. Add in soy sauce mixture, followed by noodles. Cook while stirring for 2 to 3 minutes until noodles are warmed through. Take out from the heat and toss with the remaining 1 1/2 teaspoon of sesame oil and sesame seeds.

Nutrition Information

- Calories: 673 calories;
- Sodium: 1639
- Total Carbohydrate: 117.2
- Cholesterol: 0
- Protein: 17.3
- Total Fat: 17.3

174. Japanese Onion Soup

Serving: 6 | Prep: 15mins | Ready in:

Ingredients

- 1/2 stalk celery, chopped
- 1 small onion, chopped
- 1/2 carrot, chopped
- 1 teaspoon grated fresh ginger root
- 1/4 teaspoon minced fresh garlic
- 2 tablespoons chicken stock
- 3 teaspoons beef bouillon granules
- 1 cup chopped fresh shiitake mushrooms
- 2 quarts water
- 1 cup baby portobello mushrooms, sliced
- 1 tablespoon minced fresh chives

Direction

- Mix a few of the mushrooms, celery, garlic, onion, ginger, and carrot in a big stockpot or saucepan. Add water, beef bouillon, and chicken stock; let it come to a rolling boil on high heat. Cover once boiling then turn to medium heat; cook for 45 mins.
- Put all the rest of the mushrooms into another pot. Put a strainer on top of the mushroom pot once the boiling mixture is done. Strain the cooked soup into the mushroom pot; get rid of the strained materials.
- In small porcelain bowls, serve the broth along with mushrooms and sprinkle on top with fresh chives. To make it more elegant, Asian soup spoons.

Nutrition Information

- Calories: 25 calories;
- Sodium: 257
- Total Carbohydrate: 4.4
- Cholesterol: 1
- Protein: 1.4
- Total Fat: 0.2

175. Japanese Soup With Tofu And Mushrooms

Serving: 2 | Prep: 10mins | Ready in:

Ingredients

- 3 cups prepared dashi stock
- 1/4 cup sliced shiitake mushrooms
- 1 tablespoon miso paste
- 1 tablespoon soy sauce
- 1/8 cup cubed soft tofu
- 1 green onion, chopped

Direction

- Boil stock in a medium pot. Lower heat to a simmer then put in mushrooms; cook for 3 mins. Combine soy sauce and miso paste together in a small bowl; mix into the stock with tofu. Let it simmer for 5 mins. Add green onion on top to serve.

Nutrition Information

- Calories: 100 calories;
- Total Fat: 3.9
- Sodium: 1326
- Total Carbohydrate: 4.8
- Cholesterol: 3
- Protein: 11

176.　　Jerk Chicken Pizza

Serving: 6 | Prep: 20mins | Ready in:

Ingredients

- 1 green bell pepper
- 4 teaspoons olive oil, divided
- 1 skinless, boneless chicken breast half - finely chopped
- 1 tablespoon jerk sauce, or to taste
- 3 cloves garlic, diced
- 1 portobello mushroom, finely chopped
- 1 (10 ounce) package pre-baked thin pizza crust
- 1/2 cup pizza sauce
- 1 (4 ounce) package thinly sliced salami
- 1 1/2 cups shredded mozzarella cheese

Direction

- Let your oven broiler heat. Put on a baking sheet the green pepper that has been brushed with a teaspoon olive oil. Let it broil for 5 minutes per side until the skin starts to blister. Remove from the heat and, for about 15 minutes, seal in a plastic container. Cut into strips. Then remove the skin, pulp, and seeds; dice.
- Let the oven heat to 175°C (350°F).
- Over medium heat, warm the extra olive oil in a pan. Heat through the chicken for up to 10 minutes or once its juice is clear. Stir in the garlic, roasted green pepper, portobello mushroom, and jerk sauce. Cook through and stir for 5 minutes.
- Put pizza crust on a pan then add on the sauce. Then arrange evenly the salami and chicken mixture over the sauce. Add mozzarella cheese as toppings.
- Bake pizza in the preheated oven for up to 10 minutes or once the cheese is bubbly and melted.

Nutrition Information

- Calories: 358 calories;
- Sodium: 1012
- Total Carbohydrate: 29.6
- Cholesterol: 53
- Protein: 23
- Total Fat: 16.7

177.　　Kale And Mushroom Side

Serving: 4 | Prep: 15mins | Ready in:

Ingredients

- 1 teaspoon grapeseed oil
- 1 onion, diced
- 1/2 cup sliced shiitake mushrooms
- 3 cloves garlic, minced
- 1 tablespoon butter
- 1 tablespoon wine vinegar
- 1 pinch salt and ground black pepper to taste
- 1 bunch kale leaves, torn (ribs removed and discarded)
- 1/2 teaspoon freshly grated nutmeg

Direction

- Heat oil on medium high heat in a wok; mix and cook garlic, mushrooms and onion in hot oil for 5 minutes till mushrooms are soft. Put vinegar and butter in mushroom mixture; season with pepper and salt. Toss mushroom mixture in wok for 1 minute till butter coats everything and melts.
- Turn off heat. Put kale in wok; mix and cook in hot wok for 5 minutes till kale is bright green. Use nutmeg to season kale mixture; mix.

Nutrition Information

- Calories: 127 calories;
- Cholesterol: 8
- Protein: 4.9
- Total Fat: 5

- Sodium: 75
- Total Carbohydrate: 18.5

178. Kansas Quail

Serving: 4 | Prep: 10mins | Ready in:

Ingredients

- wooden skewers
- 12 slices bacon
- 12 mushrooms

Direction

- In a bowl of water, soak wooden skewers for 10 minutes.
- Preheat the grill to medium heat. Oil the grate lightly.
- Around each mushroom, wrap 1 bacon slice. Thread onto skewers. Leave 1/2-inch space between every wrapped mushrooms.
- Cook on preheated grill, frequently rotating skewers, for 10-15 minutes until bacon is crispy.

Nutrition Information

- Calories: 161 calories;
- Total Carbohydrate: 2.2
- Cholesterol: 30
- Protein: 11.9
- Total Fat: 11.7
- Sodium: 638

179. Karen's Easy Baked Mushroom And Onion Risotto

Serving: 6 | Prep: 15mins | Ready in:

Ingredients

- 1 Reynolds® Oven Bag, large size
- 1 tablespoon flour
- 1 teaspoon salt
- 1 teaspoon pepper
- 1 cup chopped cremini mushrooms
- 1 cup Arborio rice
- 1 cup finely chopped onion
- 2 tablespoons butter, divided
- 1 cup water
- 1 cup chicken broth
- 1/3 cup Parmesan cheese, shredded
- Chopped fresh parsley (optional)

Direction

- Preheat the oven to 400 °F. Put Reynolds(R) Oven Bag in a 13x9x2-inch pan. Into the bag, put the pepper, salt and flour. Gently squeeze bag to mix the ingredients.
- Into the oven bag, put 1 tablespoon butter, rice, mushrooms and onion. Flip the bag a few times to combine the ingredients. Layer the ingredients evenly in the bag. Fold down bag opening twice to keep it open; reserve.
- In a measuring cup or medium-sized microwavable bowl, microwave chicken broth and water on high power for approximately 3 minutes till liquid is extremely hot. Carefully scoop or pour the liquid on top of the ingredients in the bag. Carefully unfold the bag opening.
- Using nylon tie, seal the bag at gathers. Make 6 half-inch slits in top near the tie.
- Bake till majority of the liquid is soaked in for 25 minutes to half an hour. Rest for 5 minutes. Carefully cut bag's top open. Into one big serving bowl, scoop the rice mixture. Mix in shredded cheese and leftover tablespoon of butter. Mix in up to cup more hot water, if necessary to make the mixture creamy. Put in more pepper and salt and jazz up with parsley, if wished.

Nutrition Information

- Calories: 212 calories;
- Total Carbohydrate: 35

- Cholesterol: 15
- Protein: 5.6
- Total Fat: 5.2
- Sodium: 652

180. Kelly's Slow Cooker Beef, Mushroom, And Barley Soup

Serving: 6 | Prep: 20mins | Ready in:

Ingredients

- 1 (32 ounce) carton beef stock
- 1 (8 ounce) can tomato sauce
- 1 cup water
- 1/2 onion, diced
- 3/4 cup diced carrots
- 1 cup barley
- 1 (6 ounce) package sliced fresh mushrooms
- 4 cloves garlic, minced
- 2 pounds beef sirloin, cut into chunks
- 1 pinch garlic salt, or to taste
- salt and ground black pepper to taste
- 2 bay leaves

Direction

- In a slow cooker, stir the beef stock, garlic, mushrooms, barley, carrot, onion, tomato sauce, and water together.
- Dust black pepper, salt, and garlic salt to season the beef chunks; add to the beef stock mixture. Put bay leaves into the slow cooker.
- Cook on Low heat for about 6 hours, until the soup is thickened and the beef is tender.
- Take out and omit the bay leaves to serve.

Nutrition Information

- Calories: 359 calories;
- Total Fat: 10.3
- Sodium: 381
- Total Carbohydrate: 31.7
- Cholesterol: 65

- Protein: 34.6

181. Keto Buffalo Cauliflower Chorizo "Mac" N Cheese

Serving: 6 | Prep: 20mins | Ready in:

Ingredients

- 1 head cauliflower, cut into florets
- 2 tablespoons coconut oil
- 1/2 pound chorizo, cut into small pieces
- 1 cup chopped mushrooms
- 1/2 onion, chopped
- 2 tablespoons butter
- 1/4 cup heavy cream
- 1 cup shredded Cheddar cheese
- 1/4 cup grated Parmesan cheese
- 1/2 cup hot pepper sauce (such as Frank's RedHot®)

Direction

- Set an oven to preheat to 165°C (325°F).
- In a microwave-safe bowl, put the cauliflower florets. Let it cook for 10 minutes in the microwave oven.
- While the cauliflower is cooking, in a pan, heat coconut oil on medium heat; then add onion, mushrooms and chorizo. Let it cook for 5-7 minutes until it becomes soft, then move to a baking dish.
- Into the cauliflower, stir the butter, cream, Cheddar cheese, and Parmesan cheese, respectively. Stir in the hot sauce and move the mixture to the baking dish with the chorizo mixture.
- Let it bake in the preheated oven for 15-20 minutes, until it becomes bubbly.

Nutrition Information

- Calories: 403 calories;
- Total Fat: 33.9

- Sodium: 1189
- Total Carbohydrate: 8.1
- Cholesterol: 80
- Protein: 17.9

182. Kevin's Asian Baked Salmon

Serving: 6 | Prep: 10mins | Ready in:

Ingredients

- 2 cups dried shiitake mushrooms
- 1 cup oyster sauce
- 1 tablespoon sherry
- 2 pounds salmon fillets

Direction

- Steep mushrooms for 20 minutes in boiling water; cut off stems and discard. Mix sherry, oyster sauce, and softened mushrooms in a mixing bowl. Allow to stand for 10 to 20 minutes.
- Set oven to 400°F (200°C) to preheat. Line aluminum foil over a large baking dish, then light grease the foil with nonstick cooking spray or olive oil.
- Arrange salmon fillets in the greased baking dish; pour mushroom mixture over fish.
- Bake for approximately 10 to 12 minutes in the preheated oven until salmon flesh is easily flaked using a fork. At the end of cooking process, broil salmon about 1 to 2 minutes to have a seared coating, if desired.

Nutrition Information

- Calories: 428 calories;
- Protein: 34.9
- Total Fat: 16.9
- Sodium: 400
- Total Carbohydrate: 38
- Cholesterol: 89

183. Killer Chicken With Mushroom, Asparagus, And Red Bell Pepper

Serving: 4 | Prep: 20mins | Ready in:

Ingredients

- 2 cups basmati rice
- 4 cups water
- 1 tablespoon vegetable oil
- 1 red onion, cut into 1/2-inch slices
- 3 1/2 pounds skinless, boneless chicken thighs, cut into 2-inch strips
- 1 tablespoon minced fresh ginger root
- 6 cloves garlic, minced
- 3 cups cremini mushrooms, cut in half
- 12 fresh asparagus, trimmed and cut into 2-inch pieces
- 2 small red bell peppers, cut into 1/2-inch strips
- 1 tablespoon fish sauce
- 1 egg
- 2 cups fresh basil leaves
- 1 cup fresh cilantro leaves, chopped
- 2 tablespoons sesame seeds, for garnish
- tamari soy sauce to taste

Direction

- In a saucepan, boil water and rice together. Lower the heat to medium-low, put a cover on and simmer for 35-40 minutes until the rice is soft and liquid is absorbed.
- Once the rice has almost done, in a big skillet, heat oil over high heat. In the hot oil, cook the onion for 2-3 minutes until tender. Add ginger, garlic and chicken to the skillet and keep stirring and cooking for 7-10 minutes until the chicken is entirely browned. Fold fish sauce, bell peppers, asparagus and mushrooms into the chicken mixture, keep cooking for 5 minutes until just hot. Crack the

egg and scramble it into the mixture. Add basil leaves to the mixture, cook for 30 seconds until the leaves have slightly wilted. Take the pan away from heat immediately. Enjoy on top of the basmati rice, drizzle tamari soy sauce over and use sesame seeds and cilantro to garnish.

Nutrition Information

- Calories: 1095 calories;
- Sodium: 610
- Total Carbohydrate: 86.7
- Cholesterol: 270
- Protein: 77.8
- Total Fat: 47.7

---

184. Korean Beef Short Rib Stew (Galbi Jjim)

Serving: 4 | Prep: 15mins | Ready in:

Ingredients

- 2 pounds Korean-style short ribs (beef chuck flanken), cut into 3-inch segments
- 4 cups water
- 6 tablespoons soy sauce
- 8 cloves garlic, minced
- 1 small onion, sliced
- 1 tablespoon rice wine
- 1 tablespoon brown sugar
- 2 carrots, cut into chunks
- 2 small potatoes, cut into chunks
- 1/2 cup fresh shiitake mushrooms, sliced
- 2 tablespoons light corn syrup
- 1 tablespoon Asian (toasted) sesame oil
- 6 chestnuts, peeled (optional)
- 6 dates, pitted (optional)
- sliced green onion

Direction

- Add cold water to cover the ribs, chill and let to soak for one hour. Drain ribs, transfer to a saucepan containing four cups of water. Heat to boil. Let the ribs cook for ten minutes. Drain and save two cups of liquid. Transfer ribs and reserved liquid into a large pot.
- In a bowl, combine together the brown sugar, rice wine, onion, garlic, and soy sauce until sugar is dissolved. Add mixture atop the broth and ribs. Mix to combine, heat to boil, decrease heat, and let to simmer for 1 1/2 hours.
- Stir in the dates, chestnuts, sesame oil, corn syrup, shiitake mushrooms, potatoes and carrots and let to simmer for about 1 hour until the veggies and meat are very tender.
- Transfer the veggies and beef into a serving dish. Decrease liquid in pot to form a thickened gravy. Add the sauce atop the veggies and ribs. Drizzle with chopped green onion and then serve.

Nutrition Information

- Calories: 749 calories;
- Total Carbohydrate: 57.5
- Cholesterol: 93
- Protein: 26.7
- Total Fat: 45.6
- Sodium: 1454

---

185. Korean Short Ribs (Kalbi Jjim)

Serving: 4 | Prep: 35mins | Ready in:

Ingredients

- 6 dried shiitake mushrooms
- 2 pounds beef short ribs
- 2 cups water
- 1 onion, sliced
- 2 tablespoons soy sauce
- 7 cloves garlic, minced
- 1 1/2 tablespoons brown sugar

- 1 tablespoon rice wine
- 1 Korean radish, peeled and cut into chunks
- 2 carrots, cut into chunks
- 6 roasted and peeled chestnuts (optional)
- 6 hard-boiled eggs, peeled (optional)
- 2 tablespoons corn syrup (mulyeot)
- 1 tablespoon sesame oil
- 1 teaspoon ground black pepper
- 1 green onion, chopped

Direction

- Soak the shiitake mushrooms for about 3 hours in bowl containing very warm water until softened. Drain off water and chop into strips.
- Soak the short ribs for 20 minutes in a bowl containing cold water and change water several times. Drain off the water and bring the ribs to room temperature for about half an hour.
- Heat water to boil in a large pot and then add short ribs. Cook for about 10 minutes until no pink color remains. Drain the ribs and then rinse under cold water. Take out any loose particles and the excess fat. Place in a large pot.
- In a bowl, combine rice wine, brown sugar, garlic, soy sauce, sliced onion and 2 cups of water. Spread on top of ribs in pot. Heat to boil. Cook for about 20 to 25 minutes. Mix in carrot, radish, and shiitake mushrooms. Decrease the heat to low and let to simmer while stirring often for about 1 hour until the short ribs become tender.
- Mix black pepper, sesame oil, corn syrup and eggs into the pot. Raise the heat to medium-high and cook while stirring often for about 15 minutes until most of the cooking liquid is evaporated. Place the short ribs onto a serving platter and then add chopped green onion on top.

Nutrition Information

- Calories: 782 calories;
- Sodium: 652

- Total Carbohydrate: 40.3
- Cholesterol: 411
- Protein: 34.2
- Total Fat: 53.5

---

186.   Lemon Mushroom Herb Chicken

Serving: 4 | Prep: 15mins | Ready in:

Ingredients

- 1 cup all-purpose flour
- 1/2 tablespoon dried thyme
- 2 tablespoons dried basil
- 1 tablespoon dried parsley
- 1 teaspoon paprika
- 1 teaspoon salt
- 1/2 teaspoon ground black pepper
- 1 teaspoon garlic powder
- 4 boneless, skinless chicken breast halves
- 1/2 cup butter
- 1 (10.75 ounce) can condensed cream of mushroom soup
- 1 (10.5 ounce) can condensed chicken broth
- 1/4 cup dry white wine
- 1 lemon, juiced
- 1 tablespoon chopped fresh parsley
- 2 tablespoons capers
- 1 tablespoon grated lemon zest

Direction

- Mix garlic powder, ground black pepper, salt, paprika, parsley, basil, flour and thyme in a bowl or shallow dish. Coat the chicken by dredging in the mixture and pat it to remove all excess flour.
- In a large skillet, melt the butter over medium heat and cook the chicken until it is not translucent anymore. Combine lemon juice, wine, chicken broth, and cream of mushroom soup together in a medium bowl; add to the chicken.

- Put a cover on the skillet and simmer until juices from the chicken run clear and the chicken is not pink anymore, 20 minutes. Add lemon zest, capers, and parsley to decorate.

Nutrition Information

- Calories: 568 calories;
- Total Carbohydrate: 36.2
- Cholesterol: 130
- Protein: 36.4
- Total Fat: 30.4
- Sodium: 1915

187. Linguine With Clams And Porcini Mushrooms

Serving: 8 | Prep: 20mins | Ready in:

Ingredients

- 1 ounce dried porcini mushrooms
- 1/4 cup olive oil
- 10 cloves garlic, minced
- 1 teaspoon dried red pepper flakes
- 36 fresh clams, cleaned
- 2 cups dry white wine
- 4 tomatoes, cubed
- 3 (8 ounce) jars clam juice
- 1 1/2 cups chopped fresh parsley
- 1 (16 ounce) package linguine pasta

Direction

- In cold water, add mushrooms and soak for 20-30 minutes to rehydrate. Dry the mushroom; chop coarsely.
- Over medium heat, put a medium saucepan and heat oil. Add red pepper, garlic and mushrooms; cook and stir until they turn browned. Mix in white wine and clams. When the clams open, transfer them to a medium bowl, remove those that don't open.

- Stir parsley, clam juice and tomatoes into the mushroom mixture. Let the mixture simmer in 15 minutes to lightly thicken.
- Boil lightly salted water in a large pot. Cook linguine until al dente, about 8-10 minutes. Drain the pasta.
- Add the clams back to the broth mixture; cook until heated through. Combine the mixture with cooked linguine thoroughly when ready to serve.

Nutrition Information

- Calories: 359 calories;
- Total Fat: 8.6
- Sodium: 209
- Total Carbohydrate: 49.2
- Cholesterol: 8
- Protein: 12

188. Loaded Sweet Potato Lasagna

Serving: 10 | Prep: 30mins | Ready in:

Ingredients

- 1/4 cup olive oil, or as needed, divided
- 1 pound ground beef
- 2 cloves garlic, minced
- 2 teaspoons Italian seasoning, divided, or to taste
- 1/2 teaspoon kosher salt, or to taste
- 1/2 teaspoon ground black pepper, or to taste
- 2 cups marinara sauce, divided
- 1 eggplant, sliced
- 2 small zucchini, sliced
- 2 Cubanelle peppers, chopped
- 2 cups sliced fresh mushrooms
- 2 small sweet potatoes, thinly sliced, or more to taste

Direction

- Put oven to 190°C (375°F). Coat a 13 in. x 9 in. pan with a tbsp. of olive oil.
- Put 1 tbsp. of oil in a big skillet on medium heat. Cook the beef; break in smaller pieces with a wooden spoon until it browns, 5 minutes. Transfer to a bowl with slotted spoon.
- Wipe the skillet with paper towel. Put in remaining 1 tbsp. of oil. Cook garlic until aromatic, 30 seconds. Put with beef. Season with salt, pepper and 1 tsp. Italian seasoning. Add 1 1/2 cups of marinara sauce. Blend well.
- Stir and cook eggplant in skillet until tender, 2 minutes a side. Sprinkle with salt. Put on a plate. Do the same with zucchini. Stir and cook mushrooms on medium heat until tender, 5 minutes. Place in a bowl. Stir and cook cubanelle peppers until soft, 3 minutes.
- Place sweet potatoes in bottom of pan. Reserve a few pieces. On top layer the eggplant, beef, zucchini, cubanelle peppers, and mushrooms. Pour the left 1/2 cup marinara sauce over. Place the reserved sweet potato slices on top. Spritz with oil, season with the remaining 1 tsp. Italian seasoning, pepper, and salt. Cover with foil.
- Bake in the oven until potatoes are soft, 45 minutes. Discard the aluminum foil; bake until golden brown, 15 minutes longer. Let it rest5 minutes then serve.

Nutrition Information

- Calories: 223 calories;
- Total Carbohydrate: 16.3
- Cholesterol: 28
- Protein: 9.8
- Total Fat: 13.5
- Sodium: 339

189. Low Calorie Vegan Chili

Serving: 6 | Prep: 20mins | Ready in:

Ingredients

- 1 (28 ounce) can diced tomatoes
- 3 cups water
- 1 (15.5 ounce) can kidney beans, drained
- 1 (15.5 ounce) can red beans, drained
- 1 yellow onion, diced
- 1 (6 ounce) can tomato paste
- 1 (6 ounce) can mushroom stems and pieces, drained
- 1/2 yellow bell pepper, diced
- 1/2 orange bell pepper, diced
- 3 tablespoons chili powder
- 2 tablespoons garlic powder
- 2 pinches salt

Direction

- In a big saucepan, mix and boil salt, garlic powder, chili powder, orange and yellow bell pepper, mushrooms, tomato paste, onion, red beans, kidney beans, water, and diced tomatoes on high heat; stir occasionally. Lower heat to medium-low. Simmer, occasionally mixing, for 30 minutes until all veggies are tender.

Nutrition Information

- Calories: 220 calories;
- Total Fat: 1.6
- Sodium: 1009
- Total Carbohydrate: 42.5
- Cholesterol: 0
- Protein: 11.9

190. Low Carb Salisbury Steak

Serving: 6 | Prep: 10mins | Ready in:

Ingredients

- Salisbury Steaks:
- 2 pounds ground beef
- 1 onion, diced

- 2 eggs
- 1 tablespoon Worcestershire sauce
- 1 tablespoon dried parsley flakes
- 2 teaspoons salt
- 1/2 teaspoon garlic powder
- 1/2 teaspoon onion powder (optional)
- 1/2 teaspoon ground black pepper
- Gravy:
- 7 tablespoons butter
- 2 cups sliced button mushrooms, or more to taste
- 1 tablespoon all-purpose flour
- 1 cup beef broth
- 1 teaspoon Worcestershire sauce
- 1/2 cup sour cream
- salt and ground black pepper to taste

Direction

- In a bowl, mix 1/2 tsp. pepper, onion powder, garlic powder, 2 tsp. salt, parsley, 1 tbsp. Worcestershire sauce, eggs, onion and ground beef. Split steak mixture to 6 portions; shape to patties.
- Heat a big skillet on medium high heat; cook patties for 5 minutes, 3 at a time, till 1 side is slightly brown. Flip; cook for 5 minutes till the other side turns brown. Repeat with leftover patties, pouring extra liquid off. Put Salisbury steaks onto a plate; cover using aluminum foil to keep the heat.
- Melt butter on medium heat in the same skillet. Add mushrooms; cook for 5 minutes till golden brown. Put mushrooms into a bowl; saving butter in skillet.
- Mix flour into butter to dissolve; add beef broth slowly, mixing for 7 minutes till thicken. Add 1 tsp. Worcestershire sauce; cook, frequently mixing, for 5 minutes till gravy begins to slightly thicken. Add sour cream; season with pepper and salt. Cook for 2 minutes, mixing till gravy is light brown and all sour cream melts.
- Mix mushrooms into gravy again; take off from heat. Cool for 2 minutes till thicken. Scoop mushrooms and gravy on steak patties.

Nutrition Information

- Calories: 536 calories;
- Total Fat: 42.9
- Sodium: 1190
- Total Carbohydrate: 7.5
- Cholesterol: 199
- Protein: 29.7

---

191.   Make Ahead Marsala Turkey Gravy

Serving: 12 | Prep: 15mins | Ready in:

Ingredients

- 2 teaspoons vegetable oil
- 3 turkey necks
- 1 onion, chopped
- 1 stalk celery, chopped
- 1 carrot, chopped
- 1/3 cup Marsala wine
- 2 quarts cold water
- 1/4 ounce dried porcini mushrooms
- 2 cloves garlic, peeled
- 1 bay leaf
- 1/4 cup butter
- 1/4 ounce dried porcini mushrooms
- 3 tablespoons flour
- 2 tablespoons heavy cream
- salt and freshly ground black pepper to taste

Direction

- Over medium-high heat, heat oil in Dutch oven. Put the turkey necks in Dutch oven and then cook for around 5-7 minutes, or until the turkey necks are golden brown. Stir in the carrot, celery, and onion; and continue to cook and mix for around five minutes, until the onion is slightly brown and soft.
- Pour in the Marsala wine over turkey necks, then turn up stove to high heat; boil mixture and scrape off brown-colored bits from the bottom of the pan. Let the turkey necks and

Marsala mixture simmer for around 3-4 minutes, until wine has been reduced by half.

- Mix in 1/4 oz. dried porcini mushrooms, bay leaf, garlic, and water. Allow mixture to boil, then reduce heat to low; simmer, skimming any foam or fat that rises to the top. Cover the Dutch oven almost completely; let the turkey necks mixture simmer for about 4-5 hours, until the meat separates from the bones. Carefully strain the resulting turkey stock into a clean container, and let the mixture cool completely, which should take about 2 hours.

- In a bowl, put 1/4 oz. of dried porcini mushrooms and pour warm water over; keep porcini mushrooms soaked for around 15 minutes, until they're soft enough to be diced. Squeeze out any excess water from the porcini mushrooms, and then drain. Set the mushrooms aside.

- Over medium heat, melt butter in a saucepan. Mix in the diced porcini mushrooms; continue to cook and stir for around five minutes, until porcini mushrooms have turned brown.

- Mix in flour into the butter and mushrooms mixture; cook and mix for around three minutes, until flour no longer appears gritty.

- Mix in turkey stock into the mixture, turning up heat to medium high, and bringing it to a simmer. Let the resulting mixture simmer for around 15-20 minutes, until sauce has thickened and has been reduced by 1/3. Mix in the cream, and season with pepper and salt, to taste.

Nutrition Information

- Calories: 163 calories;
- Total Fat: 8.9
- Sodium: 79
- Total Carbohydrate: 5.6
- Cholesterol: 68
- Protein: 13.1

---

192.   Make Ahead Turkey Gravy With Porcini Mushrooms And Marsala Wine

Serving: 16 | Prep: 5hours | Ready in:

Ingredients

- For the turkey neck stock:
- 2 teaspoons vegetable oil
- 4 turkey necks
- 1 onion, chopped
- 1 stalk celery, chopped
- 1 carrot, chopped
- 1/3 cup Marsala wine
- 2 quarts cold water
- 1 bay leaf
- 2 garlic cloves
- 1/4 ounce dried porcini mushrooms
- For the sauce:
- 1/4 ounce dried porcini mushrooms
- 1 cup hot water
- 1/4 cup butter
- 3 tablespoons all-purpose flour
- 2 tablespoons heavy cream
- salt and ground black pepper to taste

Direction

- Over medium-high heat, heat vegetable oil in a big stockpot. In hot oil, brown turkey necks for about 6 minutes on each side. Put carrots, celery, and onion. Cook for 5 to 10 minutes until the vegetables begin to soften and brown. Put into Marsala wine. At the bottom of the pan, scrape and dissolve any vegetable bits and browned meat off. Turn heat to high and cook until liquid is reduced by half.

- Stir 1/4 ounce dried porcini mushrooms, garlic cloves, bay leaves and 2 quarts of cold water in. Bring to a simmer. Reduce heat to low. Skim and dispose any foam that comes to the top as stock simmers. Partially cover, and simmer for 4 to 5 hours on very low heat. Strain solids out and to cool, set broth aside.

- In a bowl, cover 1 cup hot water to cover 1/4 ounce dried porcini. For 10 minutes, allow to rehydrate. Take mushrooms out from water and chop it finely. Over medium heat, heat 1/4 cup of butter in a big saucepan and brown mushrooms for about 10 minutes. Stir in flour into butter and mushrooms and over medium heat, cook for 3 minutes, constantly stirring. Whisk in about 1/2 cup of broth at a time. Turn heat to medium high and bring gravy to boil.

- Allow to simmer by reducing heat, and cook gravy for about 30 minutes until thickened and reduced. Stir often and stir cream in before serving. Use black pepper and salt to season.

Nutrition Information

- Calories: 140 calories;
- Sodium: 56
- Total Carbohydrate: 3.5
- Cholesterol: 65
- Protein: 12.7
- Total Fat: 7.5

---

193. Mandy's Lamb Enchiladas

Serving: 6 | Prep: 15mins | Ready in:

Ingredients

- 2 pounds ground lamb
- 1 onion, chopped
- 1 (14.5 ounce) can diced tomatoes, drained
- 1 (15.25 ounce) can red kidney beans, drained
- 1 (8 ounce) package sliced fresh mushrooms
- 1 (8 ounce) jar salsa
- 12 (8 inch) flour tortillas
- 2 cups shredded Cheddar cheese

Direction

- Preheat an oven to 175°C/350°F.

- Sauté onion and lamb for 4-5 minutes in a big skillet on medium high heat; mix in mushrooms, beans and tomatoes when lightly browned. Add 1/2 salsa; cook all together till heated through.
- Put it onto tortillas, evenly dividing; roll up tortillas. Put into 9x13-in. lightly greased baking dish. Spread leftover salsa on top; sprinkle cheese.
- Bake for 30 minutes at 175°C/350°F till cheese is bubbly and melted.

Nutrition Information

- Calories: 897 calories;
- Total Carbohydrate: 79.9
- Cholesterol: 142
- Protein: 49.6
- Total Fat: 40.7
- Sodium: 1394

---

194. Marty's Ginger Pad Thai

Serving: 4 | Prep: 45mins | Ready in:

Ingredients

- 1 (8 ounce) package rice noodles (rice vermicelli)
- 2 cups chicken stock
- 1 cup water
- 2 stalks lemongrass, chopped
- 1 cup peanuts
- 1/2 cup coconut powder
- 1 pound boneless chicken breast, sliced
- 1/4 cup oyster sauce
- 2 tablespoons fish sauce
- 2 tablespoons dark soy sauce
- 2 teaspoons salt
- 2 teaspoons ground black pepper
- 2 teaspoons peanut oil, divided
- 1/2 cup chopped ginger
- 1 small Spanish onion, chopped
- 2 jalapeno peppers, seeded and chopped

- 4 cloves garlic, chopped
- 1 habanero pepper, seeded and chopped, or more to taste
- 1 large carrot, cut into matchsticks
- 1 large yellow bell pepper, sliced
- 1 small green bell pepper, sliced
- 4 small radishes, sliced
- 1 large king oyster mushroom, sliced
- 2 tablespoons red curry paste
- 1 teaspoon curry powder, or more to taste
- 1/4 cup white wine
- 1/4 wedge lime, juiced
- 5 sprigs cilantro leaves, chopped

Direction

- In a big pot, put noodles and use lukewarm water to cover. Let submerge for half an hour till softened. Boil; cook for 3 minutes till noodles are tender yet still firm to the bite, mixing from time to time. Drain and put back to the pot.
- In a small saucepan, mix together lemongrass, a cup water and chicken stock. Boil; allow to simmer for 5 minutes till broth is aromatic. Filter out lemongrass and throw.
- Using a mortar and pestle, pound peanuts. In a big skillet or wok, toast for 2 to 3 minutes over medium heat till aromatic. Move to a bowl.
- In the wok, toast coconut for 2 to 3 minutes till aromatic and golden brown, mixing frequently. Move to a bowl.
- In a big bowl, put chicken. Cover with pepper, salt, soy sauce, fish sauce and oyster sauce.
- In the wok over medium-high heat, heat a teaspoon peanut oil. Put in ginger and chicken mixture; cook and mix for 2 minutes each side till chicken is browned. Take out of the wok.
- In the wok over medium-high heat, heat leftover 1 teaspoon peanut oil. Put in habanero pepper, garlic, jalapeno peppers and onion; sauté for 2 minutes till aromatic. Put in radishes, green bell pepper, yellow bell pepper and carrot; cook and mix for a minute. Mix in curry powder, red curry paste and mushroom for 1 to 2 minutes till well-incorporated.

- Put white wine and broth into the wok. Cook for 5 minutes till reduced. Mix in all the coconut and half of the toasted peanuts; allow to simmer for 2 minutes. Put in chicken; keep on simmering for 5 minutes till sauce has reduced to about 1 1/2 cup and chicken is not pink in the middle anymore.
- In the pot, put sauce and chicken atop noodles; put leftover peanuts. Mix for 2 to 3 minutes over low heat till well-incorporated. Add lime juice and jazz up with cilantro.

Nutrition Information

- Calories: 740 calories;
- Total Fat: 31.6
- Sodium: 2942
- Total Carbohydrate: 77.3
- Cholesterol: 59
- Protein: 37.8

195. Mary McCormack's Marinated Mushrooms

Serving: 8 | Prep: | Ready in:

Ingredients

- 1 1/2 teaspoons garlic salt
- 1 1/2 teaspoons seasoning salt
- 1/4 cup distilled white vinegar
- 1/2 cup olive oil
- 2 (8 ounce) cans mushrooms, drained

Direction

- Whisk the olive oil, vinegar, seasoned salt and garlic salt together. Spread over mushrooms and let marinate for 24 hours.

Nutrition Information

- Calories: 135 calories;
- Sodium: 750

- Total Carbohydrate: 3.2
- Cholesterol: 0
- Protein: 1.1
- Total Fat: 13.7

196. Minnesota Pork Chops

Serving: 4 | Prep: 20mins | Ready in:

Ingredients

- 6 pork chops
- salt and pepper to taste
- 1 cup uncooked wild rice
- 1 1/2 cups water
- 1 (8 ounce) can canned mushrooms
- 1 tablespoon chicken bouillon granules
- 1 (10.75 ounce) can condensed cream of mushroom soup

Direction

- Preheat the oven to 175 degrees C (350 degrees F).
- Brown the chops seasoned with pepper and salt in a skillet with a little amount of oil. Use nonstick spray to spritz a large 9x13 inch casserole dish. Evenly drizzle washed rice on bottom of dish.
- Add mushrooms and water. Drizzle with the chicken bouillon. Spread chops at the top and spoon the soup atop rice and chops. Use aluminum foil to cover the casserole and then seal tightly. Bake for about 1 1/2 hours to 2 hours or until the chops and rice become tender.

Nutrition Information

- Calories: 352 calories;
- Total Fat: 14.4
- Sodium: 791
- Total Carbohydrate: 29.3
- Cholesterol: 56

- Protein: 26.9

197. Mouth Watering Stuffed Mushrooms

Serving: 12 | Prep: 25mins | Ready in:

Ingredients

- 12 whole fresh mushrooms
- 1 tablespoon vegetable oil
- 1 tablespoon minced garlic
- 1 (8 ounce) package cream cheese, softened
- 1/4 cup grated Parmesan cheese
- 1/4 teaspoon ground black pepper
- 1/4 teaspoon onion powder
- 1/4 teaspoon ground cayenne pepper

Direction

- Set oven to 350°F (175°C) to preheat. Grease a baking sheet with cooking spray. Clean mushrooms using a damp paper towel. Gently break off mushroom stems. Chop stems very fine, removing any tough end of the stems.
- In a large skillet, heat oil over medium heat. Put chopped mushroom stems and garlic to pan and fry until moisture has evaporated, being careful not to burn the garlic. Put to one side and allow to cool. Once mushrooms and garlic are cool enough, mix in cayenne pepper, onion powder, black pepper, Parmesan cheese, and cream cheese until the mixture becomes very thick. Fill each mushroom cap with a liberal amount of stuffing mixture with a little spoon. Place the stuffed mushroom caps on the prepared baking sheet.
- Bake in the preheated oven until mushrooms are very hot and liquid begins to form under the caps, for 20 minutes.

Nutrition Information

- Calories: 88 calories;

- Sodium: 82
- Total Carbohydrate: 1.5
- Cholesterol: 22
- Protein: 2.7
- Total Fat: 8.2

198. Mushroom Bagna Cauda

Serving: 6 | Prep: 15mins | Ready in:

Ingredients

- 1 tablespoon butter
- 1 (2 ounce) can anchovy fillets, drained
- 8 cloves garlic, minced
- 1 (10 ounce) can condensed cream of mushroom soup
- 1 cup whipping cream
- 2 cups half and half

Direction

- In a sauté pan, melt butter over medium heat. Sauté anchovies and garlic for 2-3 minutes until the garlic has mellowed. Add half and half, cream, and the mushroom soup; lower the heat to low and cook for 45 minutes without boiling the mixture.

Nutrition Information

- Calories: 321 calories;
- Cholesterol: 96
- Protein: 6.4
- Total Fat: 29.4
- Sodium: 643
- Total Carbohydrate: 9.1

199. Mushroom Barley Soup

Serving: 6 | Prep: 25mins | Ready in:

Ingredients

- 1 cup barley
- 3 cups water
- 1 1/2 tablespoons olive oil
- 2 onions, chopped
- 1 carrot, thinly sliced
- 2 stalks celery, thinly sliced
- 2 (10 ounce) packages sliced mushrooms
- 5 cups beef broth
- 1/2 teaspoon salt
- 1/4 teaspoon ground black pepper

Direction

- Boil water and barley in a saucepan. Cover the saucepan. Adjust the heat to low and let it simmer for 30 minutes until tender.
- Put olive oil in a large saucepan and heat it over medium heat. Mix in carrots, celery, and onions. Cook for 10 minutes, stirring until the onion is translucent and soft. Mix in mushrooms. Cook for 5 more minutes.
- Add the beef broth. Simmer the soup over medium-high heat. Adjust the heat to medium-low and continue to simmer for 15 more minutes. Mix in barley. Season the mixture with salt and pepper before serving.

Nutrition Information

- Calories: 194 calories;
- Total Fat: 4.9
- Sodium: 882
- Total Carbohydrate: 30.5
- Cholesterol: 0
- Protein: 9.6

200. Mushroom Bok Choy Soup

Serving: 6 | Prep: 15mins | Ready in:

Ingredients

- 1/4 cup unsalted butter
- 1 head bok choy, chopped
- 1 pound white and crimini mushrooms, cut into quarters
- 4 green onions, sliced
- 2 tablespoons minced garlic, or more to taste
- 8 slices fresh ginger, quartered
- 1/4 cup lime juice
- 7 cups chicken broth
- 1/2 cup chopped fresh cilantro

Direction

- Using a stock pot on medium heat, heat the butter and mix in the mushrooms, green onions, garlic, ginger, and bok choy. Drizzle in lime juice with the mushroom mixture. Stir and cook for 2 to 3 minutes until it turns a light brown color. Adjust the heat to medium-high and pour the chicken broth in. Once it starts boiling, lower the heat and let it simmer for 5 minutes or until the vegetables become soft. Present the dish with cilantro.

Nutrition Information

- Calories: 125 calories;
- Cholesterol: 26
- Protein: 5.3
- Total Fat: 8.7
- Sodium: 1178
- Total Carbohydrate: 8.4

---

201.   Mushroom Burgers

Serving: 6 | Prep: 20mins | Ready in:

Ingredients

- 1 pound fresh mushrooms, sliced
- 1 large onion, minced
- 2 slices white bread, finely diced
- 2 tablespoons oyster sauce
- 1 egg

- salt to taste
- ground black pepper to taste

Direction

- Coat a big skillet with cooking spray and put on moderate heat. Put in onions and mushrooms, then cook and stir about 4 minutes just until mushrooms start to draw out their juices. Stir in oyster sauce and bread cubes, then cook and stir for a minute. Take mixture out of the pan and set aside to cool. Wipe pan clean.
- Beat egg and combine into the mushroom mixture, then season with pepper and salt, to taste.
- Coat cooking spray to the skillet and put on moderate heat. Scoop the mixture into skillet in 6 equal quantity. Brown one side then flip over and brown the rest side. Serve.

Nutrition Information

- Calories: 61 calories;
- Total Carbohydrate: 9.2
- Cholesterol: 31
- Protein: 4.3
- Total Fat: 1.4
- Sodium: 110

---

202.   Mushroom Cheeseburger Calzones

Serving: 4 | Prep: 30mins | Ready in:

Ingredients

- 1 pound lean ground beef
- 1 cup fresh mushrooms, chopped
- 1 small sweet onion, diced
- 1 jalapeno pepper, diced
- 1/4 cup ketchup
- 2 tablespoons prepared yellow mustard
- salt and ground black pepper to taste

- 1 (10 ounce) container refrigerated pizza dough
- 12 dill pickle slices
- 1 cup shredded American and Cheddar cheese blend
- 2 teaspoons olive oil
- 1 teaspoon sesame seeds

Direction

- Start preheating the oven to 190°C (375°F).
- Add jalapeno pepper, sweet onion, mushrooms, and ground beef to a big skillet and cook on medium heat for about 10 minutes until the mushrooms are tender and the beef is crumbly and browned. Remove the excess grease and whisk in black pepper, salt, yellow mustard, and ketchup. Take away from heat.
- On a floured work surface, roll the pizza dough out and slice in half. Scoop 1/2 of the ground beef onto each half, then add 6 dill pickle slices and 1/2 of the American-Cheddar cheese blend on top of each half. Fold the dough over the filling and use a folk to press the edges together to seal the calzones. Arrange them onto a baking sheet, spread the olive oil over the tops using a brush, then top with sesame seeds.
- Bake for about 15-20 minutes in the preheated oven until the cheese melts and the calzones become golden brown.

Nutrition Information

- Calories: 584 calories;
- Total Fat: 28.5
- Sodium: 2373
- Total Carbohydrate: 44.8
- Cholesterol: 101
- Protein: 36.3

203. Mushroom Chicken Piccata

Serving: 6 | Prep: 20mins | Ready in:

Ingredients

- 1/2 cup all-purpose flour
- 1 teaspoon salt
- 1/2 teaspoon paprika
- 1 egg
- 2 tablespoons milk
- 6 skinless, boneless chicken breast halves
- 4 tablespoons butter
- 1/2 pound fresh mushrooms, sliced
- 1/4 cup chopped onion
- 1 cup chicken broth
- 1/2 cup white wine
- 2 tablespoons lemon juice
- 1 tablespoon cornstarch
- 1 tablespoon chopped fresh parsley, for garnish

Direction

- Combine paprika, salt and flour in a bowl or a shallow dish. Combine milk and egg in a separate bowl or dish. Dredge chicken pieces to the egg mixture then transfer them to the seasoned flour mixture.
- Heat margarine or butter in a large skillet over medium-high heat. Sauté chicken pieces until they are golden brown in color. Stir in onion and mushrooms; sauté for 3-5 minutes.
- Mix together cornstarch, lemon juice, wine and broth in a medium bowl. Stir well and transfer it onto the mushrooms and chicken. Lower the heat to medium-low; simmer the mixture until juices run clear and the chicken is cooked through or for 25 minutes. Use parsley to sprinkle before serving.

Nutrition Information

- Calories: 288 calories;
- Total Fat: 10.4
- Sodium: 697

- Total Carbohydrate: 12.6
- Cholesterol: 121
- Protein: 31.1

---

204. Mushroom Chicken Tetrazzini

Serving: 4 | Prep: 15mins | Ready in:

Ingredients

- 1/2 (8 ounce) package spaghetti
- 3 skinless, boneless chicken breast halves
- 1 onion, chopped
- 8 ounces fresh mushrooms, quartered
- 1 cube chicken bouillon
- water to cover
- salt and pepper to taste
- 4 cups heavy cream
- 1/4 cup grated Parmesan cheese

Direction

- Boil a big pot with slightly salted water. Put in and cook pasta till al dente, for 8 to 10 minutes; strain. Meantime, let chicken cook in microwave till nearly cooked completely and juices run nearly clear.
- Preheat the oven to 165°C or 325°F.
- In medium size saucepan, sauté mushrooms and onion till soft. Put in bouillon, chicken, and water to submerge. Simmer on moderately low heat, seasoning to taste with pepper and salt. Put in cream and cooked spaghetti and combine everything; lastly, mix cheese in.
- In prepped oven, bake for 20 minutes to half an hour, or till cooked completely. Monitor dish midway through cooking and if wished, put in additional Parmesan cheese to taste.

Nutrition Information

- Calories: 1072 calories;

- Total Carbohydrate: 33.5
- Cholesterol: 382
- Protein: 32.5
- Total Fat: 91.4
- Sodium: 516

---

205. Mushroom Chile Relleno Casserole

Serving: 4 | Prep: 20mins | Ready in:

Ingredients

- 2 tablespoons butter
- 3 cloves garlic, minced
- 1/2 cup chopped onion
- 1/2 cup seeded and minced sweet peppers
- 1/2 cup minced green bell pepper
- 1/2 cup chopped fresh mushrooms
- 1 (16 ounce) can chopped green chiles, or to taste
- 1/2 cup stewed tomatoes with juice, chopped
- salt and freshly ground black pepper to taste
- 1 1/2 cups soy milk
- 5 eggs
- 1/2 cup all-purpose flour
- 2 tablespoons minced cilantro
- 1/8 teaspoon chili powder
- 1/8 teaspoon dried oregano
- 1/8 teaspoon ground cumin
- 1 cup shredded Cheddar-Monterey Jack cheese blend

Direction

- Start preheating the oven to 350°F (175°C). Lightly coat a 2-qt. casserole dish with oil.
- In a frying pan, heat butter over medium-low heat. Add garlic, mix in green bell pepper, sweet peppers, and onion. Cook for 5 minutes until soft. Add mushrooms and cook for 4-6 minutes until soft. Add stewed tomatoes and green chiles, cook for 3-4 minutes until thoroughly heated. Use pepper and salt to

season. On the bottom of the prepared casserole dish, spread the mixture.

- In a big bowl, combine eggs and soy milk until thoroughly mixed. Add cumin, oregano, cilantro, and flour. Use pepper and salt to season. Using a whisk, combine very well until all of the lumps have mostly gone.
- In the casserole, sprinkle over the top of the pepper mixture with 1/2 cup Cheddar-Monterey Jack cheese. Add to the egg mixture and put the leftover cheese on top.
- Put in the preheated oven and bake for 45 minutes until the sides and tops are barely crunchy and a knife will come out clean when you insert it into the middle. Allow to sit before slicing, about 10 minutes.

Nutrition Information

- Calories: 401 calories;
- Total Fat: 22.1
- Sodium: 1772
- Total Carbohydrate: 31.9
- Cholesterol: 273
- Protein: 20.9

---

206. Mushroom Cream Sauce With Shallots

Serving: 3 | Prep: 10mins | Ready in:

Ingredients

- 2 lobster mushrooms, cut into cubes
- 2 tablespoons water
- 1/3 cup heavy whipping cream
- 2 teaspoons all-purpose flour
- 2 tablespoons grated Asiago cheese
- 1/2 shallot, minced
- 1/2 teaspoon salt
- 1/2 teaspoon ground black pepper

Direction

- Place a nonstick skillet over medium heat; add mushrooms; put in water. Cook while stirring sometimes for around 5 minutes or till water is evaporated.
- Whisk flour and cream into mushrooms till flour is incorporated. Put black pepper, salt, shallot and Asiago cheese into the mushroom mixture, stirring continually. Cook while stirring for around 7 minutes or till sauce thickens.

Nutrition Information

- Calories: 123 calories;
- Total Fat: 11.1
- Sodium: 454
- Total Carbohydrate: 4.1
- Cholesterol: 40
- Protein: 2.5

---

207. Mushroom Curry With Galangal

Serving: 4 | Prep: 10mins | Ready in:

Ingredients

- 2 cups coconut milk
- 1 (2 inch) piece galangal, peeled and sliced
- 3 kaffir lime leaves, torn
- 2 teaspoons salt
- 1/3 pound sliced fresh mushrooms
- 5 Thai chile peppers, chopped
- 1/4 cup fresh lime juice
- 1 tablespoon fish sauce

Direction

- In a pot, add the galangal and coconut milk and then heat to boil. Add salt and kaffir lime leaves and simmer for ten minutes. Place in mushrooms and cook for 5 to 7 minutes until soft. Take out from the heat. Mix fish sauce and lime juice into the mixture. Transfer to a bowl and add the Thai chilies on top. Serve.

Nutrition Information

- Calories: 261 calories;
- Total Fat: 24.4
- Sodium: 1458
- Total Carbohydrate: 11.8
- Cholesterol: 0
- Protein: 4.9

208. Mushroom Gravy/Sauce

Serving: 8 | Prep: 10mins | Ready in:

Ingredients

- 2 tablespoons butter
- 1 (8 ounce) package button mushrooms, sliced
- 1/4 cup minced shallot
- 2 tablespoons all-purpose flour
- 2 teaspoons all-purpose flour
- 2 cups fat-free reduced-sodium beef broth
- 1/4 cup half-and-half
- 1/2 teaspoon ground black pepper
- 1 dash salt

Direction

- Over medium-high heat, melt butter in a heavy 12 inches skillet. Put shallot and mushrooms. Sauté for about 6 minutes until softened, stirring occasionally. Put 2 tablespoons and 2 teaspoons of flour. For about a minute, cook until incorporated. Put beef broth. Cook for about 2 minutes until thickened slightly, stirring frequently. Stir half-and-half, salt and black pepper in. Cook for 30 more seconds.

Nutrition Information

- Calories: 64 calories;

- Protein: 2.7
- Total Fat: 4.2
- Sodium: 93
- Total Carbohydrate: 4.4
- Cholesterol: 10

209. Mushroom Mint Pasta Salad

Serving: 12 | Prep: 15mins | Ready in:

Ingredients

- 1 (16 ounce) package farfalle (bow tie) pasta
- 1/4 cup olive oil, divided
- 2 (8 ounce) packages button mushrooms, sliced
- 4 onions, sliced
- 1 quart heavy cream
- 10 sprigs fresh mint
- 1 1/2 teaspoons white sugar
- 1 pinch salt
- 1 pinch ground black pepper

Direction

- Boil the lightly salted water in a large pot. Put pasta into pot and cook until al dente, about 8-10 mins, then drain. Let cool, then place into a large bowl. Mix with 3 tablespoons of the olive oil.
- In a large skillet, heat the remaining olive oil over medium heat. In the skillet, put onions and mushrooms. Cook while stirring until it is lightly brown. Add heavy cream gradually, stirring continuously. Put mint sprigs into skillet. Cook while stirring for 5 mins.
- Mix the sugar into cream sauce. Add pepper and salt to season. Using slotted spoon, discard the mint sprigs. Stir in cooked pasta until it is well coated.

Nutrition Information

- Calories: 487 calories;
- Sodium: 35
- Total Carbohydrate: 36.4
- Cholesterol: 109
- Protein: 8.7
- Total Fat: 34.9

210. Mushroom Risotto

Serving: 4 | Prep: 10mins | Ready in:

Ingredients

- 1 tablespoon olive oil
- 3 small onions, finely chopped
- 1 clove garlic, crushed
- 1 teaspoon minced fresh parsley
- 1 teaspoon minced celery
- salt and pepper to taste
- 1 1/2 cups sliced fresh mushrooms
- 1 cup whole milk
- 1/4 cup heavy cream
- 1 cup rice
- 5 cups vegetable stock
- 1 teaspoon butter
- 1 cup grated Parmesan cheese

Direction

- Put enough oil in a large skillet and heat it over medium-high heat. Cook and sauté the garlic and onion in hot oil until the garlic is lightly browned and the onion is tender. Remove the garlic, and add the salt, celery, pepper, and parsley. Add mushrooms once the celery is tender. Adjust the heat to low, and cook the mushrooms until tender.
- Stir in cream and milk, and then followed by the rice. Bring the mixture to simmer. Pour in vegetable stock, one cup at a time, until absorbed completely.
- Add butter and Parmesan cheese once the rice is cooked. Remove the mixture from the heat and serve warm.

Nutrition Information

- Calories: 439 calories;
- Cholesterol: 50
- Protein: 16.9
- Total Fat: 19.5
- Sodium: 768
- Total Carbohydrate: 48.7

211. Mushroom Stuffed Beef Rouladen

Serving: 4 | Prep: 45mins | Ready in:

Ingredients

- 3 tablespoons vegetable oil, divided
- 1 clove garlic, chopped
- 1 pound assorted mushrooms (brown, oyster, portobello), thinly sliced
- 1 pinch dried thyme
- salt and pepper to taste
- 1 egg, beaten
- 1/4 cup bread crumbs
- 8 (3 ounce) pieces top round, pounded thin
- 1/4 cup dry red wine
- 2 1/2 cups beef stock
- 1/4 cup all-purpose flour
- 1 tablespoon Dijon mustard

Direction

- In a big sauté pan, let 2 tablespoons of oil heat up over medium-high heat setting. Put in the mushrooms and garlic and mix it together. Sauté the mixture in the hot oil until the mushrooms become soft, then add in the dried thyme and mix everything together; remove the pan away from the heat and let the mixture cool down to room temperature. Once the mixture has cooled down, add in pepper and salt to taste followed by the breadcrumbs and beaten egg and mix.
- Distribute the prepared mushroom mixture evenly among each of the top round slices.

Tightly roll up each of the filled top round slices in a cylinder and use a toothpick to seal the filling inside.

- Preheat the oven to 350°F (175°C).
- In a skillet, let the remaining 1 tablespoon of oil heat up over medium-high heat setting. Let the prepared Rouladen cook in the hot oil until it turns brown in color; put the browned Rouladen in an 8x8-inch baking dish. In the same hot skillet used for the Rouladen, put in the wine and let it simmer. While the wine is simmering, mix the flour and beef stock together until it is smooth in consistency. Add the beef stock mixture into the skillet and let it get back to a simmer. Allow the mixture to cook until it is thick in consistency, then add in the Dijon mustard and mix everything together. Pour the prepared sauce on top of the browned Rouladen.
- Cover the baking dish and put it in the preheated oven; let it bake for 60-75 minutes until the meat becomes tender.

Nutrition Information

- Calories: 533 calories;
- Cholesterol: 150
- Protein: 45.9
- Total Fat: 28.9
- Sodium: 307
- Total Carbohydrate: 18.3

---

212.   Mushroom Stuffing

Serving: 14 | Prep: | Ready in:

Ingredients

- 1 pound fresh mushrooms, sliced
- 6 tablespoons butter
- 1 cup diced onion
- 1 cup chopped celery
- 1 teaspoon poultry seasoning
- 1 teaspoon salt

- 1/4 teaspoon ground black pepper
- 12 cups dried bread crumbs
- 1 1/2 cups hot chicken broth
- 2 eggs, beaten
- 2 cups diced apple without peel
- 1/4 cup chopped parsley

Direction

- Butter 1 9x13-in. casserole dish; preheat an oven to 190°C/375°F.
- Rinse, pat dry then quarter mushrooms. Heat butter in a big skillet; add celery, onion and mushrooms. Sauté for 5 minutes; discard from heat. Mix in pepper, salt and poultry seasoning.
- Mix breadcrumbs with eggs and broth in a big mixing bowl; put in parsley, mushroom mixture and apples, then mix well. Turn into the casserole dish.
- Cover; bake for 45 minutes at 190°C/375°F. Uncover; bake until brown top, about 15 minutes.

Nutrition Information

- Calories: 443 calories;
- Sodium: 899
- Total Carbohydrate: 71.7
- Cholesterol: 40
- Protein: 14.6
- Total Fat: 10.7

---

213.   Mushroom Tacos

Serving: 3 | Prep: 20mins | Ready in:

Ingredients

- 2 tablespoons olive oil
- 1 (8 ounce) package sliced mushrooms (such as Monterey Mushrooms®)
- 1 tablespoon minced garlic
- 2 zucchini, cut into chunks

- 3 tablespoons diced sun-dried tomatoes
- 1 tablespoon Worcestershire sauce
- 1 teaspoon onion powder
- 1 teaspoon salt
- 1 teaspoon ground black pepper
- 6 (6 inch) corn tortillas

Direction

- Heat up a big skillet on medium-high heat, then pour in the olive oil. Add the garlic and mushrooms, then sauté until aromatic, 1-2 minutes. Stir in pepper, salt, onion powder, Worcestershire sauce, sun-dried tomatoes, and zucchini; cook until the flavors have blended, 4-5 minutes.
- Heat up the griddle on medium-high heat and cook the corn tortillas until they toast lightly, around a minute on each side. Spoon over tortillas with the mushroom mixture.

Nutrition Information

- Calories: 244 calories;
- Total Fat: 11
- Sodium: 938
- Total Carbohydrate: 33.2
- Cholesterol: 0
- Protein: 7

---

214. Mushroom And Chickpea Tagine

Serving: 4 | Prep: 20mins | Ready in:

Ingredients

- Dukka:
- 2 teaspoons cumin seeds
- 2 teaspoons coriander seeds
- 1 teaspoon sesame seeds
- Tagine:
- 2 tablespoons olive oil
- 1 red onion, chopped

- 1 clove garlic, crushed
- 3 1/2 cups quartered chestnut mushrooms
- 1 (14 ounce) can chopped tomatoes
- 1 (14 ounce) can chickpeas, drained
- 1 (10.5 ounce) can vegetable stock
- 1/3 cup halved dried apricots
- 2 tablespoons chopped fresh parsley
- 1 tablespoon honey
- 1 tablespoon tomato puree
- 1 tablespoon lemon juice
- 1 cinnamon stick
- 2 dried bay leaves
- 1 pinch white sugar, or to taste
- salt and ground black pepper to taste
- 3/4 cup plain yogurt

Direction

- In a dry frypan, toast the sesame seeds, coriander seeds and cumin seeds on medium heat for 2-3 minutes until it becomes aromatic. In a spice grinder, place the dukka mixture and grind it until it becomes a smooth powder.
- In a big pot, heat the oil on medium heat. Put garlic and onion, then cook with cover for 3-5 minutes, stirring from time to time, until it becomes tender. Put mushrooms and 1 tsp dukka then cook for 3 minutes with cover. Take off the cover and let it cook for about 5 minutes, mixing often, until the mushroom releases most of its moisture.
- In the pot, mix the pepper, salt, sugar, bay leaves, cinnamon stick, lemon juice, tomato puree, honey, parsley, apricots, vegetable stock, chickpeas and chopped tomatoes. Let it simmer for about 15 minutes with cover, until the flavors are blended. Put 1 tsp dukka and cook for about 15 minutes, mixing often until the tagine becomes thick.
- Get rid of bay leaves and cinnamon stick. Stir in 1 tsp dukka into the yogurt then serve it alongside tagine.

Nutrition Information

- Calories: 292 calories;

- Total Carbohydrate: 45.9
- Cholesterol: 0
- Protein: 9.3
- Total Fat: 9.1
- Sodium: 667

215. Mushroom And Gorgonzola Soup

Serving: 6 | Prep: 30mins | Ready in:

Ingredients

- 2 tablespoons butter
- 1/2 onion, diced
- 2 cloves garlic, minced
- 1 pound sliced mushrooms
- 2 tablespoons butter
- 2 tablespoons all-purpose flour
- 2 (13.75 ounce) cans chicken broth
- 1 cup half-and-half cream
- 1/2 teaspoon salt
- 1/2 teaspoon dried rosemary leaves, crumbled
- 1/2 cup crumbled Gorgonzola or blue cheese
- 1 tablespoon sherry
- salt and pepper to taste
- 1/4 cup chopped fresh parsley (optional)

Direction

- In a skillet, add 2 tablespoons butter and melt over medium-high heat. Mix in mushrooms, garlic, and onions. Stir and cook for 5 minutes until the mushrooms decrease and the onions are tender. Take away from heat.
- In the meantime, in a pot, add the leftover 2 tablespoons butter and melt over medium-high heat. Mix in flour, then stir and cook for 5 minutes until the mixture is golden brown. Slowly add rosemary, 1/2 teaspoon salt, half-and-half, and chicken broth; mix to combine the ingredients. Lower the heat to medium. Mix the mushroom mixture and gorgonzola cheese into the chicken broth mixture, then

simmer the soup and cook for 10 minutes, whisking often.
- In a blender, add 1/2 of the soup. Process until smooth and put back into the pot. Mix in sherry, and use pepper and salt to season. Cook for another 5 minutes until the mixture is thick. If you want, use fresh parsley to garnish and enjoy.

Nutrition Information

- Calories: 219 calories;
- Sodium: 1057
- Total Carbohydrate: 9.6
- Cholesterol: 54
- Protein: 7.9
- Total Fat: 17

216. Mushroom And Mascarpone Ravioli

Serving: 4 | Prep: 25mins | Ready in:

Ingredients

- 1 tablespoon olive oil
- 2 large shallots, minced
- 8 ounces fresh mushrooms, chopped
- 1 tablespoon chopped fresh thyme
- 2 tablespoons minced garlic
- 1 tablespoon chopped fresh chives
- 1 (8 ounce) container mascarpone cheese
- salt and pepper to taste
- 32 (3.5 inch square) wonton wrappers
- 1 egg, beaten
- 2 tablespoons milk

Direction

- In a big skillet, heat the olive oil over medium-high heat. Put the shallots; cook and mix till beginning to brown. Lower the heat to medium and put the chives, garlic, thyme and mushrooms; keep cooking for 5 to 10 minutes till the liquid from the mushrooms has evaporated. Take off heat and reserve to cool.

- Mix together the mushroom mixture and mascarpone cheese in a medium bowl. Put with salt and pepper to taste; reserve.
- On a clean surface, lay 16 wonton wrappers out. In a small cup, mix together the milk and egg. Onto the wrappers, brush with egg wash. Place a tablespoon of the cheese mixture onto the middle of every square. With a small spoonful of the mushroom mixture, atop the cheese. Put the second wonton wrapper on top of all the filling and pinch edges to seal. Ravioli can be chilled on a baking tray with plastic wrap cover.
- Boil a big pot of lightly salted water. Put the ravioli one at a time and allow to cook till they rises to the top for 3 to 4 minutes.

Nutrition Information

- Calories: 519 calories;
- Total Fat: 32
- Sodium: 424
- Total Carbohydrate: 46
- Cholesterol: 123
- Protein: 14.9

| 217. | Mushroom Smothered Beef Burgers |

Serving: 4 | Prep: 15mins | Ready in:

Ingredients

- 1 (10.75 ounce) can Campbell's® Condensed Cream of Mushroom Soup (Regular or 98% Fat Free)
- 1 pound ground beef
- 1/3 cup Italian-seasoned dry bread crumbs
- 1 small onion, finely chopped
- 1 egg, beaten
- 1 tablespoon vegetable oil
- 1 tablespoon Worcestershire sauce

- 2 tablespoons water
- 1 1/2 cups sliced mushrooms

Direction

- In a big bowl, combine thoroughly together egg, onion, bread crumbs, beef and 1/4 cup of soup. Form the beef mixture firmly into four burgers with the thickness of 1/2 inch.
- In a 10-in. skillet, heat oil on moderately high heat. Put in burgers and cook until both sides of burgers are well browned. Get rid of any fat.
- Put into the skillet with mushrooms, water, Worcestershire and leftover soup, then heat to a boil. Lower heat to low, then place on a cover and cook until burgers are cooked through, about 10 minutes.

Nutrition Information

- Calories: 365 calories;
- Total Fat: 22.3
- Sodium: 837
- Total Carbohydrate: 15.8
- Cholesterol: 119
- Protein: 23.6

| 218. | Mushroom Walnut Loaf (Garden Loaf) |

Serving: 12 | Prep: 15mins | Ready in:

Ingredients

- 3 1/2 cups cooked brown rice
- 6 eggs, beaten
- 4 cups shredded Cheddar cheese
- 2 1/2 cups sliced fresh mushrooms
- 1 1/2 cups chopped raw walnuts
- 3/4 cup finely chopped onion
- 1 1/2 tablespoons tamari
- 1 1/2 teaspoons garlic powder

Direction

- Set the oven to 350°F (175°C) and start preheating.
- In a large bowl, mix garlic powder, tamari, onion, walnuts, mushrooms, Cheddar cheese, beaten eggs and cooked rice; combine well. Transfer to a 9x13-inch baking pan.
- Bake in the prepared oven for about 45 minutes until set.

Nutrition Information

- Calories: 358 calories;
- Total Carbohydrate: 17.6
- Cholesterol: 133
- Protein: 17
- Total Fat: 25.3
- Sodium: 397

---

219.   Mushrooms And Peas Rice

Serving: 5 | Prep: 10mins | Ready in:

Ingredients

- 8 ounces fresh mushrooms, sliced
- 1 tablespoon butter
- 1 (10.75 ounce) can condensed cream of mushroom soup
- 10 3/4 fluid ounces milk
- 1 3/4 cups instant rice
- 1 1/2 cups frozen green peas

Direction

- Sauté mushrooms with butter in a big skillet, then put aside.
- Warm milk and condensed cream of mushroom soup. Once it comes to a slow bubble, put in instant rice and cover. Allow to sit for a minimum of 5 minutes.

- While you are warming the soup mixture, place peas in the microwave to thaw at 30-second intervals. Avoid over-heating the peas.
- Once the rice is softened, stir into rice with peas and mushrooms. Use pepper and salt to season the mixture to taste.

Nutrition Information

- Calories: 269 calories;
- Cholesterol: 11
- Protein: 9.2
- Total Fat: 7.5
- Sodium: 493
- Total Carbohydrate: 41.2

---

220.   Neptune's Favor

Serving: 5 | Prep: 20mins | Ready in:

Ingredients

- 2 (10 ounce) boxes frozen chopped spinach, thawed and squeezed dry
- 1/4 cup mayonnaise
- 1/4 cup all-purpose flour
- 2 cups milk
- 3/4 teaspoon salt
- 1/4 teaspoon paprika
- 1/8 teaspoon crushed rosemary
- 1/8 teaspoon dried thyme leaves
- 2 tablespoons grated onion
- 1/2 (4 ounce) can sliced mushrooms, drained
- 2 hard cooked eggs, chopped
- 1 pound cooked Alaskan snow crab meat
- 1/2 cup shredded Swiss cheese

Direction

- Preheat an oven to 175°C/350°F then butter a square glass 8-in. glass baking dish. Put spinach onto bottom then around sides of the prepped baking dish.

- Mix flour and mayonnaise in a saucepan; mix in milk. Season with thyme, rosemary, paprika and salt. Add mushrooms and onion; simmer on medium high heat and cook till thick, constantly mixing. Mix in eggs; put into a baking dish. Sprinkle cheese and crabmeat.
- In preheated oven, bake for approximately 20 minutes till cheese is melted.

Nutrition Information

- Calories: 435 calories;
- Sodium: 947
- Total Carbohydrate: 17
- Cholesterol: 194
- Protein: 34.8
- Total Fat: 26

221. Nikki's Pork Chops With A Mushroom Cream Sauce Over White Jasmine Rice

Serving: 4 | Prep: 20mins | Ready in:

Ingredients

- Rice:
- 2 cups water
- 1 cup white jasmine rice
- 1/2 teaspoon salt
- 1 tablespoon butter
- Pork Chops:
- 4 (1/2-inch thick) pork chops
- 1 tablespoon olive oil, or to taste
- 1/2 teaspoon Creole seasoning, or to taste
- salt and ground black pepper to taste
- 1 green bell pepper, sliced
- 1/2 small onion, sliced
- Cream Sauce:
- 1/4 cup butter
- 1/2 cup sliced fresh mushrooms
- 1/4 cup chopped onion
- 2 cups half-and-half

- 1 tablespoon all-purpose flour
- 1/2 teaspoon ground paprika, or to taste

Direction

- In a saucepan, mix half teaspoon salt, rice and water; bring to a boil. Lower the heat to low; cook with a cover for about 20 minutes until rice becomes tender. Take out of the heat; add a tablespoon of butter; stir until rice becomes fluffy.
- Set the oven to 350°F (175°C) and start preheating. (If you use a countertop induction oven, set the oven to "Combo 1" setting and start preheating.)
- In a 9-inch baking pan, place pork chops (or grill pan if you use countertop induction oven). Drizzle over top with olive oil. Sprinkle pepper, salt and Creole seasoning. Place sliced onions and green bell peppers on and around pork chops.
- Bake in the prepared oven for about 20 minutes with the conventional oven and 10-15 minutes with the countertop induction oven until the inserted instant-read thermometer into the center registers at least 145°F (63°C). Use aluminum foil to cover.
- Over medium heat, in a large skillet, melt 1/4 cup butter. Add chopped onion and mushrooms; cook while stirring for about 5 minutes until onion becomes translucent. Pour in half-and-half. Slowly stir in flour; cook while stirring for about 5 minutes until sauce is thickened.
- Pour sauce on top pork chops; stir to incorporate juices in pan.
- Place pork chops back to the prepared oven; bake for 3-5 minutes until flavors combine. Serve over rice. Top with paprika.

Nutrition Information

- Calories: 673 calories;
- Protein: 31.5
- Total Fat: 38.8
- Sodium: 580
- Total Carbohydrate: 48.9

- Cholesterol: 142

222.   No Sour Cream Beef Stroganoff

Serving: 4 | Prep: 20mins | Ready in:

Ingredients

- 1 1/2 pounds ground beef
- salt to taste
- 1 tablespoon butter
- 1 (8 ounce) can mushrooms, drained
- 1 onion, chopped
- 1 clove garlic, minced
- 4 tablespoons flour
- 1/2 cup white wine
- 1 (10.5 ounce) can cream of mushroom soup
- 1/2 (10.5 ounce) can beef broth
- Worcestershire sauce to taste

Direction

- In large skillet, brown ground beef over medium heat. Season with salt. Add in butter, onion, mushrooms and garlic; cook until the onions are soft.
- Mix together flour and white wine in a small bowl. Add this mixture along with the beef broth and mushroom soup into the meat. Simmer for 10 to 15 minutes until thick. Add more broth if necessary. Season with a dash of Worcestershire sauce and serve.

Nutrition Information

- Calories: 473 calories;
- Protein: 32.4
- Total Fat: 27.6
- Sodium: 962
- Total Carbohydrate: 17.3
- Cholesterol: 111

223.   No Noodle Zucchini Lasagna

Serving: 8 | Prep: 30mins | Ready in:

Ingredients

- 2 large zucchini
- 1 tablespoon salt
- 1 pound ground beef
- 1 1/2 teaspoons ground black pepper
- 1 small green bell pepper, diced
- 1 onion, diced
- 1 cup tomato paste
- 1 (16 ounce) can tomato sauce
- 1/4 cup red wine
- 2 tablespoons chopped fresh basil
- 1 tablespoon chopped fresh oregano
- hot water as needed
- 1 egg
- 1 (15 ounce) container low-fat ricotta cheese
- 2 tablespoons chopped fresh parsley
- 1 (16 ounce) package frozen chopped spinach, thawed and drained
- 1 pound fresh mushrooms, sliced
- 8 ounces shredded mozzarella cheese
- 8 ounces grated Parmesan cheese

Direction

- Set oven temperature to 325 degrees F (165 degrees C) and leave aside for preheating.
- Cut zucchini into long slices that are as thin as possible. Add a sprinkle of salt on these slices and put aside for draining in a colander.
- Prepare the meat sauce by cooking ground beef and black pepper in a large skillet for 5 minutes on medium-high heat settings. Stir in onions and green pepper and continue cooking until meat no longer appears rare. Mix tomato sauce, tomato paste, basil, wine, and oregano into the pan, consider adding a little hot water if the sauce gets too thick in consistency. Increase the temperature to a boil

and then decrease and let simmer for 20 minutes, stirring often.

- In the meantime, combine ricotta, parsley, and egg in a bowl until evenly mixed.
- Assembly the lasagna as follows; 1/2 of the meat sauce is poured into the bottom of prepared pan and spread evenly. Add in the following arrangement, 1/2 zucchini slices, 1/2 ricotta mix, all of the spinach, and all of the mushroom, followed by 1/2 of the mozzarella cheese. Continue the arrangement with the remainder of the meat sauce, zucchini slices, ricotta mixture, and mozzarella cheese. Cover with an even spread of Parmesan cheese and a layer of foil.
- Carefully place in the oven and bake for 45 minutes. Then remove the foil, increase oven temperature to 350 degrees and bake for another 15 minutes. Set aside for 5 minutes before serving.

Nutrition Information

- Calories: 494 calories;
- Total Fat: 27.3
- Sodium: 2200
- Total Carbohydrate: 23.2
- Cholesterol: 118
- Protein: 41.3

224. Oh So Good Chicken

Serving: 5 | Prep: | Ready in:

Ingredients

- 4 teaspoons olive oil
- 6 tablespoons sour cream
- 4 ounces shredded Cheddar cheese
- 2 cups fresh sliced mushrooms
- 1 (16 ounce) jar salsa
- 2 cups cooked white rice
- 8 ounces boneless chicken breast halves, cooked and diced

Direction

- Heat oil in a skillet on medium heat then sauté mushrooms.
- Mix chicken, rice, salsa, cheese, sour cream and mushrooms. Put into greased casserole dish.
- Bake for 25-35 minutes at 175°C/350°F.

Nutrition Information

- Calories: 357 calories;
- Sodium: 717
- Total Carbohydrate: 25.4
- Cholesterol: 65
- Protein: 22.4
- Total Fat: 18.7

225. One Pot Pasta

Serving: 4 | Prep: | Ready in:

Ingredients

- 1 teaspoon olive oil
- 1/2 cup sliced onion
- 1 cup fresh sliced mushrooms
- 1 (29 ounce) can diced tomatoes
- 1 (8 ounce) can tomato sauce
- 1 cup water
- 2 teaspoons dried basil
- 1 teaspoon dried oregano
- 1 teaspoon white sugar
- 1/4 teaspoon garlic powder
- 1/4 teaspoon ground black pepper
- 8 ounces macaroni

Direction

- Spray nonstick cooking spray over a large nonstick pan. Put in oil, heat over medium flame. Put in mushrooms and onion. Cook until tender, stirring frequently, for 3-5 mins.
- Put spices, sugar, water, tomato sauce and tomatoes into skillet. Stir in pasta once the

mixture starts to boil. Lower the heat to medium-low, cover and cook for 20 mins. While cooking, stir mixture every 4-5 mins.

Nutrition Information

- Calories: 290 calories;
- Total Carbohydrate: 55.2
- Cholesterol: 0
- Protein: 10.6
- Total Fat: 2.3
- Sodium: 775

---

226. Our Favorite Beef Stroganoff

Serving: 4 | Prep: 10mins | Ready in:

Ingredients

- 1 pound ground beef chuck
- 1 small onion, chopped
- 1 clove garlic, minced, or more to taste
- 1/4 teaspoon ground thyme
- 1/4 teaspoon dried basil
- 1 dash salt and ground black pepper
- 1 (10.75 ounce) can condensed cream of mushroom soup
- 1 cup beef broth
- 1 (4.5 ounce) can mushroom pieces and stems, drained
- 1/2 cup sour cream

Direction

- Over medium-high heat, heat up a big skillet then stir in the onion and beef. Cook and stir for 5 to 7 minutes until the beef is crumbly and browned, then drain it to get rid of the grease. Add pepper, salt, basil, thyme and garlic, followed by mushrooms, beef broth and cream of mushroom soup. Lower the heat and let it simmer for about 20 minutes until the flavors

combine together. Towards the end of the cooking process, fold in the sour cream. Serve.

Nutrition Information

- Calories: 308 calories;
- Total Fat: 22.3
- Sodium: 968
- Total Carbohydrate: 9.9
- Cholesterol: 64
- Protein: 17

---

227. Owen's Chicken Rice

Serving: 10 | Prep: | Ready in:

Ingredients

- 1/2 (3 pound) whole chicken, cut into pieces
- 8 ounces Chinese-style sausages
- 1 teaspoon salt
- 1 tablespoon dark soy sauce
- 2 tablespoons sesame oil
- 1/2 slice fresh ginger root, chopped
- 12 dried shiitake mushrooms, soaked until soft
- 3 cups long-grain white rice
- 2 1/2 cups boiling water
- 3 tablespoons chopped fresh cilantro
- 3 tablespoons thinly sliced green onion

Direction

- Mix soy sauce and 1 teaspoon salt then marinate the sausages and chicken in it and put it aside.
- In a big nonstick wok, heat the sesame oil in it and stir fry the ginger in the oil until it's fragrant. Mix in the chicken and sausages and stir fry them until they are brown. Mix in the mushrooms then fry for 3 more minutes. Add the rice while stirring then add salt and pepper to season.
- Move the mixture to a rice cooker then pour in water. Once the rice has cooked, add spring

onions and chopped coriander as toppings then serve.

Nutrition Information

- Calories: 469 calories;
- Sodium: 576
- Total Carbohydrate: 49.4
- Cholesterol: 51
- Protein: 22.1
- Total Fat: 20.1

---

228. Oyster And Mushroom Stuffing

Serving: 16 | Prep: 20mins | Ready in:

Ingredients

- 1/2 cup margarine
- 1 large onion, chopped
- 2 cups chopped celery
- 1 (12 ounce) package fresh mushrooms, sliced
- 8 cups dry bread crumbs
- 1 egg, beaten
- 1 pint shucked oysters, chopped
- 1/2 cup chicken broth
- 1 teaspoon poultry seasoning
- 1 teaspoon dried sage
- 1/2 teaspoon salt
- 1/2 teaspoon ground black pepper

Direction

- Preheat an oven to 165°C/325°F.
- Melt margarine in big skillet on medium heat; mix and cook celery and onion for about 10 minutes till celery is tender. Mix mushrooms in; mix and cook for 5-8 minutes till they release their juice and tender.
- Mix oysters, egg and breadcrumbs in bowl; mix cooked veggies with margarine and juices, black pepper, salt, sage, poultry seasoning and

chicken broth in till combined well. Put stuffing in 2-qt. casserole dish.

- In preheated oven, bake for about 45 minutes till top is browned, oysters are cooked and stuffing is hot.

Nutrition Information

- Calories: 309 calories;
- Cholesterol: 30
- Protein: 12
- Total Fat: 9.7
- Sodium: 619
- Total Carbohydrate: 42.9

---

229. Paleo Chicken Marsala

Serving: 5 | Prep: 15mins | Ready in:

Ingredients

- 4 skinless, boneless chicken breast halves
- sea salt and ground black pepper to taste
- 1 tablespoon extra-virgin olive oil, or more as needed
- 2 tablespoons unsalted butter, divided
- 6 (1 ounce) slices prosciutto, cut into thirds
- 1 small shallot, minced
- 8 ounces crimini mushrooms, stemmed and halved
- 1/2 cup sweet Marsala wine
- 1/2 cup chicken stock
- 1/4 cup chopped flat-leaf parsley

Direction

- On a hard, level surface, put chicken cutlets between 2 plastic wrap sheets. Firmly pound a meat mallet's smooth side onto the meat until the thickness is 1/4-inch. Use pepper and salt to season both sides.
- In a big frying pan, heat 1 tablespoon butter and 1 tablespoon olive oil over medium-high heat until the butter melts. In the frying pan,

put the chicken cutlets; cook for 5 minutes per side until turning golden brown on both sides.

- Lower the heat to medium, pour olive oil into the frying pan if necessary. In the frying pan, put shallots and prosciutto; stir and cook for 1 minute until warmed. Mix in mushrooms and cook for 5 minutes until turning brown. Use pepper and salt to season. Add wine to the frying pan; simmer for 1 minute until the flavors blend. Pour in chicken stock; stir and simmer for 1 minute until the sauce partially decreases.
- Mix into the frying pan with 1 tablespoon of butter. Put the chicken back into the pan; simmer for 1 minute until the chicken has fully heated. Use pepper, salt, and parsley to garnish.

Nutrition Information

- Calories: 357 calories;
- Total Carbohydrate: 5.8
- Cholesterol: 97
- Protein: 28.9
- Total Fat: 20.5
- Sodium: 811

230. Pan Roasted Beef Tenderloin With Ginger Shiitake Brown Butter

Serving: 4 | Prep: 25mins | Ready in:

Ingredients

- 2 tablespoons olive oil
- 4 (8 ounce) beef tenderloin filets
- Kosher salt and freshly ground black pepper, to taste
- 3 tablespoons unsalted butter
- 2 tablespoons minced fresh ginger
- 1 tablespoon minced fresh garlic
- 1/2 cup thinly sliced fresh shiitake mushrooms

- 3 tablespoons sake
- 2 tablespoons mirin (sweetened rice wine)
- 1 tablespoon finely chopped garlic chives
- 3/4 cup unsalted butter

Direction

- Preheat oven to 200 °C or 400 °F.
- Over high heat, heat olive oil in a big ovenproof skillet until smoking lightly. Use pepper and salt to season filets to taste. Sear both sides for about 3 minutes per side until golden brown. Put into oven and cook for about 12 minutes for medium-rare to desired doneness. Once done, let it rest for 5 minutes out of the pan.
- Meanwhile, over medium-high heat, melt 3 tablespoons of butter in a saucepan. Stir garlic and ginger in. Cook for about 1 1/2 minutes until aromatic and translucent but not browned. Put shiitake mushrooms and cook until softened for 3 to 4 minutes. Put in mirin and sake. Allow to simmer until reduced by half. Melt the leftover 3/4 cup of butter, then, turn heat to medium-low. Cook for 6 to 8 minutes until the butter browns. Once done, add pepper and salt to taste, then, stir chives in. To serve, spoon sauce over steaks.

Nutrition Information

- Calories: 872 calories;
- Total Fat: 76.9
- Sodium: 189
- Total Carbohydrate: 5.2
- Cholesterol: 229
- Protein: 34.7

231. Parsley Mushroom Gravy

Serving: 4 | Prep: 5mins | Ready in:

Ingredients

- 2 tablespoons chicken drippings

- 1/4 cup all-purpose flour
- 2 cups chicken broth
- 1 cup canned sliced mushrooms, drained
- 1 tablespoon finely chopped parsley
- salt and ground black pepper to taste

Direction

- Over medium heat, heat the chicken drippings in a small saucepan. Add the flour and continue to cook for around 2-3 minutes, until mixture is golden brown, while continuously stirring mixture. Add the chicken broth and let the mixture boil. Continue to cook for around 3-5 minutes, until the gravy has thickened, while continuously stirring mixture in the process. Stir in mushrooms, parsley, salt and pepper.

Nutrition Information

- Calories: 58 calories;
- Protein: 4.7
- Total Fat: 0.5
- Sodium: 828
- Total Carbohydrate: 8.6
- Cholesterol: 3

232.　　Parsnip And Mushroom Soup

Serving: 30 | Prep: 35mins | Ready in:

Ingredients

- 1/3 cup extra-virgin olive oil
- 2 large carrots, peeled and chopped
- 2 celery ribs, chopped
- 1 white onion, peeled and chopped
- 3 large portobello mushroom caps, cleaned and chopped
- 5 (13.75 ounce) cans chicken broth
- 8 parsnips, peeled and chopped
- 2 cups fresh shiitake mushrooms, sliced

- 1/3 cup extra-virgin olive oil
- 5 cloves garlic, minced
- 1 bunch fresh tarragon
- 3 sprigs fresh thyme
- kosher salt to taste (optional)

Direction

- Into deep pot, put 1/3 cup of olive oil, and heat over moderate heat. Mix in onion, celery and carrots; cook for 5 minutes till vegetables are fork-tender. Mix in portobello mushrooms, and cook for 5 minutes longer. Add in chicken broth, and put shiitake mushrooms and parsnips. Boil the mixture, then lower heat to moderate, and simmer for 10 minutes till parsnips are tender. Take off heat.
- In blender or food processor's bowl, put 1/3 cup of olive oil. Put thyme, tarragon and garlic, and beat till well incorporated. Into the soup, mix the mixture. Season with kosher salt to taste.

Nutrition Information

- Calories: 92 calories;
- Total Fat: 5.3
- Sodium: 344
- Total Carbohydrate: 9.7
- Cholesterol: 2
- Protein: 1.5

233.　　Passover Mushroom Dressing

Serving: 6 | Prep: 30mins | Ready in:

Ingredients

- 2 cups matzo meal
- 1 tablespoon sugar
- 1 teaspoon salt
- 1 teaspoon ground black pepper, or to taste
- 1/4 teaspoon poultry seasoning

- 2 cups chicken broth
- 1/2 cup canola oil
- 2 tablespoons canola oil
- 2 tablespoons butter or margarine
- 3 cups onion, chopped
- 2 bunches green onions, chopped
- 1 (8 ounce) package sliced fresh mushrooms
- 1/2 cup chopped celery
- 4 extra large eggs
- 1 1/2 cups chicken broth

Direction

- Preheat an oven to 190°C/375°F. Mix poultry seasoning, pepper, salt, sugar and matzo meat in big mixing bowl; put aside.
- Boil 2 cups chicken broth and 1/2 cup canola oil in a small saucepan; mix into matzo mixture till moistened evenly. Put aside; let cool. Heat butter and leftover canola oil in a big cast-iron skillet on medium heat. Mix in green onion and chopped onion; cook for 7 minutes till onion is translucent and soft. Mix in celery and mushrooms; cook for 10 minutes longer till celery starts to soften.
- Whisk eggs and leftover 1 1/2 cups chicken stock; mix into cooled matzo mixture then fold in cooked veggies till mixed evenly. Put mixture in the cast-iron skillet.
- In the preheated oven, bake till brown for 50 minutes; during this time, mix once to evenly cook.

Nutrition Information

- Calories: 472 calories;
- Sodium: 495
- Total Carbohydrate: 39.6
- Cholesterol: 154
- Protein: 11.8
- Total Fat: 31.7

234. Pasta Pizzaz

Serving: 4 | Prep: 10mins | Ready in:

Ingredients

- 1 pound farfalle (bow tie) pasta
- 1/3 cup olive oil
- 1 clove garlic, chopped
- 1/4 cup butter
- 2 small zucchini, quartered and sliced
- 1 onion, chopped
- 1 tomato, chopped
- 1 (8 ounce) package mushrooms, sliced
- 1 tablespoon dried oregano
- 1 tablespoon paprika
- salt and pepper to taste

Direction

- Boil slightly salted water in a large pot, then add the farfalle pasta, cook until al dente, about 8-10 minutes, and drain.
- Melt butter with olive oil in a broad skillet above medium heat, then sauté pepper, salt, paprika, oregano, mushrooms, onion tomato, zucchini, and garlic for 15-20 minutes. Combine pasta with the sautéed vegetables and toss together.

Nutrition Information

- Calories: 717 calories;
- Total Fat: 32.9
- Sodium: 491
- Total Carbohydrate: 92.8
- Cholesterol: 31
- Protein: 18.1

235. Pasta Shells With Portobello Mushrooms And Asparagus In Boursin Sauce

Serving: 6 | Prep: 15mins | Ready in:

Ingredients

- 1 tablespoon butter
- 1 tablespoon olive oil
- 1 pound portobello mushrooms, stems removed
- 1/2 teaspoon salt
- 1 1/4 cups low-sodium chicken broth
- 1 (5.2 ounce) package pepper Boursin cheese
- 3/4 pound uncooked pasta shells
- 1 pound fresh asparagus, trimmed

Direction

- Put a big pan over medium heat, heat the olive oil and melt the butter in it. Slice the mushrooms in half and 1/4 inch thick. Cook the mushrooms until they are tender and lightly browned, about 8 minutes then add salt for seasoning. Add the Boursin cheese and chicken broth, stirring it in. Lower the heat and let the sauce simmer with constant stirring until it has blended well.
- Boil lightly salted water in a big pot then add shell pasta and cook for 5 minutes. Add the asparagus and continue cooking for 5 more minutes until the asparagus is tender and the pasta is al dente, then drain the water. Mix with the mushroom sauce then serve.

Nutrition Information

- Calories: 400 calories;
- Sodium: 388
- Total Carbohydrate: 51.6
- Cholesterol: 35
- Protein: 14.1
- Total Fat: 16.6

---

236.   Pasta And Fresh Cilantro Crunchy Stuff

Serving: 16 | Prep: 20mins | Ready in:

Ingredients

- 4 bunches cilantro leaves
- 2 bunches fresh basil, stems removed
- 3 cloves garlic
- 24 ounces freshly grated Parmesan cheese
- 1/4 cup olive oil
- salt and pepper, to taste
- 2 tablespoons olive oil
- 2 tablespoons minced garlic
- 2 pounds crimini mushrooms, sliced
- 1 (8 ounce) jar sun-dried tomatoes packed in oil, drained and chopped
- 3 (16 ounce) jars Alfredo pasta sauce
- 2 (16 ounce) packages fusilli pasta

Direction

- Set oven to 375°F (190°C) to preheat.
- Process 3 garlic cloves, basil, and cilantro together in a food processor or blender until very finely minced. In a large mixing bowl, combine herb mixture with 1/4 cup olive oil and Parmesan thoroughly; sprinkle with pepper and salt to season. Press mixture firmly into a medium glass baking dish, about 1 inch thick.
- Bake for about 5 to 7 minutes in the preheated oven until top is crispy and lightly brown. Take out of the oven, mix well, and place back into the oven until golden brown, for 5 to 7 minutes more. Take out of the oven; use a spoon to break apart; let cool.
- Meanwhile, heat olive oil over low heat in a large pan. Brown 2 tablespoons garlic lightly; mix in mushrooms, and cook until tender. Mix in Alfredo sauce and sun-dried tomatoes; cook to warm.
- Bring lightly salted water in a large pot to a boil. Put in pasta and cook until al dente, for 8 to 10 minutes; drain. Combine pasta with sauce, and scatter with crunchy stuff. Serve.

Nutrition Information

- Calories: 733 calories;
- Cholesterol: 72

- Protein: 31.9
- Total Fat: 45.4
- Sodium: 1617
- Total Carbohydrate: 53.1

237.   Pasta With Asparagus

Serving: 4 | Prep: 15mins | Ready in:

Ingredients

- 1 1/2 pounds fresh asparagus, trimmed and cut into 1 inch pieces
- 1/4 cup chicken broth
- 1/2 pound fresh mushrooms, sliced
- 8 ounces angel hair pasta
- 1 tablespoon olive oil
- 1/2 teaspoon crushed red pepper
- 1/2 cup grated Parmesan cheese

Direction

- Cook the pasta, following the directions in its package.
- In a nonstick pan, heat olive oil and sauté asparagus on medium heat for 3 minutes. Add mushroom slices and chicken broth for another 3 minutes.
- Strain the pasta and place onto a serving dish, and toss carefully with the asparagus mixture. Sprinkle with crushed red pepper and Parmesan.

Nutrition Information

- Calories: 281 calories;
- Protein: 15.5
- Total Fat: 8.4
- Sodium: 339
- Total Carbohydrate: 39.4
- Cholesterol: 9

238.   Pastini Soup

Serving: 4 | Prep: 5mins | Ready in:

Ingredients

- 1 (8 ounce) package dry pastini
- 3 cups veal stock
- 1 grilled portobello mushroom cap, sliced
- 1 tablespoon tomato paste
- 1 tablespoon red wine
- salt and pepper to taste

Direction

- Add the wine, tomato paste, mushroom, stock and pasta with pepper and salt for seasoning into a big pot and mix together. Cook over moderate-high heat for 8 to 10 minutes or until pasta is heated through but firm enough to bite.

Nutrition Information

- Calories: 229 calories;
- Sodium: 108
- Total Carbohydrate: 39.7
- Cholesterol: 46
- Protein: 11.1
- Total Fat: 2.3

239.   Peanut Sesame Chicken With Mushrooms

Serving: 6 | Prep: 15mins | Ready in:

Ingredients

- 2 cups water
- 1 cup uncooked glutinous white rice (sushi rice)
- 2 tablespoons vegetable oil
- 2 teaspoons sesame oil
- 5 green onions, chopped
- 3 cloves garlic, minced

- 3 skinless, boneless chicken breast halves - cubed
- 8 ounces fresh mushrooms, chopped
- 1 tablespoon rice vinegar
- 3 tablespoons soy sauce
- 2 tablespoons toasted sesame seeds
- 1 tablespoon cornstarch
- 2 tablespoons cold water
- 3/4 cup chopped unsalted dry-roasted peanuts

Direction

- Place rice and 2 cups water in a medium saucepan and bring to a boil. Cover, lower the heat to low and simmer for 20 minutes.
- Put sesame oil and vegetable oil in a large skillet over medium-high heat, and stir-fry the garlic and green onions until tender. Stir in the mushrooms, and chicken, and keep on stirring and cooking for about 5 minutes. Stir in the sesame seeds, soy sauce, and rice vinegar. Lower the heat to medium-low, and simmer for 20 minutes, stirring occasionally.
- Combine the 2 tablespoons cold water and cornstarch in a bowl. Mix the peanuts and cornstarch mixture into the skillet and cook over high heat for a few minutes until thickened. Place over the cooked rice to serve.

Nutrition Information

- Calories: 322 calories;
- Total Fat: 18.2
- Sodium: 485
- Total Carbohydrate: 22.1
- Cholesterol: 30
- Protein: 19.5

240.   Philly Steak And Cheese Sliders

Serving: 12 | Prep: 20mins | Ready in:

Ingredients

- 1 pound sirloin steak, cut into 1/8-inch strips
- 1 pinch meat tenderizer
- 1 splash olive oil
- 1 onion, thinly sliced
- 1/2 cup minced bell pepper
- 1 teaspoon Italian seasoning, or to taste
- ground black pepper to taste
- 2 cups canned sliced mushrooms
- 1 (12 count) package Hawaiian-style dinner rolls, sliced in half
- 8 slices provolone cheese

Direction

- Place the oven rack approximately 6-inches away from heat source and prepare the oven's broiler by preheating. In a bowl, combine meat tenderizer and steak.
- In a skillet set on medium heat, add olive oil. Add bell pepper and onion; stir and cook for approximately 3 minutes until slightly tender. Mix in steak mixture; stir and cook for approximately 3 minutes until flavors blend. Stir in pepper and Italian seasoning; mix in mushrooms. Stir and cook for approximately 3 minutes until steak is mostly browned.
- Transfer steak mixture on lower half of dinner rolls until they are covered; put provolone cheese on top. Put on a baking sheet.
- Then broil in preheated oven for 1-3 minutes until cheese is dissolved; take from the broiler. Put the dinner rolls onto dissolved provolone cheese; then broil for 1-2 minutes until tops become toasted.

Nutrition Information

- Calories: 403 calories;
- Total Fat: 7.7
- Sodium: 512
- Total Carbohydrate: 45.9
- Cholesterol: 69
- Protein: 26.2

241. Pita Bread Tofu Sandwiches

Serving: 2 | Prep: 15mins | Ready in:

Ingredients

- 1 tablespoon olive oil
- 1/2 (12 ounce) package tofu, cubed
- 6 mushrooms, sliced, or more to taste
- 1 cup chopped broccoli
- 1/2 cup sliced onion
- 2 stalks celery, chopped
- 3 tablespoons soy sauce
- 1 1/2 teaspoons cornstarch
- 2 pita bread rounds
- 1/2 cup shredded Cheddar cheese

Direction

- On medium-high heat, heat oil in a pan. Sauté celery, tofu, onion, mushrooms, and broccoli for 5 mins until tender.
- In a bowl, combine cornstarch and soy sauce. Pour mixture in the pan with tofu. Cook for 4-5 mins until thick.
- In a toaster, hear pit bread for a minute until warm. Scoop tofu mixture on pita bread. Garnish with Cheddar cheese.

Nutrition Information

- Calories: 473 calories;
- Protein: 24.5
- Total Fat: 21.3
- Sodium: 1908
- Total Carbohydrate: 48.9
- Cholesterol: 30

242. Pizza Style Portabello Mushrooms

Serving: 2 | Prep: 15mins | Ready in:

Ingredients

- 2 large portobello mushroom caps
- 1/2 cup diced tomatoes
- 2 tablespoons balsamic vinegar
- 1 tablespoon olive oil
- 1 tablespoon chopped fresh basil
- 2 cloves garlic, chopped
- 1 pinch dried parsley, or to taste
- 1 pinch red pepper flakes, or to taste
- 4 ounces shredded pepperjack cheese
- 4 ounces shredded mozzarella cheese
- 2 tablespoons sliced black olives, or to taste (optional)
- 1 tablespoon Italian-style seasoned bread crumbs, or to taste

Direction

- Preheat the oven to 175°C or 350°F. Put mushrooms in a baking pan.
- On medium heat, mix together red pepper flakes, tomatoes, parsley, balsamic vinegar, garlic, olive oil, and basil in a big skillet and cook for 5-10 minutes until heated through.
- Spread half of the tomato mixture on top of each mushroom. Top with mozzarella cheese and pepperjack cheese. Sprinkle black olives and bread crumbs on top.
- Bake in the preheated oven for 25 minutes until crispy and golden.

Nutrition Information

- Calories: 477 calories;
- Total Fat: 35.4
- Sodium: 845
- Total Carbohydrate: 12.4
- Cholesterol: 97
- Protein: 27.4

243.   Porcini Braised Boar With Artichoke And Fennel

Serving: 8 | Prep: 50mins | Ready in:

Ingredients

- 3 cups dry cannellini beans
- 1 quart chicken or pork stock
- 2 cups water
- 4 pounds wild boar (cinghiale) roast, cut into serving-size pieces
- 1/4 cup olive oil
- 8 ounces fresh porcini, chanterelles or stemmed shiitake mushrooms, thickly sliced
- 1/4 cup chopped garlic
- 1/4 cup minced fresh rosemary
- sea salt and ground black pepper to taste
- 8 large artichoke hearts, cut into eighths
- 2 large fennel bulbs, cored and thinly sliced
- 1/4 cup olive oil
- 2 tablespoons minced garlic
- 1/2 teaspoon crushed red pepper flakes
- 1/2 cup white wine
- 1/4 cup freshly squeezed lemon juice
- extra-virgin olive oil for drizzling
- 1/2 cup grated pecorino Toscano (or pecorino Romano) cheese
- 1/2 cup chopped Italian flat leaf parsley
- 1 lemon, zested

Direction

- Place the beans in much of cold water and soak them overnight.
- Drain the cannellini beans and pour them into a large Dutch oven together with water and chicken stock. Bring the mixture to a boil over high heat. Adjust the heat to medium-low. Cover the pot and simmer for 1 hour, skimming off any foam that forms. Remove the boar from the fridge and let it rest at room temperature during this time.
- Add 1/4 cup of olive oil in a large skillet and heat it over high heat until it starts to smoke.
- Add the boar pieces and sear until browned on every side. Transfer the seared boar into the top of the gently simmering beans in the pot. Heat the skillet until it smokes again. Mix in porcini mushrooms. Let them cook for 2 minutes until softened. Add 1/4 cup of the garlic. Continue cooking until the garlic turns golden brown. Sprinkle the mixture with chopped rosemary. Cook the mixture for 30 seconds longer, and then add the mushrooms into the beans and boar.
- Cover the skillet and keep simmering the boar and beans for approximately 1 1/2 hours, adding more water if necessary until they are all tender. Once they're ready, season them lightly with freshly ground pepper and sea salt to taste.
- Once the beans are nearly ready, add the artichoke hearts and some water into a large skillet. Cover the skillet and steam over high heat for about 2 minutes until just tender. Add the sliced fennel and steam the mixture for 1 minute longer. Drain in a colander. Place the skillet back into the stove.
- Adjust the heat to medium-high. Pour in 2 tbsp. of minced garlic and 1/4 cup of olive oil. Cook the mixture while frequently stirring until the garlic turns golden. Sprinkle the garlic with red pepper flakes. Add the drained vegetables. Cook and stir the vegetables for about 2 minutes until they are golden and tender. Whisk in white wine. Cook the mixture until almost evaporated. Season the mixture with salt, pepper, and lemon juice.
- To serve the dish, mound the vegetables into the middle of a large platter. Arrange the boar pieces on the top. Scoop the beans around the vegetables. Drizzle extra-virgin olive oil liberally over the mixture. Sprinkle parsley, lemon zest strands, and pecorino Toscano cheese.

Nutrition Information

- Calories: 820 calories;
- Sodium: 481

- Total Carbohydrate: 74.2
- Cholesterol: 118
- Protein: 64.7
- Total Fat: 30.3

244. Pork Chops With Garden Rice

Serving: 6 | Prep: 15mins | Ready in:

Ingredients

- 6 (1 inch thick) pork chops
- 1/2 teaspoon salt
- 1/4 teaspoon ground black pepper
- 1/2 teaspoon paprika
- 2 tablespoons olive oil
- 1 clove garlic, minced
- 1 (14 ounce) can vegetable broth
- 1 cup uncooked long grain white rice
- 1 (14.5 ounce) can Italian-style diced tomatoes, drained
- 1/2 cup chopped green bell pepper
- 1/2 cup chopped orange bell pepper
- 1/3 cup chopped green onions
- 1/2 cup thinly sliced fresh mushrooms

Direction

- Preheat an oven to 175°C/350°F.
- Season pork chops with paprika, pepper and salt. Heat oil in a skillet on medium heat; sauté garlic for 1 minute. Brown pork chops for 2 minutes per side.
- Boil rice and vegetable broth in a pot. Mix mushrooms, green onions, orange and green bell pepper and Italian-style diced tomatoes in; cook till heated through for 5 minutes. Put in a 9x13-in. baking dish; put pork chops over veggies and rice.
- Cover; in the preheated oven, bake for 1 hour till pork's internal temperature is 63°C/145°F and veggies and rice are tender.

Nutrition Information

- Calories: 366 calories;
- Total Carbohydrate: 32.1
- Cholesterol: 69
- Protein: 27
- Total Fat: 13.2
- Sodium: 496

245. Pork Chops With Mushrooms And Grape Tomatoes

Serving: 4 | Prep: 15mins | Ready in:

Ingredients

- 4 (1 1/2 inches thick) boneless pork chops
- 1 pinch seasoned salt, or to taste
- 1 pinch lemon-pepper seasoning, or to taste
- 1 tablespoon olive oil
- 1 cup white wine, divided
- 1/2 cup water
- 1 cup oyster mushrooms, pulled apart but not chopped
- 1/2 green bell pepper, diced
- 1/2 small onion, minced
- 2 cloves garlic, minced
- 1/2 cup grape tomatoes
- 1 tablespoon butter

Direction

- Season pork chops with lemon-pepper seasoning and seasoned salt.
- Over medium-high heat, in a large skillet, heat olive oil. Add seasoned pork chops; cook for 3-5 minutes on each side until golden. Pour water and half cup wine over pork chops; bring to a simmer. Cook for 8-10 minutes until the center of chops is no longer pink and the liquid has mostly evaporated. Place chops on serving plates.
- Stir garlic, onion, green bell pepper and oyster mushrooms into the skillet. Raise heat to high

and cook while stirring often for 3-5 minutes until onion softens and all liquid has evaporated. Add the remaining half cup wine, butter and tomatoes. Cook while stirring for 1-2 minutes until heated through.

- Serve tomato and mushroom mixture over pork chops.

Nutrition Information

- Calories: 454 calories;
- Total Fat: 20.3
- Sodium: 213
- Total Carbohydrate: 5.7
- Cholesterol: 126
- Protein: 48.2

---

246.   Pork With Apples And Mushrooms

Serving: 4 | Prep: 15mins | Ready in:

Ingredients

- 1 pound boneless pork tenderloin, cut into 1/2-inch thick slices
- 1/2 teaspoon dried thyme, crushed
- 1/4 teaspoon ground black pepper
- 1 tablespoon canola oil
- 1 large onion, cut in half and sliced
- 8 ounces assorted sliced mushrooms (baby bellas, shiitake, and oyster)
- 1 medium apple, sliced
- 1 (10.5 ounce) can Campbell's® Healthy Request® Condensed Cream of Mushroom Soup
- 2 tablespoons balsamic vinegar
- 3/4 cup Swanson® Natural Goodness® Chicken Broth
- 2 cups hot cooked instant brown rice

Direction

- Season pork with black pepper and thyme.

- In a nonstick 12 inch skillet, heat oil over medium-high heat, and add the pork, then cook until both sides are brown. Take out of the skillet.
- Cook onion and mushrooms in the same skillet, occasionally stirring, for 5 minutes. Stir in the apple and cook until crisp-tender, about 5 minutes. Stir in broth, vinegar, and soup, then boil. Place the pork back into the skillet and bring down heat to low. Cook while covered for 5 minutes until the pork is cooked through. Serve sauce and pork with rice.

Nutrition Information

- Calories: 376 calories;
- Total Fat: 11.1
- Sodium: 463
- Total Carbohydrate: 40.1
- Cholesterol: 66
- Protein: 27.4

---

247.   Portabella Mushroom Dressing

Serving: 8 | Prep: | Ready in:

Ingredients

- 4 stalks celery
- 1 onion, chopped
- 2 large portobello mushrooms, sliced
- 3 fresh shiitake mushrooms, stemmed and sliced
- 8 crimini mushrooms, sliced
- 2 cloves garlic, minced
- 1 (12 ounce) package dry bread stuffing mix with seasoning packet reserved
- 3 (14.5 ounce) cans chicken broth

Direction

- Preheat the oven to 175°C or 350°F.

- Cook and mix garlic, mushrooms, onion and celery for 3 minutes in a skillet. Mix in 1 can of chicken broth and cook till vegetables are soft. With bread crumb stuffing, mix mushroom mixture. Put packet of seasoning on top of dressing mixture and coat by tossing.
- Heat the rest of chicken broth in a 2-quart saucepan till hot. Put broth on top of mixture. Mix thoroughly.
- Into a 2-quart casserole dish, put the stuffing and allow to bake for 30 to 40 minutes.

Nutrition Information

- Calories: 188 calories;
- Total Fat: 1.5
- Sodium: 694
- Total Carbohydrate: 36.5
- Cholesterol: 1
- Protein: 6.6

---

248. Portobello Pesto Egg Omelette

Serving: 1 | Prep: 10mins | Ready in:

Ingredients

- 1 teaspoon olive oil
- 1 portobello mushroom cap, sliced
- 1/4 cup chopped red onion
- 4 egg whites
- 1 teaspoon water
- salt and ground black pepper to taste
- 1/4 cup shredded low-fat mozzarella cheese
- 1 teaspoon prepared pesto

Direction

- Over medium heat, heat the olive oil in a skillet. In the heated oil, cook the red onion and portobello mushroom for 3-5 minutes until mushrooms soften.

- Together in a small bowl, whisk water and the egg whites; pour the mixture over the onion and mushroom mix. Add salt and pepper to season the egg whites. Cook and stir occasionally, about 5 minutes, until the egg whites are not runny anymore. Sprinkle the mixture with mozzarella cheese; add the pesto on top. Fold the omelette in half and keep cooking for 2-3 minutes until the cheese melts.

Nutrition Information

- Calories: 259 calories;
- Total Fat: 12
- Sodium: 501
- Total Carbohydrate: 12
- Cholesterol: 19
- Protein: 28

---

249. Portobello Pot Pie

Serving: 8 | Prep: 30mins | Ready in:

Ingredients

- 2 (9 inch) unbaked pie crusts
- 6 small red potatoes
- 3 tablespoons olive oil
- 1 cup sliced onion
- 1 cup thinly sliced fresh shiitake mushrooms
- 3 1/2 cups water
- 1/4 cup tamari or soy sauce
- 5 tablespoons rice flour
- 2 portobello mushroom caps, cut into bite size pieces
- 1 teaspoon dried thyme
- 2 teaspoons dried sage
- 2 stalks celery, chopped
- 1 carrot, cubed

Direction

- Start preheating oven to 350°F (175°C). Press 1 of pie crusts into and up sides a 9-in. pie plate.

- Boil water in a saucepan. Put in potatoes. Cook for 10-15 mins or until tender. Drain, then cut into cubes. Put aside.
- In large saucepan, heat one tablespoon olive oil over low heat. Put in shiitake mushrooms and onion. Allow mushrooms to sweat with a cover, stirring occasionally, about 7 mins. Add tamari and water. Boil. Then whisk in the rice flour, stirring until no lumps remain. Let simmer.
- In a large skillet, heat the remaining olive oil over medium-high heat. Put in portobello pieces. Briefly sauté until outside of the mushrooms have browned. Put mushrooms into gravy mixture along with potatoes, celery and carrots. Simmer, stirring occasionally, about 10 mins. Season with sage and thyme. Pour into prepared crust. Add other pie crust to cover, then seal by crimping edges. Create a few slits in top of the crust to vent steam.
- Bake in prepared oven for 40 mins or until the crust turns golden brown.

Nutrition Information

- Calories: 418 calories;
- Total Fat: 20.4
- Sodium: 763
- Total Carbohydrate: 51.9
- Cholesterol: 0
- Protein: 8

250. Portobello Stacks

Serving: 4 | Prep: 20mins | Ready in:

Ingredients

- 4 portobello mushrooms
- 1 large onion, sliced 1/4 inch thick
- 1/4 cup balsamic vinegar
- 1 eggplant, sliced into 1/2 inch rounds
- 1 tomato, sliced 1/2 inch thick
- 4 slices provolone cheese

Direction

- In balsamic vinegar, marinate onions and mushrooms for 20 minutes.
- Preheat an oven to 175°C/350°F.
- In 4 stacks, layer cheese, tomato, onion, mushroom and eggplant on a nonstick baking pan.
- In the preheated oven, bake till cheese is golden brown for 30 minutes.

Nutrition Information

- Calories: 195 calories;
- Total Carbohydrate: 21.5
- Cholesterol: 20
- Protein: 12.2
- Total Fat: 8.2
- Sodium: 267

251. Portobello Stuffed Mushroom Burger

Serving: 4 | Prep: 10mins | Ready in:

Ingredients

- vegetable cooking spray
- 4 portobello mushroom caps
- 2 cups fresh spinach leaves
- 1/4 cup shredded aged Cheddar cheese
- 1/4 cup 1% cottage cheese
- 1/8 teaspoon garlic powder
- 1/8 teaspoon salt
- 4 thin, multi-grain hamburger buns

Direction

- Preheat an oven to 200 °C or 400 °F.
- With vegetable spray, coat rounded ends of mushroom caps and put on baking sheet, greased side facing down.
- In microwave-safe bowl, put the spinach, drizzle with several drops of water, and on

high, microwave for a minute. Cut cooked spinach; stir with salt, garlic powder, cottage cheese and Cheddar cheese. Onto prepped mushroom caps, spread the spinach mixture.

- In prepped oven, bake for about 12 minutes till mushrooms are soft. Put on hamburger buns and serve.

Nutrition Information

- Calories: 195 calories;
- Sodium: 433
- Total Carbohydrate: 28.4
- Cholesterol: 8
- Protein: 10.4
- Total Fat: 5

252.　　Potato Ginger Soup

Serving: 6 | Prep: 10mins | Ready in:

Ingredients

- 3 large potatoes, sliced
- 4 cups chicken broth
- 1 pound fresh mushrooms, chopped
- 3 tablespoons grated fresh ginger root
- pepper to taste
- 1/4 cup chopped green onion

Direction

- Combine potatoes, mushrooms, chicken broth and ginger in a large pot. Boil, cook for 20 mins. Add pepper to season. Working in batches, puree with a blender or in pan with an immersion blender. Enjoy hot, decorated with the green onions.

Nutrition Information

- Calories: 162 calories;
- Sodium: 16
- Total Carbohydrate: 35.5

- Cholesterol: 0
- Protein: 6.2
- Total Fat: 0.5

253.　　Potsticker Salad

Serving: 6 | Prep: 15mins | Ready in:

Ingredients

- 1 (10 ounce) package egg noodles
- 12 frozen vegetable potstickers
- 2 tablespoons vegetable oil
- 2 tablespoons water
- 1/2 cup water chestnuts, drained and sliced
- 1/2 cup baby corn
- 1 carrot, shredded
- 1 (15 ounce) can straw mushrooms
- 1/2 cup Thai peanut sauce
- 1/4 cup chopped roasted peanuts

Direction

- Boil water in a large pot and cook egg noodles until al dente or in 5-7 minutes. Drain well and put it aside.
- On medium heat, put on a large frying pan and heat oil. Add potstickers to cook with 1 or 2 turns until they become golden brown. Pour water into the pan; decrease the heat to low and continue cooking with cover until the liquid has evaporated or for another 3 minutes. Put it under cold water to rinse; drain and cut into halves.
- Combine potstickers, noodles, peanut sauce, mushrooms, carrot, baby corn and water chestnuts in a large mixing bowl. Let it chill in 1 hour. Add peanuts on top to serve.

Nutrition Information

- Calories: 408 calories;
- Protein: 15.5
- Total Fat: 13.3

- Sodium: 804
- Total Carbohydrate: 59.9
- Cholesterol: 34

254.   Poulet De Provencal

Serving: 4 | Prep: 20mins | Ready in:

Ingredients

- 2 teaspoons olive oil
- 1 teaspoon butter
- 2 1/2 tablespoons balsamic vinegar
- 2 teaspoons Dijon mustard
- 3 large cloves garlic, chopped
- 4 (4 ounce) skinless, boneless chicken breast halves, pounded flat
- 1/3 cup chicken stock
- 1 large shallot, chopped
- 2 cups cremini mushrooms, chopped
- 1/3 cup chicken stock
- 1/4 teaspoon herbes de Provence, crumbled
- 1 1/2 teaspoons balsamic vinegar
- salt and ground black pepper to taste
- 2 slices provolone cheese, halved

Direction

- Heat butter and olive oil in a big nonstick skillet on medium heat; mix garlic, Dijon mustard and 2 1/2 tablespoons of balsamic vinegar in bowl; mix chicken breast halves into mixture till coated. Put chicken with marinade in skillet; cook, occasionally turning, 5-8 minutes per side till chicken isn't pink inside. Put chicken on a platter; keep warm.
- Put 1/3 cup of chicken stock in skillet; mix to dissolve browned food bits from skillet. Mix and cook mushrooms and shallot for 5 minutes till mushrooms are tender. Mix 1 1/2 teaspoon of balsamic vinegar, herbes de Provence and 1/3 cup of chicken stock inch Cook, occasionally mixing, for 2 minutes till mushrooms are deep brown in color.

- Put chicken breasts in pan; top each with 1/2 provolone cheese slice. Cover skillet; let cheese melt then serve with mushrooms.

Nutrition Information

- Calories: 249 calories;
- Total Carbohydrate: 8.1
- Cholesterol: 77
- Protein: 30.1
- Total Fat: 10
- Sodium: 388

255.   Purple Yam Pancakes

Serving: 6 | Prep: 20mins | Ready in:

Ingredients

- Spicy Mushroom Sauce:
- 1 tablespoon vegetable oil
- 12 large mushrooms, finely chopped
- 1/2 large onion, chopped
- 2 tablespoons butter
- 6 large tomatoes
- 1 large bell pepper, cut into chunks
- 1/2 large onion
- 5 large fresh hot chile peppers, stemmed
- 2 pickled jalapeno peppers
- 1 cup chopped fresh parsley
- 1/2 cup chopped fresh cilantro
- 2 cloves garlic
- 1 cube vegetable bouillon (such as Maggi®)
- 1 teaspoon dried thyme
- 1 teaspoon ground cumin
- 1 teaspoon cayenne pepper
- 1 pinch salt and freshly ground black pepper to taste (optional)
- 1 1/4 cups vegetable broth
- 2 tablespoons dark soy sauce
- water as needed
- Pancakes:
- 3 purple yams, cut into wedges

- 2 cups all-purpose flour
- 1 onion
- 2 eggs
- 2 teaspoons salt
- 1 teaspoon garlic powder
- 1 red bell pepper, chopped
- 1 teaspoon paprika
- 1 teaspoon chile powder
- 1 teaspoon ground black pepper
- 1 tablespoon vegetable oil, or to taste
- 1/2 pound ground beef
- 1/2 pound ground chicken

Direction

- In skillet, heat a tablespoon of oil over moderately-low heat. Cook and mix mushrooms and half chopped onion for 5 to 10 minutes till tender and clear. Put the butter.
- In blender, mix garlic, cilantro, parsley, jalapeno peppers, chili peppers, onion, bell pepper chunks and tomatoes; process till nearly smooth.
- To skillet of mushrooms, mix black pepper, salt, cayenne pepper, cumin, thyme, vegetable bouillon cube and blended tomato mixture and mix till thoroughly incorporated. Put sufficient water, soy sauce and vegetable broth to create sauce. Place cover and let simmer for 30 to 35 minutes till sauce has thickens.
- In food processor bowl, mix garlic powder, 2 teaspoons salt, eggs, 1 onion, flour and purple yams; pulse till combined. Into batter, fold the red bell pepper with spatula and add 1 teaspoon of black pepper, chili powder and paprika to season. Stir till well incorporated.
- In skillet, heat a tablespoon of oil over moderately-high heat. Onto skillet, drop the batter by big spoonfuls. Over every pancake, scoop some ground chicken and some ground beef; top with several additional spoonfuls of batter. Let pancakes cook for 3 to 5 minutes till equally browned. Turn and cook for 2 to 3 minutes till browned on another side. Place cover on skillet and cook pancakes on low heat for 5 minutes till chicken and beef are cooked

completely. Redo with the rest of batter. Serve along with mushroom sauce.

Nutrition Information

- Calories: 640 calories;
- Cholesterol: 118
- Protein: 30.6
- Total Fat: 19.1
- Sodium: 1470
- Total Carbohydrate: 91.8

256.   Quiche With Leeks, Mushrooms And Sweet Potatoes

Serving: 6 | Prep: 20mins | Ready in:

Ingredients

- 2 teaspoons olive oil
- 1 onion, chopped
- 1/2 teaspoon dried thyme
- 2 leeks, white part only, chopped
- 6 ounces mushrooms, chopped
- 1/2 sweet potato, peeled and diced
- 5 eggs
- 1/3 cup sour cream
- 1/2 teaspoon salt
- 1 cup heavy whipping cream
- 1 tablespoon finely shredded Asiago cheese

Direction

- Set the oven to 175°C (350°F) to preheat. Lightly coat a 9-inch pie dish with oil.
- Over medium heat, put olive oil in a skillet and add in onion. Cook while stirring them for around 2 minutes then put in mushrooms and leeks, and thyme. Continue stirring and cooking for 5 to 8 minutes, or until the onions are well cooked.
- Put in sweet potato, cook while stirring for about 15 minutes or until the sweet potato

softens. Put the mixture in the greased pie dish.

- In a food processor, add cream, salt, sour cream and eggs; blend them well together until smooth. Transfer them to the pie dish and gently pour over the onion mixture. Put on top some Asiago cheese.
- Bake the quiche for 45-50 minutes in the preheated oven, or until the outside is golden brown and the center feel gently firm. Set aside to warm for a few minutes. Cut into pieces and serve.

Nutrition Information

- Calories: 298 calories;
- Protein: 8.8
- Total Fat: 23.6
- Sodium: 307
- Total Carbohydrate: 14.5
- Cholesterol: 216

---

257. Quick Brown Rice And Mushroom Pilaf

Serving: 8 | Prep: | Ready in:

Ingredients

- 2 tablespoons olive oil
- 1 small onion, chopped
- 1/4 cup celery, chopped
- 1 1/2 cups sliced mushrooms
- 1 (14.5 ounce) can chicken broth
- 2 cups Minute® Brown Rice, uncooked
- 1/2 cup chopped walnuts, toasted
- 2 tablespoons fresh parsley, chopped

Direction

- In a medium saucepan, heat oil over medium heat and add the celery and onions, then cook for 3 minutes, stirring sometimes, until tender-crisp.

- Add the mushrooms and cook, occasionally stirring, for 3 minutes until mushrooms become tender. Add the broth, stir, and set to boil.
- Stir in the rice and cover, then bring heat down to medium-low and simmer for 5 minutes. Take off the heat and let sit for 5 minutes. Add parsley and walnuts, lightly mixing.

Nutrition Information

- Calories: 163 calories;
- Cholesterol: 1
- Protein: 3.4
- Total Fat: 9.1
- Sodium: 227
- Total Carbohydrate: 19.7

---

258. Quick Chicken Zingarella

Serving: 8 | Prep: | Ready in:

Ingredients

- 4 boneless skinless chicken breasts, cut into 1-inch cubes
- 1 (28 ounce) jar spaghetti sauce
- 1 (14 ounce) jar roasted Italian cherry peppers, drained and chopped
- 5 fresh mushrooms, sliced
- 1 onion, chopped
- 3 cloves garlic, minced
- 2 tablespoons brown sugar
- 1/4 cup red wine
- 1/4 cup olive oil
- 1 (16 ounce) package linguini pasta

Direction

- Heat oil in big skillet on medium heat. Add garlic, onions and mushrooms; sauté till tender. Add chicken; cook till not pink anymore. Mix in brown sugar, wine and pasta

sauce; simmer for 15 minutes. Add the drained and sliced roasted red peppers; simmer for 5 more minutes.
- Meanwhile, follow the package directions to cook pasta; drain. Serve the sauce over the pasta.

Nutrition Information

- Calories: 454 calories;
- Total Fat: 11.8
- Sodium: 697
- Total Carbohydrate: 62.3
- Cholesterol: 36
- Protein: 21.1

---

259. Quick And Easy Greek Spaghetti

Serving: 4 | Prep: 15mins | Ready in:

Ingredients

- 1 (8 ounce) package spaghetti
- extra-virgin olive oil, or as needed
- 1 (10 ounce) bag fresh spinach
- 1 (8 ounce) package sliced fresh mushrooms
- 1/4 cup red wine vinegar
- 1/4 cup balsamic vinegar
- 2 (14.5 ounce) cans diced tomatoes
- 1/4 cup chopped fresh basil
- 1 tablespoon chopped fresh parsley
- 1 (6 ounce) can sliced black olives, drained (optional)
- 2 ounces crumbled feta cheese, or to taste

Direction

- Allow lightly salted water in a big pot to come to a rolling boil. At a boil, cook spaghetti for 12 minutes until soft yet firm to the bite, tossing sometimes. Strain and put aside.
- In a big saucepan, heat olive oil over medium heat. In the hot oil, stir and cook mushrooms

and spinach for 10 minutes until they release their liquid. Add balsamic vinegar and red wine vinegar, boil it. Mix black olives, parsley, basil and tomatoes into the boiling mixture, keep stirring and cooking for another 10 minutes until the flavors combine.
- Stir into the tomato mixture with the cooked spaghetti and lower the heat to medium-low. Simmer the sauce and pasta for 8-10 minutes until the flavors combine, mix feta cheese into the pasta. Sprinkle additional feta cheese over and enjoy.

Nutrition Information

- Calories: 413 calories;
- Total Fat: 11.7
- Sodium: 1095
- Total Carbohydrate: 60.7
- Cholesterol: 13
- Protein: 16.1

---

260. Rabbit Loin Cigars

Serving: 1 | Prep: 15mins | Ready in:

Ingredients

- 2 teaspoons vegetable oil
- 1 cup morel mushrooms
- 1 teaspoon minced shallot
- salt and pepper to taste
- 1/4 sheet frozen puff pastry, thawed
- 3 spears white asparagus, trimmed
- 1/2 cup beef or veal demiglace
- 1 tablespoon butter
- 6 ounces rabbit loin
- 1 egg yolk, beaten

Direction

- Pre heat oven to 175 degrees C (350 degrees F). Use the parchment paper to line the baking sheet.

- Heat oil on medium high heat in a small-sized skillet. Put in pepper, salt, shallot and mushrooms. Cook and whisk for 5-10 minutes till mushrooms break down into a paste. Take out of the heat and let it cool down slightly.
- Lay sheet of the puff pastry out onto a clean working surface and roll out to fit rabbit loin's length. Spread over the surface with mushroom paste. Add rabbit loin onto middle and arrange asparagus alongside the rabbit. Roll pastry around asparagus and rabbit into one tight-closed cylinder, pinching ends to seal. Add onto prepped baking sheet, and use the egg yolk to brush pastry's top.
- Bake in the preheated oven for 10-13 minutes till pastry turns deep golden-brown. Take out of oven and allow it to stand for 5 minutes. Meat should have the internal temperature of no less than 65 degrees C (145 degrees F).
- When rabbit is cooking, heat demi-glace on medium heat in a small-sized skillet. Once becoming melted and hot, whisk in butter till the butter melts and then take out of the heat.
- To serve, halve the pastry crosswise, and put into middle of a serving plate. Sprinkle sauce around the plate.

Nutrition Information

- Calories: 845 calories;
- Total Fat: 57.1
- Sodium: 335
- Total Carbohydrate: 38.9
- Cholesterol: 323
- Protein: 44.7

---

261.   Rachel's Turkey Loaf

Serving: 6 | Prep: 15mins | Ready in:

Ingredients

- 1 pound ground turkey
- 2 eggs, lightly beaten

- 1/2 cup chopped fresh mushrooms (optional)
- 1 1/2 cups Italian seasoned bread crumbs
- 1 (1 ounce) envelope dry onion soup mix
- 2/3 cup ready-to-serve creamy tomato soup, divided
- 1/4 cup ketchup, divided
- 1/4 cup barbeque sauce, divided
- 2 tablespoons Worcestershire sauce, divided
- chili powder to taste

Direction

- Set the oven to 350°F (175°C) and start preheating.
- Mix a tablespoon Worcestershire sauce, 2 tablespoons barbeque sauce, 2 tablespoons ketchup, 1/3 cup creamy tomato soup, soup mix, bread crumbs, mushrooms, eggs and turkey in a bowl. Mold the mixture into a loaf shape; transfer to a baking dish. Top with chili powder.
- Mix the rest of each of Worcestershire sauce, barbeque sauce, ketchup and creamy tomato soup in another bowl. Put aside.
- Bake loaf in the prepared oven for 45 minutes. Pour sauce on top; keep baking 15 minutes until it reaches a minimum internal temperature of 165°F (74°C).

Nutrition Information

- Calories: 308 calories;
- Total Fat: 9.5
- Sodium: 1282
- Total Carbohydrate: 34
- Cholesterol: 118
- Protein: 22.2

---

262.   Refreshing Salad With Grilled Oyster Mushrooms

Serving: 4 | Prep: 15mins | Ready in:

Ingredients

- 16 ounces fresh oyster mushrooms, stemmed and sliced
- 1/4 cup olive oil, divided
- salt to taste
- 1 cucumber, halved and sliced
- 2 tomatoes, halved and quartered
- 1 onion, sliced and separated into rings
- 1 green bell pepper, seeded and sliced
- 2 carrots, shredded
- 1 avocado, cut into 1/2-inch chunks
- 2 tablespoons fresh lemon juice, or to taste

Direction

- Put the rack of the oven approximately 6-in. from the heat source and turn on the oven's broiler to preheat.
- In a bowl, combine mushrooms with 1 pinch of salt and 2 tablespoons olive oil. Put in an oven-safe pan.
- Put in the preheated oven and broil for 5-10 minutes until crunchy, checking frequently.
- In a big serving bowl, mix together avocado, carrots, green bell pepper, onion, tomatoes, and cucumber; mix lightly.
- Add lemon juice and the leftover olive oil to the salad, then sprinkle salt over to taste. Mix to blend.
- Top the salad with mushrooms; mix again.

Nutrition Information

- Calories: 312 calories;
- Total Fat: 22.2
- Sodium: 80
- Total Carbohydrate: 25.2
- Cholesterol: 0
- Protein: 6.8

263. Rib Eye Steak And Mushroom Risotto

Serving: 6 | Prep: 15mins | Ready in:

Ingredients

- salt and ground black pepper to taste
- 2 (8 ounce) boneless rib-eye steaks
- 1 tablespoon canola oil
- 3 tablespoons olive oil, divided
- 1 (16 ounce) package white mushrooms, thinly sliced
- 1 (16 ounce) package cremini mushrooms, thinly sliced
- 3 shallots, diced
- 3 cloves garlic, minced
- 1 1/2 cups Arborio rice
- 1/2 cup dry white wine
- 6 cups low-sodium chicken broth, divided
- 1/4 cup butter
- 2 tablespoons finely chopped fresh chives
- sea salt to taste
- freshly ground black pepper to taste

Direction

- In a water bath, preheat the sous vide cooker to 56 °C or 132 °F, following manufacturer's directions.
- Sprinkle pepper and salt onto steaks to season and put in a heavy-duty or vacuum-seal freezer bag. Enclose. Into the water bath, lower the bag and set the timer to 2 hours.
- Take steaks out of the bag and put on plate lined with paper towel. Blot dry carefully on each side.
- In heavy skillet on moderately-high heat, heat the canola oil till it begins to smoke. Put in the steaks. Cook till well browned on each side, turning after every 15 to 30 seconds, for 90 seconds in total. Turn the steaks onto a plate; allow to sit for 10 minutes. Thinly cut against the grain.
- In a heavy big saucepan, heat 2 tablespoons of olive oil on moderately-high heat. Mix in cremini mushrooms and white mushrooms; cook for 3 minutes till tender. Turn the mushrooms including their liquid onto a bowl.
- In the same saucepan, heat the leftover tablespoon of olive oil over moderately-low heat. Put in garlic and shallots. Let cook for 3

minutes, mixing continuously, till shallots are soft. Put in rice and raise the heat to moderate. Cook and mix for 3 to 4 minutes till rice is pale golden with almost clear edges.

- Into the rice mixture, add the wine; let cook for 6 minutes, mixing continuously, till fully soaked in. Put in half cup of chicken broth; mix for 3 minutes till soaked in. Put in the rest of the broth, half cup at a time, mixing risotto constantly for an additional 15 to 20 minutes till liquid is soaked in and rice is soft but firm to the bite.
- Take risotto off the heat. Mix in the mushrooms including their liquid, freshly ground pepper, sea salt, chives and butter. Put risotto on a plate together with steak strips.

Nutrition Information

- Calories: 549 calories;
- Protein: 21.8
- Total Fat: 24.5
- Sodium: 305
- Total Carbohydrate: 56.8
- Cholesterol: 51

---

264. Roasted Asparagus And Mushrooms

Serving: 6 | Prep: 10mins | Ready in:

Ingredients

- 1 bunch fresh asparagus, trimmed
- 1/2 pound fresh mushrooms, quartered
- 2 sprigs fresh rosemary, minced
- 2 teaspoons olive oil
- kosher salt to taste
- freshly ground black pepper to taste

Direction

- Heat the oven beforehand to 230 °C or 450 °F. Use vegetable cooking spray to lightly spray on a cookie sheet.
- In a bowl, put the mushrooms and asparagus then drizzle with olive oil. Season with pepper, salt and rosemary then toss well. On the prepared pan, lay the mushrooms and asparagus in an even layer. Roast for about 15 minutes in the preheated oven until the asparagus becomes tender.

Nutrition Information

- Calories: 38 calories;
- Total Fat: 1.8
- Sodium: 84
- Total Carbohydrate: 4.3
- Cholesterol: 0
- Protein: 2.8

---

265. Roasted Eggplant And Mushrooms

Serving: 2 | Prep: 10mins | Ready in:

Ingredients

- 1 medium eggplant, peeled and cubed
- 2 small zucchini, cubed
- 1/2 small yellow onion, chopped
- 1 (8 ounce) package mushrooms, sliced
- 1 1/2 tablespoons tomato paste
- 1/2 cup water
- 1 clove garlic, minced
- 1/2 teaspoon dried basil
- salt and pepper to taste

Direction

- Set the oven to 230°C or 450°F.
- In a 2-qt. casserole dish, add mushrooms, onion, zucchini and eggplant. Mix together water and tomato paste in a small bowl, then

stir in pepper, salt, basil and garlic. Drizzle over the vegetables and blend well.

- In the preheated oven, bake until eggplant is softened while stirring from time to time, or for 45 minutes. If the vegetables start to stick, put in additional water as needed, however, vegetables should be fairly dry, with lightly browned edges.

Nutrition Information

- Calories: 118 calories;
- Total Fat: 1.1
- Sodium: 111
- Total Carbohydrate: 25.8
- Cholesterol: 0
- Protein: 6.6

---

266.   Roasted Pork Chops With Tomatoes, Mushrooms, And Garlic Sauce

Serving: 6 | Prep: 25mins | Ready in:

Ingredients

- 1 pound roma tomatoes, quartered
- 1 pound sliced button mushrooms
- 5 cloves garlic, chopped
- 2 tablespoons extra virgin olive oil
- salt and pepper to taste
- Spice Rub
- 1 teaspoon salt
- 1/2 teaspoon ground black pepper
- 1/4 teaspoon ground cumin
- 1/4 teaspoon ground coriander
- 1/4 teaspoon dried oregano leaves
- 1/4 teaspoon dried marjoram leaves
- 1/4 teaspoon dried thyme leaves
- 1/4 teaspoon dried rosemary, crushed
- 1/4 teaspoon dried sage leaves, crushed
- 1/4 teaspoon dried basil leaves
- 1/4 teaspoon garlic powder

- 1/4 teaspoon onion powder
- 1/4 teaspoon ground paprika
- 1/4 teaspoon white sugar
- 1/4 teaspoon crushed red pepper
- 2 1/4 pounds pork chops

Direction

- Start preheating oven to 425°F (220°C).
- Toss olive oil, garlic, mushrooms and tomatoes in a 9x13-in. baking dish and season to taste with pepper and salt. Using hands to lightly mix to coat oil over all the ingredients. Spread the edges of dish with tomato-mushroom mixture, retaining middle free for pork chops.
- In a bowl, combine crushed red pepper, sugar, ground paprika, onion powder, garlic powder, basil, sage, rosemary, thyme, marjoram, oregano, ground coriander, cumin, half teaspoon of black pepper and one teaspoon of salt to create the spice rub.
- Sprinkle spice rub over pork chops, working the rub well into both sides of meat. Put pork chops into middle of baking dish, putting mushroom and tomato mixture around.
- In the prepared oven, roast for 45-50 mins or until mushrooms become tender and the middle of pork is no longer pink. An instant-read thermometer should register 145°F (63°C) when inserted into middle of a chop. Place the pork chops onto the serving dish. Pour all pan juices and roasted tomato-mushroom mixture over top. Enjoy!

Nutrition Information

- Calories: 314 calories;
- Total Fat: 13.3
- Sodium: 457
- Total Carbohydrate: 7.1
- Cholesterol: 98
- Protein: 40.8

267. Roasted Veggies With Couscous

Serving: 8 | Prep: 10mins | Ready in:

Ingredients

- 1 large zucchini, thickly sliced
- 4 ounces button mushrooms, quartered
- 1 red bell pepper, chopped
- 1 tablespoon olive oil
- 3 cups water
- 1 teaspoon salt
- 2 tablespoons olive oil
- 2 cups couscous
- 2 tablespoons balsamic vinegar

Direction

- Set the grill to high heat for preheating, either indoor or outdoor.
- Coat the vegetables lightly with olive oil. Arrange the vegetables on the grill. Let them cook, turning over occasionally until the vegetables are just tender.
- Meanwhile, boil couscous, 1 tbsp. of olive oil, water, and salt in a large pot. Remove the pot from the heat after boiling. Allow it to stand for 5 minutes. Use a fork to fluff it once done. Allow the couscous to cool to room temperature.
- Spoon the couscous on a plate. Place the veggies on its top. Drizzle over the balsamic vinegar and a small amount of olive oil.

Nutrition Information

- Calories: 224 calories;
- Sodium: 301
- Total Carbohydrate: 36.8
- Cholesterol: 0
- Protein: 6.6
- Total Fat: 5.5

268. Roasted Wild Mushrooms And Potatoes

Serving: 4 | Prep: | Ready in:

Ingredients

- 2 pounds new potatoes (such as Yukon Gold), halved
- 2 tablespoons olive oil, or more if needed
- salt to taste
- 1 teaspoon olive oil
- 2 ounces pancetta, chopped
- 1/4 pound king trumpet mushrooms, cut into chunks
- 1/4 pound chanterelle mushrooms, cut into chunks
- 1/4 pound nameko mushrooms, trimmed
- 1/4 pound clamshell (shimeji) mushrooms, trimmed
- 3 tablespoons sherry vinegar
- 2 tablespoons chopped fresh tarragon
- 2 cloves garlic, minced
- 1 tablespoon olive oil (optional)

Direction

- Preheat the oven to 200°C or 400°F.
- Into a big roasting pan, put the potatoes and sprinkle 2 tablespoons of olive oil on top. Scatter salt over and stir to cover potatoes in olive oil and salt. Flip, cut sides facing up.
- In the prepped oven, roast for half an hour.
- Meanwhile, into a big skillet, put a teaspoon of olive oil over medium heat and let pancetta cook in the hot oil for 5 minutes, mixing frequently, till pancetta releases some fat and resembles a cooked ham. Mix in clamshell mushrooms, nameko, chanterelle and king trumpet, putting a pinch of salt as it cooks.
- Raise the heat to high and let mushrooms cook for 10 minutes till mushrooms start to brown and most of the juices steams off.
- Raise the oven heat up to 220°C or 425°F.
- In the baking dish, mix the potatoes; add pancetta and mushrooms to potatoes. Put back to the oven and let bake for 10 minutes; mix

and keep baking for 10 minutes longer till potatoes are tender, soft and browned. Allow to slightly cool for 10 minutes.

- Sprinkle sherry vinegar on top of mushrooms and potatoes, scatter 1 tablespoon of olive oil, garlic and tarragon on top, and combine by tossing. Taste and alter the seasoning. Put to serving platter.

Nutrition Information

- Calories: 335 calories;
- Sodium: 168
- Total Carbohydrate: 44.9
- Cholesterol: 5
- Protein: 9.7
- Total Fat: 13.7

269.   Rolled Flank Steak

Serving: 6 | Prep: 45mins | Ready in:

Ingredients

- 1 (2 pound) beef flank steak
- 1/4 cup soy sauce
- 1/2 cup olive oil
- 2 teaspoons steak seasoning
- 8 ounces thinly sliced provolone cheese
- 4 slices thick cut bacon
- 1/2 cup fresh spinach leaves
- 1/2 cup sliced crimini mushrooms
- 1/2 red bell pepper, seeded and cut into strips

Direction

- Arrange the flank steak onto a cutting board with the short end closest to you. Beginning from one of long sides, slice through meat horizontally to within half an in. of opposite edge. You could also tell the butcher to butterfly flank steak for you instead of chopping it on your own.

- Combine steak seasoning, olive oil and soy sauce in a gallon-size resealable plastic bag. Let the flank steak marinate in fridge for 4 hours to overnight.
- Preheat the oven to 175 degrees C (350 degrees F). Grease a glass baking plate.
- Lay out flank steak flat in front of you along with grain of meat running from the left side to right side. Layer provolone across steak, leaving a one-in. border. Arrange mushrooms, red pepper, spinach and bacon across cheese which covered the steak in stripes running with same direction as meat's grain. Roll flank steak up and away from you, so that once the roll is sliced into pinwheel-shape, each filling ingredients is visible. Roll them firmly, but be careful not to squeeze fillings out of ends. When rolled, tie every 2 in. with the kitchen twine.
- Add into the prepped baking dish, and bake in the preheated oven till the internal temperature reads 65 degrees C (145 degrees F) or for 60 minutes. Take out of oven and allow it to stand for 5-10 minutes prior to slicing into one-in. slices. Ensure to take out the twine prior to serving!

Nutrition Information

- Calories: 472 calories;
- Protein: 31.4
- Total Fat: 36.9
- Sodium: 1422
- Total Carbohydrate: 3
- Cholesterol: 67

270.   Rosemary Chicken Stew

Serving: 8 | Prep: 25mins | Ready in:

Ingredients

- 2 pounds boneless skinless chicken breasts, cut into bite-size pieces

- 1 (10 ounce) package fresh mushrooms, sliced
- 3 medium onions, sliced
- 1 (16 ounce) can diced tomatoes with juice
- 1 pound carrots, sliced
- 4 celery ribs, sliced
- 1 pound dried great Northern beans, soaked overnight
- 6 cloves garlic, chopped
- 1 1/2 teaspoons dried rosemary
- water
- salt and pepper to taste
- cornstarch

Direction

- Over medium heat, place onions, mushrooms and chicken in a big stock pot. Mix in celery, carrots and tomatoes. Stir in rosemary, garlic, beans, and just enough water not to fully cover. Bring mixture to a low simmer, cook about 2-3 hours until chicken is soft. Add salt and pepper to taste. If required to thicken, stir in cornstarch.

Nutrition Information

- Calories: 365 calories;
- Total Fat: 6.6
- Sodium: 216
- Total Carbohydrate: 42.3
- Cholesterol: 57
- Protein: 34.7

---

271.   Salisbury Steak With Mushrooms

Serving: 4 | Prep: 15mins | Ready in:

Ingredients

- 1 pound lean ground beef
- 1/3 cup dry bread crumbs
- 1/4 cup chopped onions
- 1 egg, beaten

- 1 teaspoon salt
- 1/4 teaspoon ground black pepper
- 2 cups beef broth
- 1 large onion, thinly sliced
- 1 cup sliced mushrooms
- 3 tablespoons cornstarch
- 3 tablespoons water

Direction

- In a bowl, mix black pepper, salt, egg, chopped onion, breadcrumbs and ground beef together until evenly combined. Form the beef mixture into 4 patties about 3/4-inch thick.
- In a big skillet over medium heat, fry the patties for about 10 minutes until both sides are browned. Mix in the mushrooms, onion and beef broth and bring it to a boil. Adjust the heat to low and cover it up. Let it simmer for about 10 minutes more until there is no hint of pink in the center of the patties. Move the patties onto a platter and keep warm.
- Bring the onion mixture to a boil. In a small bowl, stir water and cornstarch together then mix it into the onion mixture. Cook and stir for about 1 minute until the onion gravy thickens. Pour the gravy over the patties. Serve.

Nutrition Information

- Calories: 323 calories;
- Protein: 26.6
- Total Fat: 15.8
- Sodium: 1129
- Total Carbohydrate: 17.2
- Cholesterol: 115

---

272.   Saucy Chicken Cordon Bleu

Serving: 5 | Prep: | Ready in:

Ingredients

- 4 skinless, boneless chicken breast halves
- 4 slices ham
- 4 slices Swiss cheese
- 1 cup all-purpose flour
- 1 teaspoon salt
- 1/2 teaspoon ground black pepper
- 1/2 teaspoon paprika
- 2 eggs, beaten
- 1/3 cup milk
- 1 cup dry bread crumbs
- 1/4 cup olive oil
- 1 (10.75 ounce) can condensed cream of mushroom soup
- 1/2 pound fresh mushrooms, sliced
- 1/4 teaspoon garlic powder
- 1/8 teaspoon curry powder
- 1/4 cup white wine
- 1/2 cup sour cream
- 2 sprigs fresh parsley, for garnish

Direction

- Set the oven to 350°F or 175°C for preheating.
- Flatten the chicken breasts, making sure you do not break the meat through. Roll each slice of ham in a cheese slice, and then roll them up in chicken breasts. Put flour in a bowl or shallow dish, and then season it with paprika, pepper, and salt. In another bowl or dish, whisk milk and eggs together. Dredge the chicken rolls into the seasoned flour, and then into the egg mixture. Dredge them lastly into the bread crumbs. Put oil into a large skillet and heat it. Add the chicken and fry until golden brown; put aside.
- For the sauce, mix garlic powder, wine, sour cream, soup, curry powder, and mushrooms in a large bowl. Mix them all together. Arrange the browned chicken into a 9x13-inches baking dish. Pour sauce mixture all over the chicken. Let it bake inside the preheated oven for 15-20 minutes. Garnish this dish with fresh parsley sprigs.

Nutrition Information

- Calories: 667 calories;
- Sodium: 1480
- Total Carbohydrate: 45.7
- Cholesterol: 175
- Protein: 43.7
- Total Fat: 33

---

273.   Sausage Mushroom Quiche

Serving: 6 | Prep: 20mins | Ready in:

Ingredients

- 1 pound small fresh button mushrooms
- 1 pound ground pork breakfast sausage
- 1/2 cup chopped fresh parsley
- 3 eggs
- 1 cup half-and-half cream
- 1/2 cup grated Parmesan cheese
- 1/4 teaspoon salt
- 1 (9 inch) unbaked 9 inch pie crust

Direction

- Preheat oven to 400°F or 200°C. Snip off the stems of the mushroom and cut any large pieces in half.
- In a big pan, crush the sausage and add the mushrooms. Cook on medium-high heat until all the liquid from the mushrooms has evaporated and both mushrooms and meat have lightly browned. Remove the grease then add parsley.
- In a big bowl, whisk the eggs then add the cheese, cream and salt. Pour egg mixture into the pan with the sausage and mushroom. Blend well. Scoop mixture into the pie shell.
- Bake for 25-30 minutes until the filling is firm and crust is well browned. Set aside for 10 minutes before serving.

Nutrition Information

- Calories: 612 calories;
- Sodium: 1101
- Total Carbohydrate: 20.6
- Cholesterol: 167
- Protein: 19.9
- Total Fat: 50.3

274. Sausage And Kale Soup

Serving: 8 | Prep: 20mins | Ready in:

Ingredients

- 1 pound Italian sausage links, halved lengthwise
- 2 large carrots, chopped
- 1 small onion, chopped
- 2 cloves garlic, minced
- 6 cups chicken broth
- 1 cup chopped portobello mushroom caps
- 1 cup chopped cauliflower
- 2 cups coarsely chopped kale
- 1 bay leaf
- 1/2 teaspoon oregano

Direction

- Heat a big pot on medium heat; cook sausages in pot, 3-5 minutes per side, till browned. Put sausages on cutting board for cooling. Keep sausage drippings in the pot.
- Cook and mix onion and carrots in the reserved sausage drippings for 5-7 minutes till onion is translucent. Mix garlic into onion and carrot mixture; mix and cook for 10-15 seconds. Put chicken broth into pot; boil while scraping browned food bits off from the bottom of pan using a wooden spoon.
- Put sausage back in broth with oregano, bay leaf, kale, cauliflower and mushrooms; mix. Lower heat to low; simmer for 15 minutes till veggies are tender but still firm enough to keep their shape. Put sausages on cutting board; slice into 1-in. half-moons. Put back into the soup; simmer for 5 more minutes.

Nutrition Information

- Calories: 173 calories;
- Total Carbohydrate: 8.2
- Cholesterol: 26
- Protein: 9.7
- Total Fat: 11.3
- Sodium: 1217

275. Sauteed Sugar Snap Peas With Mushrooms

Serving: 2 | Prep: 5mins | Ready in:

Ingredients

- 2 tablespoons olive oil
- 4 fresh mushrooms, or more to taste, sliced
- salt to taste
- 20 sugar snap peas, or more to taste

Direction

- Prepare a sauté pan, heat over medium heat. Add olive oil. Use salt for seasoning mushrooms and sauté with olive oil for approximately 5 minutes till tender.
- During the time mushrooms are cooking, add water into a small pot and bring to a boil. Put sugar snap peas in; allow to cook for 1-2 minutes till bright green. Using a slotted spoon, remove sugar snap peas out of water and toss snap peas with mushrooms for 1-2 minutes in the pan. Use salt for seasoning and serve right away.

Nutrition Information

- Calories: 537 calories;
- Sodium: 80
- Total Carbohydrate: 72.9
- Cholesterol: 0
- Protein: 21.6

- Total Fat: 13.6

276.   Sauteed Swiss Chard With Mushrooms And Roasted Red Peppers

Serving: 4 | Prep: 20mins | Ready in:

Ingredients

- 3 tablespoons olive oil
- 1 cup sliced fresh mushrooms
- 1/2 onion, finely chopped
- 3 cloves garlic, minced
- 1 bunch Swiss chard, chopped
- 1/2 roasted red pepper, chopped
- 1 teaspoon dried oregano
- 1 teaspoon dried basil
- salt and ground black pepper to taste
- 1/2 cup white wine

Direction

- On medium heat, heat olive oil in a big pan. Cook and stir garlic, onion, and mushrooms for about 5mins until the mushrooms are soft and the onion is translucent. Mix in black pepper, Swiss chard, salt, red pepper, basil, and oregano. Cook for about 3mins until the Swiss chard wilts. Mix in white wine; cook for another 3-4mins until the Swiss chard is tender.

Nutrition Information

- Calories: 150 calories;
- Total Fat: 10.4
- Sodium: 205
- Total Carbohydrate: 7.8
- Cholesterol: 0
- Protein: 2.3

277.   Savannah's Best Marinated Portobello Mushrooms

Serving: 2 | Prep: 10mins | Ready in:

Ingredients

- 1/2 cup cooking wine
- 1 tablespoon olive oil
- 2 tablespoons dark soy sauce
- 2 tablespoons balsamic vinegar
- 2 cloves garlic, minced
- 2 large portobello mushroom caps

Direction

- Preheat the oven to 200°Celsius or 400°F.
- Stir garlic, wine, balsamic vinegar, olive oil, and soy sauce in a baking dish. Put the mushroom caps in the marinade with its top-side down; let the mushrooms marinate for 15 minutes.
- Cover the dish and place in the preheated oven; bake for 25 minutes. Flip the mushrooms and keep on baking for 8 minutes.

Nutrition Information

- Calories: 112 calories;
- Total Carbohydrate: 4.5
- Cholesterol: 0
- Protein: 1.3
- Total Fat: 6.8
- Sodium: 1286

278.   Savory French Crepes

Serving: 4 | Prep: 30mins | Ready in:

Ingredients

- 2 eggs
- 1 1/2 cups milk

- 2 tablespoons butter
- 1/4 cup buckwheat flour
- 3/4 cup all-purpose flour
- 1 pinch salt
- 3 tablespoons butter
- 1/2 cup cremini mushrooms, sliced
- 1/2 cup oyster mushrooms, sliced
- 1 cup diced tomatoes
- 2 cups baby spinach leaves
- 4 teaspoons butter, divided
- 1 cup shredded Gruyere cheese, divided

Direction

- In a blender, mix milk, eggs, and 2 tablespoons of butter. Add all-purpose flour, buckwheat flour, and a dash of salt. Puree until the mixture becomes smooth. Let batter rest overnight in the refrigerator.
- In a big skillet melt 3 tablespoons of butter on medium-high heat. Stir cremini mushrooms in and cook for 10 minutes until they turn golden brown. Add the spinach and tomatoes; stir and cook for 3-4 minutes until spinach wilts. Set aside.
- In a large skillet, melt 1 teaspoon of butter on medium heat. Depending on pan size, put about 1/4 cup of batter in the hot pan and make sure to distribute the batter evenly by immediately tilting and swirling the skillet. Cook for 3-4 minutes until edges start to turn brown and center becomes set. In the center of each crepe, sprinkle 1/4 of filling and sprinkle on 3 tablespoons Gruyere cheese on each. Set aside remaining cheese. Over the filling, fold the crepes in thirds to form triangles. With the remaining Gruyere cheese on top, serve crepes.

Nutrition Information

- Calories: 507 calories;
- Sodium: 369
- Total Carbohydrate: 30.7
- Cholesterol: 186
- Protein: 20.9
- Total Fat: 34.1

---

279.   Savory Italian Sausage Sauce

Serving: 4 | Prep: 20mins | Ready in:

Ingredients

- 2 tablespoons olive oil
- 4 cloves garlic, minced
- 1 pound Italian sausage
- 4 green onions, chopped
- 1 (8 ounce) package fresh mushrooms, sliced
- 1 tablespoon dried basil
- 1 tablespoon dried oregano
- 1 (15 ounce) can tomato sauce
- 1 (14.5 ounce) can stewed tomatoes
- 1 (6 ounce) can tomato paste
- 1/2 cup water
- 1/2 cup red wine
- 1 teaspoon red pepper flakes
- 2 tablespoons white sugar
- salt and pepper to taste

Direction

- In a big skillet, heat olive oil over medium-high heat and sauté garlic until browned. Place in the sausage and cook, crumbling the meat, until browned evenly.
- Stir in the oregano, basil, and mushrooms, and then cook for 5 minutes. Stir in tomato paste, stewed tomatoes, and tomato sauce, and then add the sugar, red pepper flakes, red wine, and water. Season to taste with pepper and salt. Bring heat down to low and simmer for a minimum of 1 hour.

Nutrition Information

- Calories: 495 calories;
- Total Fat: 29.2
- Sodium: 2063
- Total Carbohydrate: 36.3

- Cholesterol: 45
- Protein: 21.1

---

280.   Seafood Lasagna II

Serving: 8 | Prep: 30mins | Ready in:

Ingredients

- 9 lasagna noodles
- 1 tablespoon butter
- 1 cup minced onion
- 1 (8 ounce) package cream cheese, softened
- 1 1/2 cups cottage cheese
- 1 egg, beaten
- 2 teaspoons dried basil leaves
- 1/2 teaspoon salt
- 1/8 teaspoon freshly ground black pepper
- 2 (10.75 ounce) cans condensed cream of mushroom soup
- 1/3 cup milk
- 1/3 cup dry white wine
- 1 (6 ounce) can crabmeat, drained and flaked
- 1 pound cooked small shrimp
- 1/4 cup grated Parmesan cheese
- 1/2 cup shredded sharp Cheddar cheese

Direction

- Boil pot with lightly salted water. Cook pasta till al dente for 8-10 minutes; drain. Rinse under cold water. Preheat an oven to 175°C/350°F.
- Cook onion in butter in a skillet on medium heat till tender; take off heat. Mix pepper, salt, basil, egg, cottage cheese and cream cheese in.
- Mix shrimp, crabmeat, wine, milk and soup in medium bowl.
- On bottom of a 9x13-in. baking dish, lay 3 cooked lasagna noodles. Spread 1/3 onion mixture on noodles. Spread 1/3 soup mixture on onion layer. Repeat soup, onion and noodle layers 2 times. Put Parmesan and Cheddar cheese on top.

- In preheated oven, bake till bubbly and heated through for 45 minutes.

Nutrition Information

- Calories: 471 calories;
- Sodium: 1205
- Total Carbohydrate: 29.9
- Cholesterol: 206
- Protein: 33
- Total Fat: 23.5

---

281.   Seared Salmon With Indian Inspired Cream Sauce

Serving: 4 | Prep: 45mins | Ready in:

Ingredients

- 4 (6 ounce) fillets fresh salmon
- salt and black pepper to taste
- 1 tablespoon butter
- 2 medium onions, diced
- 8 cloves garlic, minced
- 1 cup chopped portobello mushrooms
- 1 cup fresh porcini mushrooms, cleaned and sliced
- 1/2 cup diced fennel bulb
- 1/2 cup diced celery
- 1 teaspoon curry powder
- 1/2 teaspoon saffron
- 2 cups chicken broth
- 1 cup heavy cream
- 1 tablespoon butter
- 4 sprigs chopped fresh parsley for garnish
- 4 lemon slices for garnish
- 2 tablespoons thinly sliced green onion for garnish

Direction

- Sprinkle salt and pepper into each of the fillets to season it; put them aside.

- In a large saucepan, melt 1 tbsp. of butter over medium heat. Mix in onions. Cook for 5-7 minutes until they turn translucent and soften. Add the garlic and cook them for 1 more minute. Mix together celery with onion, fennel, and mushrooms. Let them cook for 5-7 minutes until the vegetables have softened. Season the mixture with salt, pepper, curry powder, and saffron. Cook the mixture for 2 more minutes. Pour in chicken broth. Cook the mixture while occasionally stirring it for another 5 minutes. Mix in heavy cream. Simmer the mixture for 5 minutes.
- In the meantime, put 1 tbsp. of butter in a large skillet and melt it over medium heat. Place the salmon fillets in the pan, positioning them skin-side down. Adjust the heat to high and sear the fillets for 2 minutes per side.
- Spoon the mushroom sauce over the bottom of the serving platter for preparation. Top the sauce with the salmon fillets. Drizzle fillets with more sauce. Garnish them with lemon slices, green onions, and parsley.

Nutrition Information

- Calories: 599 calories;
- Sodium: 665
- Total Carbohydrate: 16.5
- Cholesterol: 182
- Protein: 34.3
- Total Fat: 44.7

---

282.   Sensational Sirloin Kabobs

Serving: 8 | Prep: 15mins | Ready in:

Ingredients

- 1/4 cup soy sauce
- 3 tablespoons light brown sugar
- 3 tablespoons distilled white vinegar
- 1/2 teaspoon garlic powder

- 1/2 teaspoon seasoned salt
- 1/2 teaspoon garlic pepper seasoning
- 4 fluid ounces lemon-lime flavored carbonated beverage
- 2 pounds beef sirloin steak, cut into 1 1/2 inch cubes
- 2 green bell peppers, cut into 2 inch pieces
- skewers
- 1/2 pound fresh mushrooms, stems removed
- 1 pint cherry tomatoes
- 1 fresh pineapple - peeled, cored and cubed

Direction

- Stir together distilled white vinegar, soy sauce, light brown sugar, seasoned salt, garlic powder, garlic pepper seasoning, and lemon-lime soda. Keep half of the mixture for basting later. Drop steak in a large zip-top plastic bag and pour the remaining marinade over the meat. Close the bag and marinate in the fridge for 8 hours or even overnight.
- Boil water in a saucepan and blanch green peppers for a minute. Drain and set aside.
- Pre-heat grill on high. Alternately cue the mushrooms, green peppers, steak, tomatoes, and pineapples onto skewers. Dispose of the marinade.
- Grease the grates lightly. Grill the kabobs for 10 minutes or until cooked to liking. Turn and baste often at the last five minutes of grilling.

Nutrition Information

- Calories: 326 calories;
- Total Fat: 17.4
- Sodium: 608
- Total Carbohydrate: 19.2
- Cholesterol: 76
- Protein: 24

283.   Sensational Steak Sandwich

Serving: 4 | Prep: 30mins | Ready in:

Ingredients

- 2 tablespoons olive oil
- 1 pound thinly sliced sirloin steak strips
- 8 ounces sliced fresh mushrooms
- 1 green bell pepper, seeded and cut into strips
- 1 medium onion, sliced
- 10 slices provolone cheese
- 1 loaf French bread
- 1 (14 ounce) can beef broth
- 1/2 teaspoon salt
- 1/2 teaspoon ground black pepper
- 1/2 teaspoon garlic powder
- 2 tablespoons Worcestershire sauce
- 1/8 teaspoon red pepper flakes
- 1/4 cup Pinot Noir or other dry red wine
- 1/2 cup prepared horseradish (optional)
- 1/2 cup brown mustard (optional)

Direction

- In a large skillet, heat the oil over medium heat. Put in the beef, then cook until browned. Put in the onion, bell pepper and mushrooms; cook and mix for around 5 minutes, until beginning to turn tender.
- In a slow cooker, blend the red wine, red pepper flakes, Worcestershire sauce, pepper, salt, and beef broth. Move the vegetables and beef to the slow cooker, then stir to combine. Cook while covered on High for 3 - 4 hours, till the beef becomes extremely softened.
- Preheat the oven to 425° F (220° C). Drain the liquid from the slow cooker, reserve for dipping. Cut lengthwise the French bread loaf like a submarine sandwich. Mix the mustard and horseradish together; spread onto the inner of the loaf. On both sides of the loaf, position slices of provolone cheese, fill with vegetables and beef. Seal the loaf, then wrap aluminum foil around the entire sandwich.

- In the preheated oven, bake for 10 - 15 minutes. Bake without the aluminum foil for crunchier bread. Cut into servings. Serve with the juices reserved from the slow cooker as dipping.

Nutrition Information

- Calories: 908 calories;
- Total Fat: 40.6
- Sodium: 2586
- Total Carbohydrate: 78.8
- Cholesterol: 109
- Protein: 55.7

284.   Sesame Cabbage And Mushrooms

Serving: 4 | Prep: 15mins | Ready in:

Ingredients

- 2 1/2 tablespoons dark sesame oil, divided
- 6 ounces shiitake mushroom caps, sliced
- 4 cups thinly sliced napa cabbage
- 1 tablespoon reduced-sodium soy sauce
- 1/4 teaspoon freshly ground black pepper
- 1/4 cup cilantro leaves
- 2 tablespoons toasted sesame seeds

Direction

- Set a large skillet over high heat. Put in 2 tablespoons sesame oil; whirl to coat. Stir-fry mushrooms for about 4 minutes, until browned. Put in cabbage; stir-fry for 2 minutes.
- Take the skillet away from heat. Stir in black pepper, soy sauce, and 1 1/2 teaspoon sesame oil until well mixed. Place sesame seeds and cilantro on top.

Nutrition Information

- Calories: 133 calories;
- Total Fat: 10.9
- Sodium: 151
- Total Carbohydrate: 6.4
- Cholesterol: 0
- Protein: 2.9

285. Shiitake Delight

Serving: 2 | Prep: 10mins | Ready in:

Ingredients

- 2 tablespoons olive oil
- 4 cloves garlic
- 8 shiitake mushrooms, chopped
- 1 cup vegetable broth
- 2 tablespoons butter
- Italian seasoning to taste
- salt to taste

Direction

- Heat olive oil over medium heat in a skillet; cook garlic just until golden. Toss in mushroom pieces; cook until softened, for 10 minutes.
- Pour in broth. Mix in butter until melted. Sprinkle with salt and Italian seasoning to season.

Nutrition Information

- Calories: 273 calories;
- Protein: 2.5
- Total Fat: 25.3
- Sodium: 328
- Total Carbohydrate: 8.5
- Cholesterol: 31

286. Shiitake Mushroom, Sun Dried Tomato Pesto, And Shrimp Pasta

Serving: 4 | Prep: 10mins | Ready in:

Ingredients

- 1 (16 ounce) package farfalle (bow-tie) pasta
- 1/4 cup butter
- 1/4 cup olive oil
- 2 tablespoons minced garlic
- 1 cup sliced shiitake mushrooms
- 1/2 cup sliced yellow onion
- 1 pound cooked shrimp, peeled and deveined
- 1 (14 ounce) can diced tomatoes
- 1/2 cup sun-dried tomato pesto
- 1/2 cup white wine
- 2 tablespoons lemon juice
- 1/2 cup half-and-half
- 1/2 cup shredded Parmesan cheese, plus more for topping
- 1/4 cup chopped flat-leaf parsley
- 1 teaspoon red pepper flakes
- 1 teaspoon freshly ground black pepper
- 1 teaspoon sea salt

Direction

- In a large pot, boil lightly salted water. Cook bow-tie pasta at a boil for approximately 12 minutes, stirring occasionally, till cooked through yet still firm to the bite; drain.
- Over medium heat, heat a skillet; add olive oil and butter. Cook and stir garlic in the hot butter-oil for around 1 minute till fragrant. Put in onion and mushrooms; cook and stir for approximately 5 minutes till softened.
- Mix diced tomatoes, shrimp, lemon juice, wine, and pesto into mushroom-onion mixture; simmer for 10 minutes. Take away skillet from heat; add Parmesan cheese, half-and-half, red pepper flakes, parsley, salt, and black pepper and mix till sauce is combined well.

- In a serving bowl, place pasta. Spoon sauce over pasta and add extra Parmesan cheese on top.

Nutrition Information

- Calories: 959 calories;
- Total Fat: 40.6
- Sodium: 1152
- Total Carbohydrate: 96.8
- Cholesterol: 272
- Protein: 46.7

---

287. Shredded Roast Spaghetti Sauce

Serving: 28 | Prep: | Ready in:

Ingredients

- 4 pounds bone-in pork roast
- 3 teaspoons salt
- 1/4 cup all-purpose flour
- 1/4 cup olive oil
- 2 cups hot water
- 3 cloves crushed garlic
- 1 onion, chopped
- 2 bay leaves
- 1 teaspoon celery salt
- 1 teaspoon ground black pepper
- 2 teaspoons white sugar
- 1/2 teaspoon crushed red pepper flakes
- 1 teaspoon Italian-style seasoning
- 1/4 teaspoon monosodium glutamate (MSG)
- 1/2 teaspoon dried oregano
- 1/2 teaspoon dried basil
- 1/2 teaspoon dried parsley
- 1/2 teaspoon dried rosemary, crushed
- 1/8 teaspoon ground nutmeg
- 4 (6 ounce) cans tomato paste
- 1 quart water
- 1 cup red wine
- 1/2 cup sliced black olives

- 1 cup fresh sliced mushrooms
- 8 anchovy fillets, mashed (optional)

Direction

- Add salt to pork roast to taste, dip in flour. In a big pot, heat the oil. Slowly brown roast on all sides of the pork in hot oil. Put in hot water, cook slowly while covered until the meat is almost falls apart for about 3 hours. Use a folk to tear meat into small pieces.
- In the same pot, put in the anchovy fillets (if you want), mushrooms, olives, wine, water, tomato paste, nutmeg, rosemary, parsley, basil, oregano, monosodium glutamate, seasoning, chile pepper, sugar, black pepper, celery salt, bay leaves, onion, and garlic. Mix the ingredients together, set the heat to low, cover the pot tightly and simmer the mixture for two hours, stir occasionally. Uncover, then keep cooking until the thickness reaches the consistency you want.

Nutrition Information

- Calories: 243 calories;
- Total Fat: 18.1
- Sodium: 599
- Total Carbohydrate: 6.9
- Cholesterol: 48
- Protein: 11.9

---

288. Shrimp Cognac And Baked Cheese Grits

Serving: 12 | Prep: 30mins | Ready in:

Ingredients

- 6 cups water
- 3/4 teaspoon salt
- 2 cups yellow grits
- 1 3/4 teaspoons salt
- 1/2 teaspoon ground black pepper

- 1/2 cup unsalted butter
- 2 tablespoons minced garlic
- 1 (8 ounce) package shredded Cheddar cheese
- 3 eggs
- 1 cup whole milk
- 1/4 cup clarified butter
- 2 tablespoons minced garlic
- 1 leek, halved and cut into 1/4-inch pieces
- 2 ounces fresh morel mushrooms, chopped
- 3 ounces fresh oyster mushrooms, chopped
- 3 ounces fresh chanterelle mushrooms, chopped
- 2 tomatoes, peeled, seeded, and chopped
- 1 tablespoon Creole seasoning
- 1/2 cup cognac
- 1/2 cup shrimp stock
- 1/3 cup veal stock
- 1 pound peeled and deveined gulf shrimp
- 2 tablespoons chopped fresh thyme
- 3 tablespoons unsalted butter
- salt and black pepper to taste

Direction

- Start preheating the oven to 350°F (175°C). Oil a 9x13-in. baking dish.
- In a big pot, boil 3/4 teaspoon of salt and water. Stir in grits and boil again. Lower the heat to low; cook for 30 minutes until the grits are very thick and soft, whisking often. Take away from heat, then mix in Cheddar cheese, 2 tablespoons garlic, 1/2 cup butter, 1/2 teaspoon of pepper, and 1 3/4 teaspoons of salt until the cheese melts. In a bowl, whisk milk with eggs until smooth; mix into the grits until evenly blended. Add to the prepared baking dish.
- Put in the preheated oven and bake for 1 hour until the top turns golden brown and the middle of the grits are hot.
- In the meantime, in a skillet, heat clarified butter over medium heat. Mix in 2 tablespoons of garlic and cook for 2 minutes until turning golden. Add leeks, and cook for another 1 minute. Mix in Creole seasoning, tomatoes, chanterelle mushrooms, oyster mushrooms, and morel mushrooms; stir and cook for 3

minutes until the mushrooms start to render their liquid. Add cognac and simmer for 2 minutes, then add veal stock and shrimp stock. Simmer again and cook until the liquid has decreased by 1/2. Mix in 3 tablespoons of butter, thyme, and the shrimp. Stir and cook over low heat for 4 minutes until the shrimp is not opaque anymore; use pepper and salt to season.
- Enjoy the mushroom sauce and shrimp with the baked grits.

Nutrition Information

- Calories: 425 calories;
- Total Carbohydrate: 26.9
- Cholesterol: 165
- Protein: 18.4
- Total Fat: 24.1
- Sodium: 846

289.   Shrimp Stuffed Mushrooms

Serving: 10 | Prep: 15mins | Ready in:

Ingredients

- 2 pounds large mushrooms
- 3/4 pound cooked baby shrimp
- 1 cup crushed bacon flavored crackers
- 1 cup cream cheese, softened
- 1/2 cup shredded sharp Cheddar cheese

Direction

- Heat oven to 220°C (425°F) beforehand. Grease a medium baking dish lightly.
- Cut stems from mushrooms. Chop stems finely, and put aside. In the baking dish, place caps cavity side up.
- Mix together cream cheese, crushed bacon flavored crackers, cooked baby shrimp, and mushroom stems in a medium bowl.

- Generously stuff mushroom stem mixture into mushroom caps. Place sharp Cheddar cheese on top.
- In the preheated oven, allow to bake till cheese browned lightly and melted for 8-10 minutes.

Nutrition Information

- Calories: 191 calories;
- Sodium: 214
- Total Carbohydrate: 7.5
- Cholesterol: 83
- Protein: 13.2
- Total Fat: 12.5

---

290.   Shrimp And Mushroom Linguini With Creamy Cheese Herb Sauce

Serving: 4 | Prep: 15mins | Ready in:

Ingredients

- 1 (8 ounce) package linguini pasta
- 2 tablespoons butter
- 1/2 pound fresh mushrooms, sliced
- 1/2 cup butter
- 2 cloves garlic, minced
- 1 (3 ounce) package cream cheese
- 2 tablespoons chopped fresh parsley
- 3/4 teaspoon dried basil
- 2/3 cup boiling water
- 1/2 pound cooked shrimp

Direction

- Boil a large pot with mildly salted water. Put in linguini and cook for 7 minutes until tender. Drain.
- In the meantime, heat 2 tablespoons butter in a large skillet on medium-high heat. Put in mushrooms; cook while stirring until soft. Place onto a plate.

- Melt half cup of butter with the minced garlic in the same pan. Pour in the cream cheese, use a spoon to break it up as it melts. Mix in the basil and parsley. Simmer for 5 minutes. Stir in boiling water until sauce is smooth. Mix in cooked mushrooms and shrimp; heat sauce through.
- Mix linguini with shrimp sauce, serve right away.

Nutrition Information

- Calories: 601 calories;
- Total Fat: 38.3
- Sodium: 403
- Total Carbohydrate: 44
- Cholesterol: 210
- Protein: 23.2

---

291.   Simple Fried Morel Mushrooms

Serving: 4 | Prep: 20mins | Ready in:

Ingredients

- 1 pound fresh morel mushrooms - dirt gently brushed off and mushrooms halved lengthwise
- 1 cup all-purpose flour
- 1 cup vegetable shortening
- salt to taste

Direction

- In a big bowl, cover halved morel mushrooms in cold, lightly salted water. Keep in fridge to loosen dirt for 5 minutes. Pour salted water off. Rinse. Repeat 2 times. The mushroom crevices could have insects or tiny stones. Rinse mushrooms thoroughly one last time. Drain mushrooms on paper towels.
- In a shallow bowl, put flour.

- In a big skillet, heat vegetable shortening until very hot.
- Roll the mushrooms into flour. Tap excess off. Lay mushrooms gently in hot shortening.
- Pan Fry for 5-8 minutes until flour coating is crisp and its golden brown, turning often. On paper towels, drain morels. Use salt to taste.

Nutrition Information

- Calories: 185 calories;
- Total Carbohydrate: 29.2
- Cholesterol: 0
- Protein: 5.9
- Total Fat: 5.3
- Sodium: 39

292. Sirloin Tips And Mushrooms

Serving: 6 | Prep: 15mins | Ready in:

Ingredients

- 3 tablespoons olive oil
- 3 cloves garlic, minced
- 1 1/2 pounds beef sirloin
- 1 (16 ounce) can mushrooms, with liquid
- 1 (8 ounce) can tomato sauce
- salt to taste
- freshly ground pepper, to taste
- 3/4 cup red wine

Direction

- Slice the beef into cubes. Heat olive oil in a large skillet over medium/high heat and brown the beef cubes together with garlic.
- Put in red wine, pepper, salt, tomato sauce, mushrooms with liquid. Cook until the beef cubes become tender, half an hour. If desired, while cooking, pour in a bit more wine.

Nutrition Information

- Calories: 257 calories;
- Total Fat: 13.5
- Sodium: 556
- Total Carbohydrate: 7.1
- Cholesterol: 49
- Protein: 21.7

293. Slovak Sauerkraut Christmas Soup

Serving: 10 | Prep: 15mins | Ready in:

Ingredients

- 1 (32 ounce) package sauerkraut, chopped
- 2 1/2 quarts chicken broth
- 6 black peppercorns
- 4 bay leaves
- salt to taste
- 2 cups dried forest mushroom blend
- 3/4 pound Hungarian style dry paprika sausage
- 3/4 pound smoked ham
- 3/4 cup chopped pitted prunes
- 2 tablespoons vegetable oil
- 1 large onion, finely chopped
- 2 tablespoons all-purpose flour
- 2 teaspoons sweet Hungarian paprika
- 1 cup water
- 1 cup sour cream

Direction

- In a large pot, put the mushrooms, salt, bay leaves, peppercorns, chicken broth, and sauerkraut; allow to boil. Add the entire piece of ham and the sausage. Allow to simmer on medium heat for 1 1/2 hours. After the first hour, put in the prunes.
- Take the meat out from the soup and put aside. Discard the bay leaves.
- In a large skillet, heat the oil on medium. Add in the onion and fry until translucent. Use

paprika and flour to dust on the onion; stir and cook for 1 minute. Use a fork to stir in water slowly to avoid forming lumps. Allow to boil and thicken. Add into the soup pot. Cube the ham and sausage and put into the soup, stir. Allow to boil and cook for 10 more minutes.

- Transfer into bowls and place a dollop of sour cream on top to serve.

Nutrition Information

- Calories: 386 calories;
- Total Carbohydrate: 21.4
- Cholesterol: 53
- Protein: 15.5
- Total Fat: 26.5
- Sodium: 1326

---

294. Slow Cooker Chicken And Mushroom Stew

Serving: 6 | Prep: 20mins | Ready in:

Ingredients

- 1/2 cup all-purpose flour
- 1 teaspoon dried basil
- 1 teaspoon dried thyme
- 1 teaspoon dried rubbed sage
- 1 teaspoon ground black pepper
- 5 chicken thighs, quartered
- 1 tablespoon olive oil, or as needed
- 1 large yellow onion, diced
- 1 large bell pepper, diced
- 8 ounces chorizo sausage, thinly sliced
- 2 cloves garlic, crushed
- 1 (8 ounce) package sliced fresh mushrooms
- 1 cup chicken stock
- 1 (10.75 ounce) can cream of mushroom soup
- 1 (10.75 ounce) can cream of celery soup
- 1 cup sour cream
- 2 teaspoons Cajun seasoning

- 1 teaspoon cayenne pepper

Direction

- In a large resealable bag, combine black pepper, sage, thyme, basil, and flour; put chicken in bag and seal, shake to evenly coat the chicken.
- In a large skillet placed over medium heat, heat olive oil. Cook and stir onion and bell pepper for 5 to 10 minutes until lightly soft. Add garlic and chorizo sausage; cook and stir until sausage is done, approximately 5 minutes. Remove mixture to a slow cooker and throw mushrooms on top.
- In the same skillet, cook and stir coated chicken (with all the flour included), adding more oil if required, 5 to 10 minutes until chicken is browned. Transfer to the slow cooker.
- In the same skillet, pour chicken stock and heat to a boil, while scraping with a wooden spoon to remove the browned bits of food from the bottom of the skillet. Pour all brown bits and liquid into slow cooker.
- In a bowl, combine cayenne pepper, Cajun seasoning, sour cream, cream of celery soup and cream of mushroom soup; scoop into slow cooker.
- Cook on High for 2 hours; lower setting to Low and continue to cook for 4 more hours.

Nutrition Information

- Calories: 554 calories;
- Total Fat: 37.3
- Sodium: 1577
- Total Carbohydrate: 23.7
- Cholesterol: 115
- Protein: 31

295.   Smothered Pork Chops With Bourbon And Mushrooms

Serving: 4 | Prep: 10mins | Ready in:

Ingredients

- 4 (8 ounce) center-cut pork chops
- salt and ground black pepper to taste
- 2 tablespoons vegetable oil
- For the Sauce:
- 2 tablespoons butter
- 2 cups thinly sliced onion
- 1 (8 ounce) package thinly sliced baby bella mushrooms
- 1 teaspoon white sugar
- 1/4 cup bourbon
- 1 1/2 cups beef broth
- 1/2 cup heavy cream
- salt and ground black pepper to taste

Direction

- Start preheating oven to 375°F (190°C).
- Add pepper and salt to season the pork chops. In a frying pan, heat oil over medium-high heat. Put in pork chops; then cook for 3-4 mins on each side or until browned. In a baking dish (about 9x13-inch), put the browned chops. Wipe out all the residual oil from pan.
- In the same pan, melt butter over medium heat. Put in sugar, mushrooms, and onion. Cook while stirring for one minute. Turn the heat to medium-low and cover pan. Simmer the mixture for 10 mins or until the onions have softened. Uncover the pan; stir mixture, scraping up any browned bits from bottom. Keep cooking the onions for 3 more mins.
- Add bourbon to onion mixture and cook for 3-4 mins or until mostly evaporated. Put in cream and broth; then simmer. Cook about 10 mins; transfer over browned chops in baking dish. Wrap in aluminum foil.
- Bake in prepared oven for 25 to 30 mins or until an instant-read thermometer registers 145°F (63°C) when inserted into pork.

Nutrition Information

- Calories: 509 calories;
- Protein: 32.4
- Total Fat: 33.4
- Sodium: 472
- Total Carbohydrate: 11.2
- Cholesterol: 126

296.   So Shiitake Wontons

Serving: 10 | Prep: 45mins | Ready in:

Ingredients

- 2 large eggs, divided
- 1 tablespoon water
- 1 1/4 pounds ground pork
- 1 (8 ounce) package shiitake mushrooms, stemmed and diced
- 1 tablespoon soy sauce
- 1/2 teaspoon sesame oil
- 1 1/2 teaspoons cornstarch
- 1 teaspoon onion powder
- waxed paper
- 4 cups chicken broth
- 1 (16 ounce) package wonton wrappers

Direction

- Into a small bowl, separate an egg white; stir in water. Set egg yolk aside.
- In a bowl, mix sesame oil, soy sauce, shiitake mushrooms, pork, the leftover a whole egg and an egg yolk. Combine using hand till just incorporated. Put in the onion powder and cornstarch; combine filling evenly.
- Line waxed paper on a baking sheet.
- Separate and put the wonton wrappers onto the work area. Onto the middle of one wrapper, put a rounded dollop of filling. Moisten edges slightly with mixture of egg white. Fold a corner over filling towards the opposing corner to make a triangle; press to seal. Moisten edges once more and gather in

corners to make a little purse-like pouch. On the prepped baking sheet, put the wonton. Repeat with the rest of wrappers and filling.

- In a big pot, let chicken broth come to boil. Carefully drop in the wontons; cook for approximately 5 minutes till clear.

Nutrition Information

- Calories: 281 calories;
- Total Fat: 10.2
- Sodium: 778
- Total Carbohydrate: 28.3
- Cholesterol: 80
- Protein: 16.7

297.   South Dakota Wild Mushroom Dip

Serving: 12 | Prep: 5mins | Ready in:

Ingredients

- 1 tablespoon butter
- 1 cup sliced mushrooms, such as oyster, portobello or shiitake
- 1/4 cup chopped onion
- 1/2 cup milk
- 1/2 cup water
- 1 (.87 ounce) package McCormick® Brown Gravy Mix
- 1 cup shredded Monterey Jack cheese, divided

Direction

- Set the oven to 350°F. In a large skillet, melt butter over medium-high heat. Add onion and mushrooms, stir and cook until softened.
- In a small bowl, stir Gravy Mix, water and milk. Mix into mushroom mixture. Cook over medium heat until the gravy comes to a boil, stirring often. Lower heat to simmer. Mix in 3/4 cup cheese. Simmer for 1-2 minutes or

until the gravy slightly thickens and cheese is melted.

- Spoon the mixture into 1-quart baking dish. Sprinkle the remaining 1/4 cup cheese on top.
- Bake in the oven until cheese is melted, 5-10 minutes. Serve with crusty bread, fries or onion rings.

Nutrition Information

- Calories: 59 calories;
- Total Fat: 4.2
- Sodium: 180
- Total Carbohydrate: 2.3
- Cholesterol: 12
- Protein: 2.9

298.   Southern Style Fried Mushrooms

Serving: 2 | Prep: 15mins | Ready in:

Ingredients

- 2 cups vegetable oil for frying
- 1/4 cup red cooking wine
- 2 teaspoons water
- 1/2 cup all-purpose flour
- 1 teaspoon chopped fresh parsley
- 3/4 teaspoon minced garlic
- 1/2 teaspoon kosher salt
- ground black pepper to taste
- 10 button mushrooms
- 2 tablespoons grated Parmesan cheese

Direction

- In a large saucepan or deep-fryer, heat oil to 350 °F (175 °C).
- Whisk water, wine, parsley, flour, garlic, pepper, and salt together in one bowl until no lumps are visible and well combined. Plunge every mushroom one by one into the mixture to coat. Put the coated mushrooms carefully

into the hot oil, prevent mushrooms from touching and sticking together while cooking. Cook for around 5 to 6 minutes until golden brown. Take away from oil and place on a plate lined with paper towels to drain. Scatter Parmesan cheese over and serve.

Nutrition Information

- Calories: 382 calories;
- Total Fat: 24.1
- Sodium: 741
- Total Carbohydrate: 33.2
- Cholesterol: 4
- Protein: 7

299.　　Special Vegan Chili

Serving: 4 | Prep: 20mins | Ready in:

Ingredients

- 1 tablespoon canola oil
- 1/2 cup chopped red bell pepper
- 1/3 cup chopped yellow onion
- 1/3 cup minced carrot
- 2 cloves garlic, minced
- 1/3 cup minced cremini mushrooms
- 1 (19 ounce) can mixed beans, drained
- 1 1/2 cups canned diced tomatoes, with juices
- 1 tablespoon chili powder
- 1 1/2 teaspoons ground flax seeds
- 1/2 teaspoon ground cumin
- 1/2 teaspoon dried oregano
- 2 pinches ground black pepper

Direction

- In a big skillet, heat oil on medium-heat. Sauté garlic, carrot, onion, and red bell pepper for 8-10 minutes until lightly toasted. Add mushrooms and cook for a minute.
- Put red bell pepper mixture in a pot. Stir in black pepper, oregano, cumin, flax seeds, chili

powder, diced tomatoes with juice, and mixed beans; mix well. Let it boil. Simmer, uncovered, for 30 minutes while stirring occasionally until flavors have blended.

Nutrition Information

- Calories: 198 calories;
- Cholesterol: 0
- Protein: 9.4
- Total Fat: 4.4
- Sodium: 693
- Total Carbohydrate: 28.6

300.　　Spicy Beef Sloppy Joes

Serving: 6 | Prep: 20mins | Ready in:

Ingredients

- 2 pounds lean ground beef
- 2 (16 ounce) jars salsa
- 3 cups sliced fresh mushrooms
- 1 1/2 cups shredded carrots
- 1 1/2 cups finely chopped red or green bell pepper
- 1/3 cup tomato paste
- 2 teaspoons dried basil, crushed
- 1 teaspoon dried oregano, crushed
- 1/2 teaspoon salt
- 1/4 teaspoon cayenne pepper
- 4 cloves garlic, minced
- 6 kaiser rolls, split and toasted
- 1 Reynolds® Slow Cooker Liner

Direction

- Cook the beef on medium heat in a skillet until it turns brown, stirring to crumble the meat into pieces. Drain off the fat.
- Use a Reynolds® Slow Cooker Liner to line a 5- or 6-quart slow cooker. Open the slow cooker liner and arrange it inside a slow cooker bowl. Fit the liner against the sides and

bottom of the bowl snugly; then pull the top of the liner to overlap the rim of the bowl.

- In the slow cooker, mix beef with the remaining ingredients excluding kaiser rolls.
- Put a cover on and cook for 8-10 hours on Low or 4-5 hours on High.
- Remove the lid carefully to release the steam. Remove sloppy joes right out of the slow cooker to serve, topping each Kaiser roll with meat. Don't transport or lift the liner containing food. Allow the slow cooker to cool completely, remove all excess liquid, then take the liner out and toss.

Nutrition Information

- Calories: 500 calories;
- Total Fat: 20.8
- Sodium: 1539
- Total Carbohydrate: 40.6
- Cholesterol: 105
- Protein: 38.7

301. Spinach Stuffed Mushrooms

Serving: 30 | Prep: 20mins | Ready in:

Ingredients

- 1/4 cup olive oil
- 30 large whole fresh mushrooms, stems removed
- 1 egg
- salt and ground black pepper to taste
- 1 teaspoon minced garlic
- 1 (10 ounce) package frozen chopped spinach, thawed and drained
- 1/4 cup grated Parmesan cheese
- 1/4 cup shredded Gouda cheese
- 1/4 cup shredded mozzarella cheese
- 1/4 cup dry bread crumbs
- 1/4 cup grated Parmesan cheese

Direction

- Set the oven to 375°F (190°C), and start preheating.
- In muffin pans, lightly brush 30 cups with olive oil. Brush all sides of the mushrooms with the remaining olive oil, then lay them into the muffin cups, gill sides facing up.
- Bake the mushrooms in the oven for about 12 minutes until just tender. While baking, in a mixing bowl, beat garlic, salt and egg. Mix in bread crumbs, mozzarella cheese, Gouda cheese, 1/4 cup of Parmesan cheese and drained spinach until well combined.
- Take the mushrooms out of the oven, and drain any gathered liquid. Stuff the spinach mixture into the mushroom caps, and place back in the muffin pan. Sprinkle the remaining 1/4 cup Parmesan cheese over mushrooms.
- Put into the oven, and bake for about 10 minutes, until the stuffing is hot and turns golden brown.

Nutrition Information

- Calories: 41 calories;
- Protein: 2.4
- Total Fat: 3
- Sodium: 129
- Total Carbohydrate: 1.9
- Cholesterol: 9

302. Spinach And Mushroom Casserole

Serving: 6 | Prep: 20mins | Ready in:

Ingredients

- 2 tablespoons butter
- 1 pound fresh mushrooms, sliced
- 2 (10 ounce) packages fresh spinach, rinsed and stems removed
- 1 teaspoon salt

- 4 tablespoons butter, melted
- 1/4 cup finely chopped onion
- 1 1/2 cups shredded Cheddar cheese, divided

Direction

- Turn oven to 350°F (175°C) to preheat. Lightly oil a 2-quart casserole dish.
- In a large skillet, melt 2 tablespoons butter over medium heat. Sauté mushrooms in melted butter for about 8 to 10 minutes until softened.
- In the meantime, put spinach into a large pot. Cook over medium heat until wilted; drain, pressing or squeezing to remove excess liquid. Transfer spinach to the prepared baking dish; top with 1/2 of the cheese, onion, 4 tablespoons melted butter, and salt. Place mushrooms in a layer on top of spinach and scatter with the remaining cheese.
- Bake for 20 minutes in the preheated oven.

Nutrition Information

- Calories: 257 calories;
- Total Carbohydrate: 7.5
- Cholesterol: 60
- Protein: 11.3
- Total Fat: 21.5
- Sodium: 721

---

303. Spinach And Mushroom Quesadillas

Serving: 16 | Prep: 10mins | Ready in:

Ingredients

- 1 (10 ounce) package chopped spinach
- 2 cups shredded Cheddar cheese
- 2 tablespoons butter
- 2 cloves garlic, sliced
- 2 portobello mushroom caps, sliced
- 4 (10 inch) flour tortillas

- 1 tablespoon vegetable oil

Direction

- Following directions on package, prepare spinach. Drain and dry by patting.
- Set oven to 3500F (1750C) and preheat. On one side of each tortilla, sprinkle half cup of cheese. On baking sheets, put tortillas cheese side up, and bake until cheese is melted, about 5 minutes.
- In a skillet, melt the butter over medium heat. Mix in mushrooms and garlic, and cook for about 5 minutes. Stir in spinach, and continue cooking for 5 minutes. On the cheese side of each tortilla, pour an equal amount of the mixture. Fold the tortillas in half over the filling.
- In a separate skillet, heat oil on medium heat. Put quesadillas one by one into the skillet, and cook each side for 3 minutes, until golden brown. Cut each quesadilla into 4 wedges and serve.

Nutrition Information

- Calories: 154 calories;
- Total Fat: 9.5
- Sodium: 247
- Total Carbohydrate: 10.9
- Cholesterol: 22
- Protein: 6.7

---

304. Spinach And Mushroom Salad

Serving: 4 | Prep: 15mins | Ready in:

Ingredients

- 4 slices bacon
- 2 eggs
- 2 teaspoons white sugar
- 2 tablespoons cider vinegar

- 2 tablespoons water
- 1/2 teaspoon salt
- 1 pound spinach
- 1/4 pound fresh mushrooms, sliced

Direction

- Put bacon in a big, deep skillet. Cook over moderately high heat until equally browned. Crumble and set aside, save 2 tbsp. bacon fat.
- In a saucepan, add eggs, and pour in cold water to cover totally. Bring water to a boil. Cover, take away from heat, and allow eggs to stand in hot water for about 10 to 12 minutes. Take the eggs out of hot water, cool, peel and slice into wedges.
- Bring 2 tbsp. bacon fat back to the skillet, then stir in salt, water, vinegar and sugar, keep it warm.
- Rinse and remove stems from spinach, dry completely and crumble into pieces in a salad bowl. Drizzle the warm dressing over and toss well to coat.
- Place bacon and mushrooms on top of the salad, decorate with egg.

Nutrition Information

- Calories: 126 calories;
- Total Carbohydrate: 7.5
- Cholesterol: 103
- Protein: 10.6
- Total Fat: 6.8
- Sodium: 625

305.   Steak Salad (Ranen Salad)

Serving: 4 | Prep: 30mins | Ready in:

Ingredients

- 1 1/2 pounds beef sirloin steak
- 8 cups romaine lettuce, torn into bite-size pieces

- 6 roma (plum) tomatoes, sliced
- 1/2 cup sliced fresh mushrooms
- 3/4 cup crumbled blue cheese
- 1/4 cup walnuts
- 1/3 cup vegetable oil
- 3 tablespoons red wine vinegar
- 2 tablespoons lemon juice
- 1/2 teaspoon salt
- 1/8 teaspoon ground black pepper
- 3 teaspoons Worcestershire sauce
- 1/8 teaspoon liquid smoke flavoring

Direction

- Set the oven to broiler setting and start preheating. Broil steak for 3 to 5 minutes each side or until steak reaches desired doneness. Cool then cut into bite-size slices.
- Lay out mushrooms, tomatoes and lettuce on chilled platters. Sprinkle with walnuts and blue cheese. Add steak slices on top.
- Whisk together smoke flavoring, Worcestershire sauce, pepper, salt, lemon juice, vinegar and oil in a small bowl. Pour over salad.

Nutrition Information

- Calories: 586 calories;
- Protein: 36.3
- Total Fat: 45.6
- Sodium: 760
- Total Carbohydrate: 8.6
- Cholesterol: 110

306.   Steak Tips With Mushroom Sauce

Serving: 6 | Prep: 10mins | Ready in:

Ingredients

- 2 1/2 pounds sirloin tips, uncut
- 1/2 (750 milliliter) bottle Burgundy wine

- 2 (14.5 ounce) cans beef broth
- 4 portobello mushroom caps, sliced
- 1/4 cup butter
- 1 clove garlic, chopped
- 1/2 teaspoon dried thyme
- 1/4 teaspoon salt, or to taste
- 1/2 teaspoon ground black pepper, or to taste
- 1 shallot, finely chopped
- 2 tablespoons all-purpose flour

Direction

- Preheat an outdoor grill for medium-high heat. In a large skillet, melt butter over medium-high heat. Sauté the shallot until transparent, then put in mushrooms, cook while covered for around 5 minutes until darkened. Take the mushrooms away from pan, and leave aside. Deglaze the pan with one can of beef broth, and burgundy wine. Raise the heat, then boil. Let the mixture boil till it lessens by 1/3.
- Grill the sirloin tips to the wanted doneness. Spice with pepper if wanted and salt. Transfer to a plate, and leave aside.
- Once the sauce is reduced, mix in the remaining can of beef broth and garlic. Set to a boil again, then keep cooking for another 5 - 10 minutes. Sauce will become thin like au jus. Fold in flour, then cook till the sauce reaches the desired thickness. Taste and modify seasoning if needed. Mix in the mushrooms. Spoon mushroom sauce over the tips to serve.

Nutrition Information

- Calories: 455 calories;
- Protein: 35.2
- Total Fat: 25.4
- Sodium: 672
- Total Carbohydrate: 9.3
- Cholesterol: 121

307.   Steak And Ale Pie With Mushrooms

Serving: 8 | Prep: 45mins | Ready in:

Ingredients

- 1 1/4 pounds cubed beef stew meat
- 1 onion, diced
- 1 (12 fluid ounce) can pale ale or lager beer
- 2 cloves garlic, minced
- 1/2 teaspoon dried thyme
- 1 1/2 teaspoons chopped fresh parsley
- 2 tablespoons Worcestershire sauce
- salt and pepper to taste
- 2 cups peeled and cubed potatoes
- 1 1/2 cups quartered fresh mushrooms
- 1 tablespoon all-purpose flour
- 1 pastry for double-crust pie

Direction

- In a large saucepan, add the ale, onion, and beef stew meat. Simmer over low heat for around 30 minutes, till the meat becomes softened.
- Preheat the oven to 400° F (200° C).
- Season the beef with pepper, salt, Worcestershire sauce, parsley, thyme, and garlic. Blend in the mushrooms and potatoes. Simmer, covered, over medium heat for 10 - 15 minutes, till potatoes become softened enough to pierce with a fork. In a small bowl, whip a small amount of the sauce and flour together, then mix into the beef. Simmer till partially thickened.
- Press one pie crust into the bottom and up the sides of a 9-inch pie plate. Fill the crust with hot beef mixture then top with the leftover pie crust. To vent steam, cut slits in the top crust then crimp the edges to seal altogether.
- In the preheated oven, bake for 35 - 40 minutes till the gravy is bubbling and the crust becomes golden brown.

Nutrition Information

- Calories: 473 calories;
- Total Fat: 28.7
- Sodium: 319
- Total Carbohydrate: 32.4
- Cholesterol: 47
- Protein: 17.5

308. Steak And Kidney Pie With Bacon And Mushrooms

Serving: 8 | Prep: 50mins | Ready in:

Ingredients

- 1/2 pound beef kidney
- 1 tablespoon vegetable oil
- 1/4 cup all-purpose flour
- salt and pepper to taste
- 1 pound beef for stew, cut in 1 inch pieces
- 4 slices thick sliced bacon, cut into 1 inch pieces
- 1 medium onion, chopped
- 1 (6 ounce) package sliced mushrooms
- 1/2 cup beef stock
- 1/2 cup red wine
- 4 large potatoes, peeled, cut into 1-inch chunks
- 2 tablespoons butter
- 1/2 cup milk
- 1 (17.25 ounce) package frozen puff pastry, thawed
- 1 egg, beaten with 2 teaspoons water

Direction

- Split the kidney in half then take the skins and tubes off. Rinse using cold water then pat to dry. Dice the kidney into 1/2 cubes. Use a big and heavy pot and pour in the vegetable oil, set the heat to medium high. Season the flour with salt and pepper using a bowl. Mix the kidney and stew meat in the flour then shake the excess off. Sear the meat in the hot oil until it becomes brown then remove. Add the bacon to the pot. Cook the bacon until it becomes crisp. Add in the mushroom and onion and cook for 2 minutes to soften. Pour the beef stock in, browned meat and the wine. Let it boil while stirring constantly for about 5 to 10 minutes. When it start thickens, lower the heat and simmer for one and a half to two hours or until the meat becomes tender. Take it away from the heat and let it cool to room temperature.
- Put the potatoes in a sauce pan then fill it with water just enough to cover the potatoes. Heat over high heat until it boils. Lower the heat to medium low and let it simmer for 20 minutes until it tenders. Drain the water out then mash with milk and butter. Add salt and pepper to taste. Set aside to cool.
- Prepare the oven and preheat to 375°F or 190°C.
- Place one sheet of puff pastry into a 9-inch pie dish and press it. Trim the edges to make it fit. Fill with cooled meat mixture. Top it with the mashed potatoes about an inch thick then take the remaining sheet of puff pastry and place it on top. Trim the excess pastry around the edges then flute the edges using a fork. Apply the top with beaten egg.
- Let it bake in the preheated oven between 20 to 25 minutes or until crust becomes golden brown.

Nutrition Information

- Calories: 767 calories;
- Total Fat: 42.6
- Sodium: 539
- Total Carbohydrate: 65.9
- Cholesterol: 190
- Protein: 27.9

309. Stir Fry Ramen

Serving: 4 | Prep: 35mins | Ready in:

Ingredients

- Sauce:
- 1/2 cup hoisin sauce
- 1/2 cup water
- 1 tablespoon cornstarch
- 1 teaspoon white sugar
- 1/2 teaspoon grated fresh ginger
- 1/4 teaspoon red pepper flakes
- kosher salt and freshly ground black pepper to taste
- 4 cups water
- 2 (3 ounce) packages ramen noodles (without flavor packet)
- Stir-Fry:
- 2 teaspoons peanut oil
- 1 bunch asparagus, cut diagonally into 1-inch pieces
- 2 carrots, peeled and sliced diagonally
- 1/2 onion, sliced
- 3 cloves garlic, pressed
- 1 cup thinly sliced cooked chicken
- 2 cups sliced napa cabbage
- 1 cup sliced mushrooms

Direction

- Sauce: whisk black pepper, salt, red pepper flakes, ginger, sugar, cornstarch, water and hoisin sauce in a bowl.
- Boil water in a big pot. Cook ramen noodles till tender, occasionally mixing, for 3 minutes; drain.
- In a nonstick skillet, heat peanut oil on medium high heat. Add garlic, onion, carrots and asparagus. Sauté for 3-5 minutes till slightly tender. Put chicken. Toss for 2 minutes till warmed through. Add mushrooms and cabbage. Put sauce in. Toss till coated. Lower heat to low. Cook, covered, for 3-5 more minutes till flavors merge.
- On noodles, serve sautéed asparagus mixture.

Nutrition Information

- Calories: 423 calories;
- Sodium: 867
- Total Carbohydrate: 55.3

- Cholesterol: 28
- Protein: 18.2
- Total Fat: 15.3

310.   Strip Steak With Red Wine Cream Sauce

Serving: 6 | Prep: 15mins | Ready in:

Ingredients

- 1 tablespoon vegetable oil
- 2 red onions, sliced
- 1 (8 ounce) package button mushrooms, sliced
- 1 tablespoon vegetable oil
- 6 New York strip steaks
- salt and ground black pepper to taste
- 1 cup red Zinfandel wine
- 1 cup beef broth
- 2 tablespoons Dijon mustard
- 1 cup heavy whipping cream

Direction

- Set the heat to medium-high, then heat a tablespoon of vegetable oil in a skillet. Cook the red onions by stirring in with the mushrooms for 10 minutes until they soften. Take a bowl and place the mixture in it.
- Use a tablespoon of vegetable oil to coat a skillet that's set on medium-high heat. Use paper towels to pat the steaks dry, then add a pinch of salt and black pepper to taste. Add each steak onto the skillet and cook, making sure the outsides turn brown while the insides depend on your preferred doneness. If you want medium, you would opt to cook each side for 5 minutes. Transfer the steaks from the skillet.
- In the same skillet, add red Zinfandel wine and remove any leftover browned bits of steak. Add some Dijon mustard and beef broth while whisking them into the wine. Then, let it boil. Cook and occasionally stir the mixture for 5 minutes until it looks slightly reduced.

Carefully pour in the cream by whisking, and let the sauce stand for another 5 minutes to thicken. Combine the meat and mushrooms with the sauce. Serve with sauce on top of the steaks.

Nutrition Information

- Calories: 649 calories;
- Protein: 69.3
- Total Fat: 33.9
- Sodium: 413
- Total Carbohydrate: 7.5
- Cholesterol: 200

311. Stuffed Cod Wrapped In Bacon

Serving: 8 | Prep: 15mins | Ready in:

Ingredients

- 8 (6 ounce) fillets cod
- 2 tablespoons sesame oil
- 2 tablespoons chili sauce
- 8 slices bacon
- 1 leek, chopped
- 1 ounce enoki mushrooms

Direction

- Preheat an outdoor grill to high heat. While the grill is heating up, steep some toothpicks inside the water.
- On each fish fillet, spread a thin layer of chili sauce and sesame oil on 1 side. At one end, add in a couple of mushrooms and some leeks. Roll towards the other end. Use a bacon slice to wrap each roll, and secure using 2 toothpicks.
- Put on the preheated grill, and cook while covered for 5 minutes. Pay attention to the bacon grease flare-ups. Flip over, and cook for

5 minutes longer, till fish could be simply flaked and bacon is crisp.

Nutrition Information

- Calories: 231 calories;
- Total Fat: 8.4
- Sodium: 393
- Total Carbohydrate: 3
- Cholesterol: 72
- Protein: 33.9

312. Stuffed Morel Mushrooms

Serving: 12 | Prep: 20mins | Ready in:

Ingredients

- 6 large fresh morel mushrooms
- 1 (8 ounce) package cream cheese at room temperature
- 1/2 (8 ounce) package imitation crabmeat, minced
- 1 teaspoon finely chopped green onion, or to taste
- 1/4 cup dry breading mix (such as Drake's Crispy Frymix®)
- 2 cups vegetable oil for frying, or as needed

Direction

- Clean whole morel mushrooms of dirt and grit gently; in a colander, place mushrooms, stem sides down and allow about 5 minutes to drain.
- Cut bottoms of hollow stems to have enough room for filling.
- Stir green onion, crabmeat, and cream cheese till combined evenly in bowl.
- Scoop the mixture in a resealable, heavy plastic bag. Force the cream cheese mixture into a corner of the bag. Cut a small snip off the bag's corner.

- Insert the trimmed end of the plastic bag into each mushroom's hollow stem and fill the mushroom with the blend of cream cheese.
- In a shallow bowl, place dry breading mix. Roll in the dry mix the stuffed mushrooms; tap off excess breading.
- In a large saucepan or deep-fryer, heat vegetable oil to 350 °F (175 °C).
- Deep-fry the stuffed mushrooms for around 3 to 4 minutes until the mushrooms are soften and the breading is golden brown. Place on paper towels to drain.

Nutrition Information

- Calories: 117 calories;
- Sodium: 193
- Total Carbohydrate: 4.1
- Cholesterol: 22
- Protein: 2.5
- Total Fat: 10.2

313.   Stuffed Mushrooms II

Serving: 24 | Prep: | Ready in:

Ingredients

- 1 pound fresh mushrooms, stems removed
- 1 (12 ounce) package chicken-flavor stuffing mix
- 1 (10.75 ounce) can condensed cream of mushroom soup
- 10 3/4 fluid ounces milk

Direction

- Prepare the oven by preheating to 350°F (175°C). Prepare one 9x13-inch baking dish that is greased.
- Ready stuffing based on package directions.
- Stuff mushrooms with stuffing and layer in baking dish.

- Use one can of milk to dilute can of soup. Place over the mushrooms, cover, and bake for 25 minutes.

Nutrition Information

- Calories: 75 calories;
- Total Carbohydrate: 12.2
- Cholesterol: 1
- Protein: 3.2
- Total Fat: 1.6
- Sodium: 348

314.   Stuffed Mushrooms III

Serving: 4 | Prep: 10mins | Ready in:

Ingredients

- 8 large fresh mushrooms
- 1 tablespoon olive oil
- 2 cups ricotta cheese
- 3/4 cup grated Parmesan cheese
- 3/4 cup shredded mozzarella cheese
- 4 tablespoons pesto

Direction

- Set the oven to 375°F (190°C), and start preheating.
- Rinse the mushrooms, discard the stems, hollow out and brush olive oil inside and out.
- Mix together pesto and cheese in a medium-size mixing bowl, reserving 1/4 cup Parmesan cheese for later. Fill the mushroom caps with the cheese-pesto mixture. On a cookie sheet, place the caps. Sprinkle the reserved Parmesan cheese over the mushrooms.
- Bake in the oven for 25 - 30 minutes, or until the cheese is bubbly and brownish.

Nutrition Information

- Calories: 261 calories;

- Total Fat: 20.7
- Sodium: 540
- Total Carbohydrate: 3.7
- Cholesterol: 38
- Protein: 16.1

315. Stuffed Mushrooms, Leeks, White Beans And Pecans

Serving: 8 | Prep: 10mins | Ready in:

Ingredients

- 16 ounces button or cremini mushrooms
- Salt to taste
- 2 ribs chopped celery
- 1 leek, white and light green parts only, cleaned
- 1 large clove garlic
- 2 tablespoons extra virgin olive oil, divided
- 1/2 teaspoon sea salt
- 1/3 cup toasted chopped pecans
- 1/3 cup panko bread crumbs
- 1/2 cup grated Parmesan cheese, plus additional for garnish
- 1/2 cup canned cannellini beans, rinsed and drained
- 1/2 teaspoon red pepper flakes
- 1/2 teaspoon fresh ground black pepper
- 1/3 cup grated fontina cheese, for garnish
- finely chopped flat-leaf parsley, for garnish
- Reynolds Wrap® Aluminum Foil

Direction

- Set the oven to 350°F, and start preheating. Line Reynolds Wrap(R) Aluminum Foil on a baking sheet. Grease or spray the foil. Wipe clean the mushrooms with a damp paper towel and cut the stems. Arrange the mushrooms upside down on the baking sheet and scatter a pinch of salt. Bake for 10 minutes, until just soften.
- Finely chop the garlic, leeks and celery. In a saucepan, heat 1 tablespoon of the olive oil over medium heat. Once warmed, add in sea salt and leek mixture. Sauté for about 5-6 minutes until softened.
- Mix black pepper, pepper flakes, beans, Parmesan, panko breadcrumbs and pecans together in another bowl. Stir to blend, use the back of a spoon to slightly mash the beans. Add in the remaining tablespoon oil and leek mixture, stir again. The filling mixture can be made an hour in advance.
- Generously stuff the mushroom caps with vegetable mix. Sprinkle the grated fontina and a bit of extra Parmesan on top. Bake for 10 more minutes or until the top is just golden. Garnish with parsley and serve warm.

Nutrition Information

- Calories: 148 calories;
- Total Carbohydrate: 10.6
- Cholesterol: 10
- Protein: 6.7
- Total Fat: 10
- Sodium: 316

316. Stuffed Red Peppers With Quinoa, Mushrooms, And Turkey

Serving: 8 | Prep: 30mins | Ready in:

Ingredients

- 2 cups water
- 1 cup uncooked quinoa
- 1 tablespoon olive oil
- 1 onion, diced
- 1 pound ground turkey
- salt and ground black pepper to taste
- 12 mushrooms, chopped, or more to taste
- 1 (24 ounce) jar tomato sauce, or more to taste
- 1 (6 ounce) can tomato paste

- 8 large red bell peppers - tops, seeds, and membranes removed
- 1 (8 ounce) package shredded Cheddar cheese, or to taste

Direction

- Boil quinoa and water in a saucepan. Lower heat to medium low and cover; simmer for 15-20 minutes till quinoa is tender.
- Heat olive oil on medium heat in a big skillet. Add onion; cook for 5 minutes till soft. Add turkey; season with pepper and salt. Mix and cook for 5-7 minutes till turkey isn't pink. Add mushrooms; cook for 5 minutes till soft.
- Preheat an oven to 175°C/350°F.
- Put cooked turkey mixture into big bowl. Add tomato paste, tomato sauce and cooked quinoa. Mix well; as needed, add extra tomato sauce till filling has a casserole-consistency.
- Put red bell peppers into baking dish; in each, put even filling amount.
- In preheated oven, bake for 45 minutes then remove from oven. Put cheddar cheese over each stuffed pepper. Bake for 10 minutes till cheese melts.

Nutrition Information

- Calories: 389 calories;
- Cholesterol: 71
- Protein: 25.8
- Total Fat: 17.4
- Sodium: 850
- Total Carbohydrate: 34.6

317. Suki's Spinach And Feta Pasta

Serving: 4 | Prep: 25mins | Ready in:

Ingredients

- 1 (8 ounce) package penne pasta

- 2 tablespoons olive oil
- 1/2 cup chopped onion
- 1 clove garlic, minced
- 3 cups chopped tomatoes
- 1 cup sliced fresh mushrooms
- 2 cups spinach leaves, packed
- salt and pepper to taste
- 1 pinch red pepper flakes
- 8 ounces feta cheese, crumbled

Direction

- Boil a large pot of lightly salted water. In boiling water, cook pasta till al dente; let drain.
- In the meantime, in a large skillet, heat olive oil over medium-high heat; add in garlic and onion, and cook until they have the color of golden brown. Stir in spinach, mushrooms, and tomatoes. Add red pepper flakes, pepper, and salt to season. Cook for an addition of 2 minutes, till spinach is wilted and tomatoes are heated through. Lessen heat to medium, stir in pasta and feta cheese, and cook till heated through.

Nutrition Information

- Calories: 451 calories;
- Sodium: 656
- Total Carbohydrate: 51.8
- Cholesterol: 50
- Protein: 17.8
- Total Fat: 20.6

318. Sunday Brunch Bake

Serving: 12 | Prep: 15mins | Ready in:

Ingredients

- 12 eggs
- 1/3 cup BREAKSTONE'S or KNUDSEN Sour Cream
- 1 (16 ounce) package breakfast pork sausage

- 1 cup sliced fresh mushrooms
- 1 onion, chopped
- 2 tomatoes, chopped
- 1 (8 ounce) package KRAFT Finely Shredded Triple Cheddar Cheese

Direction

- Heat the oven to 400 °F.
- Using a whisk, mix sour cream and eggs till well incorporated. Put into a 13x9-inch baking dish coated with cooking spray. Bake till egg mixture is softly set, about 10 minutes. In the meantime, in big skillet over moderate heat, cook the onions, mushrooms and sausage for 6 to 8 minutes or till sausage is cooked, mixing from time to time. Drain.
- Lower oven heat to 325 °F. Scoop tomatoes on top of egg layer; top with cheese and sausage mixture.
- Bake till middle is firm, about 30 minutes.

Nutrition Information

- Calories: 249 calories;
- Total Fat: 20.2
- Sodium: 529
- Total Carbohydrate: 3.2
- Cholesterol: 180
- Protein: 14.4

319.   Sunday Lunch Soup

Serving: 8 | Prep: 45mins | Ready in:

Ingredients

- 2 skinless, boneless chicken breast halves
- 5 cups water
- 2 onions, chopped
- 2 cloves garlic, crushed
- 1 green chile pepper, seeded and diced
- 4 potatoes, chopped
- 1 zucchini, chopped

- 8 mushrooms, sliced
- 1 (10.75 ounce) can tomato puree
- 1 (11 ounce) can sweet corn, drained
- 1/4 medium head cabbage, finely chopped
- 2 carrots, chopped
- 2 stalks celery, chopped
- 2 cubes chicken bouillon
- 2 tablespoons mixed spice
- 1 1/4 cups heavy cream
- paprika, for garnish

Direction

- In a big saucepan, cover chicken with 5 cups of water; boil for nearly 30 minutes. Drain, saving liquid, cut chicken.
- In the saucepan, place green chile pepper, garlic, onions, and nearly 2 tablespoons reserved liquid over medium heat. Cook and stir slowly until tender, about 5 minutes. While gradually pouring in the rest of liquid, stir in celery, carrots, cabbage, sweet corn, tomato puree, mushrooms, zucchini, potatoes, and chopped chicken, one at a time. Add any remaining liquid, blend in mixed spice and chicken bouillon; heat to a boil. Decrease heat, let simmer 1-2 hours, mixing from time to time.
- Mix in heavy cream, combining well before serving. Put in a sprinkling of paprika to serve.

Nutrition Information

- Calories: 326 calories;
- Total Fat: 14.9
- Sodium: 620
- Total Carbohydrate: 38.2
- Cholesterol: 68
- Protein: 13.1

320. Super Crispy Roasted Goose

Serving: 12 | Prep: 1hours | Ready in:

Ingredients

- 1 (10 pound) fresh goose
- 1 1/2 cups wild rice
- 5 cups cold water
- 1 tablespoon butter
- 1 onion, chopped
- 2 1/2 cups fresh sliced shiitake mushrooms
- 1 egg
- 1 tablespoon poultry seasoning
- salt and freshly ground black pepper to taste
- 2/3 cup dry sherry
- 2 cups giblet gravy

Direction

- Using a skewer, gently prick all sides of the goose, making sure not poking in the flesh. Fill a pot large enough to hold the goose with water until two-thirds full; boil. Fully soak bird neck side down for 60 seconds until goose bumps appear on the goose. Flip tail side of the goose downwards, then repeat the process. Take goose out of the pot and drain. Set goose with its breast side facing upwards on a rack in a large roasting pan. Refrigerate while uncovered for 24-48 hours until skin is dried.
- In order to cook rice on the night prior to roasting the goose, put rice into a pot filled with 5 cups of water; boil. Lower to low heat, simmer, covered, for 45 minutes. Leave in the fridge overnight.
- Set oven to 175°C (or 350°F) and start preheating.
- In a skillet, heat butter on medium heat until melted; cook onion until softened. Stir in egg, mushrooms and cooked rice. Season pepper, salt and poultry seasoning all over the mixture. Sprinkle the inside and out of the goose with pepper and salt. Pack stuffing into the goose cavities. Use kitchen twine to enclose cavities, then arrange goose, breast side facing downwards, on a rack in a roasting pan.
- Roast bird in prepared oven, 90 minutes, without opening the oven door while cooking. Take bird out of the oven, removing fat that has accumulated in the bottom of the pan with a baster. Flip over to back surface in the roasting pan, keep roasting for another 60 minutes until a meat thermometer inserted to test its internal temperature registers at least 82°C (or 180°F).
- Switch oven to 200°C (or 400°F). Take goose out of the oven and place to a larger pan. Put back into the oven for another 15 minutes until browned and crisp. Remove goose form the oven, then uncover and rest for half an hour before taking out the stuffing.
- Bring the first roasting pan to 2 burners to prepare gravy. Stir in two-thirds cup of dry sherry, then use a wooden spoon to scrape the pan. Mix giblet broth and drippings to make a gravy to serve over stuffing and goose.

Nutrition Information

- Calories: 517 calories;
- Sodium: 418
- Total Carbohydrate: 17.7
- Cholesterol: 153
- Protein: 37.6
- Total Fat: 31.4

321. Super Easy Slow Cooker Chicken

Serving: 4 | Prep: 15mins | Ready in:

Ingredients

- 1 (10.75 ounce) can condensed low fat cream of chicken and herbs soup
- 1 (4 ounce) can mushroom pieces, drained
- 1/2 red onion, chopped

- 1 1/2 pounds skinless, boneless chicken breast halves - cut into strips
- 1 dash Marsala wine

Direction

- In a slow cooker, combine wine, chicken, onion, mushroom pieces, and soup.
- Cook on Low setting for 2 and a half hours to 3 hours.

Nutrition Information

- Calories: 234 calories;
- Total Fat: 5.7
- Sodium: 684
- Total Carbohydrate: 8.2
- Cholesterol: 91
- Protein: 34.9

322.   Sweet Maple Pork Chops

Serving: 6 | Prep: 20mins | Ready in:

Ingredients

- 1 egg, lightly beaten
- 1 quart heavy cream, divided
- salt to taste
- ground black pepper to taste
- 6 boneless pork chops
- 1/2 cup quick cooking oats
- 1 quart vegetable oil for frying
- 1 tablespoon butter
- 1 large onion, cut into 1 inch chunks
- 1 clove garlic, diced
- 3/4 cup maple syrup
- 6 ounces sliced fresh mushrooms
- 2 tablespoons chopped fresh basil leaves

Direction

- In a shallow bowl, mix pepper, salt, 3 cups of the heavy cream and egg. Season pork chops with pepper and salt, then dip in cream mixture. Coat by dredging in oats. Repeat to completely coat the chops.
- In a skillet, heat oil over medium-high heat. Place coated chops in hot oil with tongs. Fry until both sides are browned. Discard from the heat. Put aside.
- In a skillet, melt butter over medium heat (if oil has been drained, use the same pan). Cook garlic, onion, and pork chops until the onion becomes tender. Add maple syrup. Mix in basil and mushrooms. Season with pepper and salt. Lower the heat, cover and cook until the pork chops are done, about 10 mins. Discard the chops from the skillet, saving the sauce.
- Mix remaining cream with the reserved sauce into skillet. Boil. Cook while stirring until thickened. Place over pork chops to serve.

Nutrition Information

- Calories: 943 calories;
- Total Carbohydrate: 39
- Cholesterol: 285
- Protein: 18.8
- Total Fat: 81
- Sodium: 115

323.   Swiss Style Veal And Mushrooms

Serving: 4 | Prep: 10mins | Ready in:

Ingredients

- 1 3/4 cups Swanson® Chicken Stock
- 1 (10.75 ounce) can Campbell's® Condensed Cream of Potato Soup
- 1 teaspoon dried thyme leaves, crushed
- 1 1/2 pounds veal for stew
- 1 (8 ounce) package sliced mushrooms
- 8 green onions, sliced
- 2 tablespoons all-purpose flour
- 1/4 cup water
- 1 cup shredded Swiss cheese

- Hot cooked egg noodles
- Freshly ground black pepper

Direction

- In a 3 1/2-quart slow cooker, combine green onions, mushrooms, veal, thyme, soup and the stock. Cook with a cover on low until the veal is fork-tender, 7-8 hours.
- In a small bowl, combine water and flour until smooth. Mix the flour mixture into the cooker. Raise the heat to high. Cook with a cover until boiled and thickened, 5 minutes.
- Mix in cheese. Pour over noodles to serve. Use black pepper to season.

Nutrition Information

- Calories: 651 calories;
- Protein: 53.1
- Total Fat: 21.4
- Sodium: 1003
- Total Carbohydrate: 59.9
- Cholesterol: 228

---

324. Take Out Fake Out Pollo Con Crema

Serving: 12 | Prep: 25mins | Ready in:

Ingredients

- 4 large skinless, boneless chicken breast halves - cubed
- salt and pepper to taste
- 2 tablespoons extra virgin olive oil, divided
- 1 (8 ounce) package sliced fresh mushrooms
- 2 large red bell peppers, cut into chunks
- 1 large yellow onion, sliced
- 2 cloves garlic, minced
- 1/4 cup butter
- 1/4 cup all-purpose flour
- 1 1/2 cups low-sodium chicken broth
- 1 1/2 cups heavy cream
- 1/4 cup sour cream
- 3 tablespoons ketchup, or to taste
- 2 dashes hot pepper sauce (such as Frank's RedHot®), or to taste
- 1 teaspoon ground cumin
- 1/2 teaspoon ground dried Anaheim or California chiles (optional)
- 12 (6 inch) flour tortillas

Direction

- Sprinkle pepper and salt on chicken cubes. Heat 1 tbsp. olive oil in big skillet on medium heat; mix and cook for 5-10 minutes till chicken juices run clear. Put chicken in bowl. Heat 1 tbsp. olive oil in skillet on medium heat; mix and cook garlic, onions, bell peppers and mushrooms for 10 minutes till veggies start to brown. Put veggies in bowl with chicken.
- Melt butter on medium high heat in same skillet; whisk flour in. Cook mixture for 2 minutes till roux gives off toasted fragrant and lightly browned; whisk broth in. Simmer; whisk till thick. Lower heat to low; whisk ground dried chiles, cumin, hot sauce, ketchup, sour cream and cream in. Cover; simmer for 15 minutes till flavors blend and thick, occasionally mixing. Mix veggies and chicken in gently; serve rolled in the flour tortillas.

Nutrition Information

- Calories: 397 calories;
- Total Fat: 23.3
- Sodium: 348
- Total Carbohydrate: 24.5
- Cholesterol: 100
- Protein: 22.2

325. Tammi's Crawfish Etoufee

Serving: 6 | Prep: 15mins | Ready in:

Ingredients

- 1/2 cup butter
- 1/4 cup olive oil
- 1 tablespoon garlic powder
- 1 cup sliced fresh mushrooms
- 1 pound frozen raw crawfish
- 1 cup chopped green onion
- 1/2 cup grated Parmesan cheese
- 1/4 cup minced fresh parsley
- 1 cup half-and-half
- 1 teaspoon crushed red pepper
- 1 teaspoon Creole-style seasoning
- salt to taste
- ground black pepper to taste

Direction

- Heat olive oil and butter in a large pan over medium heat. Cook mushrooms and garlic powder in the hot oil for 3-5 minutes, until the mushrooms are softened.
- Throw in onions and crawfish. Lower the temperature to low. Cook for 5 more minutes.
- Mix in parsley, parmesan cheese, and half-and-half. Let it simmer for another 5 minutes. Throw in creole seasoning and crushed red pepper. Season with salt and pepper.

Nutrition Information

- Calories: 363 calories;
- Protein: 14.9
- Total Fat: 31.8
- Sodium: 401
- Total Carbohydrate: 5.7
- Cholesterol: 140

326. Teriyaki And Pineapple Chicken

Serving: 8 | Prep: 15mins | Ready in:

Ingredients

- 2 tablespoons vegetable oil
- 1 pound skinless, boneless chicken breasts, cut into cubes
- 1 green bell pepper, sliced thin
- 1 yellow bell pepper, sliced thin
- 1 red bell pepper, sliced thin
- 1 1/4 cups sliced fresh mushrooms
- 1 onion, chopped
- 1 cup teriyaki sauce
- 1 (8 ounce) can pineapple chunks, undrained
- 1 teaspoon garlic powder
- 1 teaspoon crushed red pepper
- 1/4 cup all-purpose flour

Direction

- Heat oil in a large pan or wok over medium-high heat. Cook chicken for 7-10 minutes until the center is no longer pink and the juices run clear.
- Put green, yellow and red bell peppers, onion, mushrooms, pineapple chunks with the juice and teriyaki sauce with the garlic powder, and crushed red pepper into the pan. Cook on medium heat. Let it simmer. Add and stir in flour. Simmer for 15 more minutes, until thick.

Nutrition Information

- Calories: 187 calories;
- Total Fat: 5.5
- Sodium: 1413
- Total Carbohydrate: 18.1
- Cholesterol: 35
- Protein: 16.3

327.   Terrific Turkey Tetrazzini

Serving: 8 | Prep: | Ready in:

Ingredients

- 3 pounds turkey, cooked
- 1 pound sliced mushrooms
- 6 tablespoons butter or margarine
- 6 tablespoons flour
- 1 cup chicken broth
- 2 cups Kikkoman PEARL Original Soymilk
- 1 pound spaghetti
- 1 cup Parmesan cheese
- Salt and pepper to taste

Direction

- Slice the turkey into bite-sized portions. In a saucepan, liquify the butter, then mix in flour; let cook till it begins to bubble. Slowly put the chicken stock, mixing till sauce thickens, then put the soymilk, cheese, pepper and salt. Put the mushrooms and turkey and gently simmer.
- Meantime, let the pasta cook following packaging directions, allow to drain and mix into turkey mixture. Put into a baking dish that is non-stick. Let bake at 450°F till heated completely and the cheese has melted.

Nutrition Information

- Calories: 680 calories;
- Total Carbohydrate: 52.1
- Cholesterol: 161
- Protein: 65.3
- Total Fat: 21.9
- Sodium: 340

328.   Thai Shrimp Curry With A Kick

Serving: 4 | Prep: 15mins | Ready in:

Ingredients

- 24 uncooked large shrimp, peeled and deveined
- 1/4 teaspoon salt
- 1/8 teaspoon cayenne pepper
- 2 tablespoons extra-virgin olive oil
- 1/2 cup finely diced red onion
- 3 cloves garlic, minced
- 2 teaspoons freshly grated gingerroot
- 1 lime, juiced
- 1 (8 ounce) package sliced fresh mushrooms
- 1 (14.5 ounce) can Hunt's® Diced Tomatoes, drained
- 1 cup chicken broth
- 1/4 teaspoon crushed red pepper flakes
- 1 (14 ounce) can coconut milk
- 1 tablespoon fish sauce
- 8 leaves Thai basil, chopped
- 1 teaspoon curry powder
- 1/4 cup chopped fresh cilantro (optional)
- 1 lime, quartered (optional)

Direction

- Sprinkle cayenne pepper and salt on shrimp.
- Heat olive oil in big pan on medium heat. Add red onion; cook for a minute. Add ginger and garlic; cook for 30 seconds. Add shrimp and lime juice; cook for 1 minute per side till shrimp is pink. Put shrimp in small bowl.
- Put crushed red pepper, chicken broth, mushrooms and diced tomatoes into pan; cook for 5 minutes till mushrooms start to soften. Add Thai basil, fish sauce, curry powder and coconut milk; cook till heated through. Put shrimp back into pan; cook for 1 minute more.
- Serve with lime wedge; if desired, garnish with cilantro.

Nutrition Information

- Calories: 406 calories;
- Protein: 26.2
- Total Fat: 29.2
- Sodium: 1221
- Total Carbohydrate: 14.4

- Cholesterol: 193

329. Thai Stuffed Tofu

Serving: 4 | Prep: 30mins | Ready in:

Ingredients

- 2 (12 ounce) packages extra firm tofu
- 1/4 cup dried shiitake mushrooms
- 1 zucchini, coarsely chopped
- 1 onion, halved
- 3 cloves garlic
- 1 jalapeno pepper, seeded and coarsely chopped
- 1 egg
- 2 tablespoons soy sauce
- 2 tablespoons minced fresh ginger, or to taste
- 1 tablespoon cornstarch
- 1 tablespoon hoisin sauce
- 1/4 cup shredded cabbage
- 1/4 cup vegetable oil, divided

Direction

- Strain tofu; cut each piece into 4 squares; then, cut each square into 2 triangles diagonally. Set triangles aside.
- In a bowl of hot water, put shiitake mushrooms; let rehydrate for around 20 minutes, or till plump and moist. Cut out the woody stems; chop finely.
- In a food processor, put jalapeno pepper, garlic, onion and zucchini; process till a paste forms and transfer into a bowl, then mix in hoisin sauce, cornstarch, ginger, soy sauce, egg and the shiitake mushrooms. Fold in shredded cabbage.
- Place a large skillet with 2 tablespoons of vegetable oil on medium heat. Using paper towels, pat the tofu triangles dry; pan-fry in hot oil for 2-3 minutes per side, or till browned on all sides except from 1 narrow side for the stuffing. Take the tofu triangles away; allow to cool till easy to handle.
- Cut a slit into the unbrowned side of a tofu triangle, using a sharp paring knife; scoop out the center of the tofu, using a grapefruit spoon, keeping the walls of the triangle around 1/4-in. thick. Fill the stuffing generously into each triangle, using a spoon, allowing the stuffing to mound out of the tofu piece.
- Place the skillet with remaining 2 tablespoons of vegetable oil on medium heat; place the tofu triangles into the hot oil, stuffing sides down, and pan-fry for around 5 minutes, or till the stuffing is hot and set inside and the stuffing edge is browned. Turn the triangles on their sides; refry in the hot oil to rewarm, 1-2 minutes.

Nutrition Information

- Calories: 374 calories;
- Cholesterol: 47
- Protein: 21
- Total Fat: 25.1
- Sodium: 555
- Total Carbohydrate: 22.5

330. The Very Best Spaghetti Sauce

Serving: 12 | Prep: 30mins | Ready in:

Ingredients

- 18 roma (plum) tomatoes
- 2 (6 ounce) cans tomato paste
- 1/2 cup butter
- 4 cloves garlic, minced
- 5 bay leaves
- 1 large white onion, chopped
- 1 large zucchini, chopped
- 1 green bell pepper, chopped
- 1 red bell pepper, chopped
- 1 (8 ounce) package fresh mushrooms, sliced
- 2 tablespoons dried oregano

- 1 tablespoon Italian seasoning
- 2 teaspoons chili powder
- 1/4 cup brown sugar
- 1 (15 ounce) container ricotta cheese

Direction

- Boil a big pot of lightly salted water. Put in tomatoes and cook for 10 minutes. Drain and use cold water to rinse. Skin the tomatoes, put back into the pot then mash them. Mix in 2 cups of water and tomato paste. Cover and allow it to simmer on low heat.
- Meanwhile, in a big skillet, melt butter over medium heat. Sauté bay leaves and garlic for a minute. Mix in onions then sauté until translucent. Mix in mushrooms, red and green bell peppers and zucchini. Cook slowly and stir for 5 to 7 minutes.
- Mix the vegetables into the tomato sauce. Put in brown sugar, chili powder, Italian seasoning and oregano. Simmer for 6 to 8 hours over low heat. Ten minutes before serving, mix in the ricotta cheese.

Nutrition Information

- Calories: 193 calories;
- Total Fat: 11.2
- Sodium: 335
- Total Carbohydrate: 19.1
- Cholesterol: 31
- Protein: 7.4

331.   Tiffany's Sauteed Mushrooms

Serving: 2 | Prep: 10mins | Ready in:

Ingredients

- 1 teaspoon olive oil
- 1 (4 ounce) can sliced mushrooms
- 1/2 cup diced red onion

- 1 clove garlic, minced
- 1 1/2 tablespoons balsamic vinegar
- 1 1/2 tablespoons Worcestershire sauce
- salt and ground black pepper to taste
- 1/2 teaspoon white sugar

Direction

- In a saucepan, heat olive oil on moderate heat, then put in black pepper, salt, Worcestershire sauce, balsamic vinegar, garlic, onion and mushrooms. Bring the mixture to a simmer and cook for 10 minutes, until the liquid reduces by 2/3, then sprinkle over with sugar. Cook and stir for 1-3 minutes, until sugar has dissolved.

Nutrition Information

- Calories: 75 calories;
- Total Carbohydrate: 12.6
- Cholesterol: 0
- Protein: 1.7
- Total Fat: 2.6
- Sodium: 371

332.   Tom Szaller's Great Pan Or Bird Stuffing

Serving: 25 | Prep: 45mins | Ready in:

Ingredients

- 6 ounces sliced bacon
- 1 pound ground pork sausage
- 1 1/2 pounds sweet onions, peeled and chopped
- 2 green bell peppers, chopped
- 2 red bell peppers, chopped
- 1 cup fresh mushrooms, sliced
- 1/2 cup butter
- 1 tablespoon ground black pepper
- 2 tablespoons celery salt
- 1 tablespoon seasoning salt

- 2 1/2 tablespoons poultry seasoning
- 1 tablespoon dried basil
- 2 tablespoons garlic powder
- 4 cups water
- 3 (1 pound) loaves white bread, torn into pieces

Direction

- Preheat an oven to 175°C/350°F.
- Put bacon in a big deep skillet. Cook till evenly browned on medium high heat. Drain and crumble; put aside.
- Put sausage in a big Dutch oven. Cook till evenly browned on medium high heat, mixing to crumble. Drain.
- Put bacon, water, garlic powder, basil, poultry seasoning, seasoning salt, celery salt, pepper, butter, red and green bell peppers, mushrooms and onions into the sausage. Boil; mix and cook till veggies are soft for 10-20 minutes.
- Put bread in the mixture slowly, blending thoroughly till all pieces get coated. Put in a big baking dish or 2 medium baking dishes.
- In the preheated oven, bake till top starts to brown for 40-60 minutes.

Nutrition Information

- Calories: 258 calories;
- Total Carbohydrate: 32.6
- Cholesterol: 23
- Protein: 8.3
- Total Fat: 10.5
- Sodium: 1080

---

333. Tuna Mushroom Casserole

Serving: 6 | Prep: 10mins | Ready in:

Ingredients

- 2 cups bow tie pasta
- 2 (5 ounce) cans tuna, drained
- 1 (10 ounce) can mushrooms, drained
- 1 (10.5 ounce) can condensed cream of mushroom soup
- 1 1/3 cups milk
- 1/2 teaspoon salt
- 1/4 teaspoon freshly ground black pepper
- 1 cup dry bread crumbs
- 3 tablespoons melted butter
- 2 teaspoons dried thyme, crushed

Direction

- Preheat the oven to 175 °C or 350 °F. Oil a 1-quart casserole dish.
- Boil a big pot of lightly salted water. Put in pasta and let cook till al dente for 8 to 10 minutes; drain.
- Put together pepper, salt, milk, and mushroom soup in a mixing bowl. Combine well. Then mix in pasta, mushrooms and tuna. Combine well. Into the greased casserole dish, put the mixture.
- Mix together thyme, butter and bread crumbs in a separate mixing bowl. Combine thoroughly. Scatter over tuna mixture.
- Without cover, bake in a prepped oven for 40 minutes till golden brown and bubbling.

Nutrition Information

- Calories: 298 calories;
- Total Fat: 11.5
- Sodium: 932
- Total Carbohydrate: 30.7
- Cholesterol: 32
- Protein: 18.3

---

334. Tuna Noodle Casserole From Scratch

Serving: 6 | Prep: 30mins | Ready in:

Ingredients

- 1/2 cup butter, divided
- 1 (8 ounce) package uncooked medium egg noodles
- 1/2 medium onion, finely chopped
- 1 stalk celery, finely chopped
- 1 clove garlic, minced
- 8 ounces button mushrooms, sliced
- 1/4 cup all-purpose flour
- 2 cups milk
- salt and pepper to taste
- 2 (5 ounce) cans tuna, drained and flaked
- 1 cup frozen peas, thawed
- 3 tablespoons bread crumbs
- 2 tablespoons butter, melted
- 1 cup shredded Cheddar cheese

Direction

- Preheat the oven to 190 ° C or 375 ° F. Using a tablespoon of butter, butter one medium size baking dish.
- Boil a big pot of slightly salted water. Put in egg noodles, let cook till al dente, for 8 to 10 minutes, and allow to drain.
- In skillet, liquify a tablespoon of butter on moderately-low heat. Mix in garlic, celery and onion, and cook till tender, for 5 minutes. Raise the heat to moderately-high, and stir in the mushrooms. Keep cooking and mixing for 5 minutes, or till most of liquid has vaporized.
- In a medium size saucepan, liquify 4 tablespoons of butter, and mix in flour till smooth. Slowly mix in milk, and keep cooking till sauce become smooth and thickened slightly, for 5 minutes. Add pepper and salt to season. Mix in cooked noodles, mushroom mixture, peas and tuna. Turn onto baking dish. In small bowl, liquify leftover 2 tablespoons of butter, stir together with bread crumbs, and scatter on top of casserole. Put cheese on top.
- In the prepped oven, bake till slightly browned and bubbly, for 25 minutes.

Nutrition Information

- Calories: 546 calories;
- Cholesterol: 121
- Protein: 27.2
- Total Fat: 31.2
- Sodium: 786
- Total Carbohydrate: 39.9

---

335.   Turkey Casserole

Serving: 6 | Prep: 20mins | Ready in:

Ingredients

- 1 cup diced celery
- 5 tablespoons butter
- 1 onion, chopped
- 1/2 green bell pepper, chopped
- 6 tablespoons all-purpose flour
- 1 (10.75 ounce) can cream of mushroom soup
- 1 (10.75 ounce) can milk
- 1 (6 ounce) can mushrooms
- 3 cups diced cooked turkey
- 1 (4 ounce) jar chopped pimento peppers
- 1/2 cup slivered almonds
- salt to taste
- 1 cup soft bread crumbs
- 1 cup shredded Cheddar cheese

Direction

- Set an oven to 190°C (375°F) and start preheating.
- Boil a large pot of lightly salted water; cook celery in the boiling water for 5-10 minutes, until it becomes tender; drain the celery.
- In a skillet, heat the butter over medium heat; stir and cook bell pepper and onion in the heated butter for 5-10 minutes until they become soft. Beat the flour into the onion mixture until flour and butter form a paste. Put in mushrooms, milk, and mushroom soup; cook and stir from time to time for 5-10 minutes until the mixture becomes smooth.

- Stir salt, almonds, pimento peppers, celery and turkey into the mushroom soup mixture; stir and cook for 5 minutes, until heated through. Add the mixture to a 2-quart casserole dish; put Cheddar cheese and breadcrumbs on top.
- In the prepared oven, bake for 30-40 minutes, until the cheese melts and casserole bubbles.

Nutrition Information

- Calories: 475 calories;
- Total Fat: 28.4
- Sodium: 773
- Total Carbohydrate: 22.7
- Cholesterol: 102
- Protein: 32.2

336.   Turkey Filled Omelette

Serving: 1 | Prep: 15mins | Ready in:

Ingredients

- 1 tablespoon olive oil
- 2 teaspoons unsalted butter
- 1 tablespoon chopped fresh shiitake mushroom
- 1 shallot, finely chopped
- 1/4 teaspoon salt
- 1 fresh sage leaf, minced
- 1/4 teaspoon crushed red pepper flakes
- 1/4 cup shredded cooked turkey
- 1 teaspoon dry vermouth (optional)
- 2 eggs, chilled
- 1 pinch ground white pepper
- 2 teaspoons olive oil
- 1 tablespoon creme fraiche

Direction

- In a skillet, heat butter and 1 tablespoon of olive oil over medium-low heat, stir in sage, red pepper flakes, salt, shallot and shitake mushroom. Cook for about 5 minutes until

shallot becomes translucent, remember to stir while cooking. Mix in vermouth and turkey, stir for 1 to 2 minutes just to heat them up; remove from heat.
- In a bowl, beat the eggs with a fork until well combined, sprinkle with a pinch of salt and white pepper to taste. In an omelet pan, heat 2 teaspoons of olive oil over medium heat until hot, pour beaten eggs into the pan. Gently stir the eggs with a spatula for 1 to 2 minutes just until they start to set; shake the pan in order that the bottom is fully covered with eggs. Use the spatula to smooth out the surface of the partially set eggs, cook just until the bottom is hardened and the top is still slightly tender, turn off the heat.
- Tuck the turkey filling into the center of omelet, remember to fill about the middle third of the omelet; use small dollops of crème fraiche to dot. Do not overfill omelet. Fold the upper third of the egg over filling using a spatula, gently tip the skillet and shake omelet towards the edge of the skillet. Fold omelet over filling one more time with spatula to form into a loose cigar shape. Gently slide the omelet onto a serving plate and serve.

Nutrition Information

- Calories: 578 calories;
- Sodium: 761
- Total Carbohydrate: 12.1
- Cholesterol: 439
- Protein: 25.1
- Total Fat: 48.1

337.   Turkey Lettuce Wraps With Shiitake Mushrooms

Serving: 4 | Prep: 40mins | Ready in:

Ingredients

- 2 cups water

- 2 ounces mai fun (angel hair) rice noodles
- 1 teaspoon vegetable oil
- 4 shiitake mushrooms, sliced
- 2 teaspoons vegetable oil
- 1 (16 ounce) package ground turkey
- 6 green onions, chopped
- 1/4 cup chopped water chestnuts
- 4 teaspoons finely minced fresh ginger root
- 2 teaspoons minced garlic
- 3 tablespoons soy sauce
- 2 tablespoons brown sugar
- 1 tablespoon rice vinegar
- 1 teaspoon sesame oil
- 1 teaspoon finely grated orange zest
- 12 leaves green leaf lettuce
- Toppings
- 1/2 cup bean sprouts
- 1 carrot, grated
- 1/2 cup salted peanuts
- 1/2 cup chopped fresh cilantro
- 1/2 cup sweet chili sauce

Direction

- Boil 2 cups of water in a small saucepan. Turn heat off. Mix in rice noodles. Cover and let noodles soak for 5-7 minutes until soft. Rinse using cold water. Thoroughly drain.
- In a big skillet, heat 1 teaspoon oil on medium-high heat. Cook mushrooms in hot oil for about 2 minutes until soft and brown. Take mushrooms out of pan. Put aside.
- Heat leftover 2 teaspoons oil in the pan. Sauté turkey in oil for 5-7 minutes until it's not pink. Mix in green onions, garlic, ginger, and water chestnuts. Keep cooking for a minute. Mix in brown sugar, soy sauce, and reserved mushrooms. Briefly simmer to merge flavors. Take pan off heat. Mix in orange zest, sesame oil, and rice vinegar.
- Put a little turkey filling on every lettuce leaf to make lettuce wraps. Place cooked noodles on top of each one. Add a sprinkle of cilantro, peanuts, carrots, and bean sprouts. Use sweet chili sauce as a dip.

Nutrition Information

- Calories: 481 calories;
- Total Fat: 22.4
- Sodium: 1284
- Total Carbohydrate: 43.5
- Cholesterol: 84
- Protein: 29.9

338.   Turkey Mushroom Gravy

Serving: 20 | Prep: 30mins | Ready in:

Ingredients

- 2 cups unsalted butter
- 1 pound portobello mushrooms, wiped clean with paper towels
- 2 pounds whole white mushrooms, wiped clean with paper towels
- 1 cup all-purpose flour
- 4 (14.5 ounce) cans chicken broth
- 1 1/2 cups turkey pan drippings
- 2 cups chopped onions
- 1 cup chopped celery
- salt and pepper to taste
- 1/4 teaspoon cayenne pepper

Direction

- Over medium-low heat, melt butter in a big stock pot and cook the mushrooms for 1 to 1 1/2 hours until they are browned and the butter is clear. Take the mushrooms out, then, chop them coarsely. Set it aside. In the stock pot, there should be about 1 cup of butter left. Mix the flour into the butter and over low heat, cook gently for about 20 minutes until the flour mixture turns mahogany brown in color. Mix the chicken broth in. To thicken the stock, let the mixture simmer.
- With a saucepan, pour the turkey drippings in, then, over medium-low heat, cook and stir the celery and onions in the drippings for about 20 minutes until the onions begin to turn brown.

Stir the vegetables and drippings into the thickened stock. Let the gravy boil gently, reduce the heat and to blend the flavors, simmer for about 20 minutes. Stir the chopped mushrooms in. Season to taste with cayenne pepper, black pepper and salt.

Nutrition Information

- Calories: 347 calories;
- Protein: 3
- Total Fat: 34
- Sodium: 12
- Total Carbohydrate: 9.1
- Cholesterol: 64

---

339.   Turkey Tetrazzini

Serving: 6 | Prep: 25mins | Ready in:

Ingredients

- 2 (8 ounce) packages angel hair pasta
- 1/4 cup butter
- 2/3 cup sliced onion
- 1/4 cup all-purpose flour
- 2 cups milk
- 1 teaspoon salt
- 1/4 teaspoon ground white pepper
- 1/2 teaspoon poultry seasoning
- 1/4 teaspoon ground mustard
- 1 cup shredded sharp Cheddar cheese, divided
- 2 tablespoons chopped pimento peppers (optional)
- 1 (4.5 ounce) can sliced mushrooms
- 1 pound cooked turkey, sliced

Direction

- Preheat oven to 200 °C or 400 °F. In a big pot, let lightly salted water boil. Put pasta and cook until almost tender or for 4 minutes. Drain it.

- Over medium heat, melt butter in a saucepan. Put onion, then cook and stir until tender. Mix the flour in until blended. Stir milk in gradually to avoid lumps from forming. Use mustard, poultry seasoning, pepper and salt to season. Over medium heat, cook it until the mixture thickens, stirring constantly. Move it away from heat and add pimento and 2/3 cup of cheese. Keep on stirring until cheese melts. In cheese sauce, put undrained mushrooms.
- At the bottom of 9x13 inch baking dish, put a layer of pasta. Put a layer of turkey to cover and put a layer of cheese sauce. Repeat the layers. Over top, sprinkle remaining 1/3 cup of cheese.
- In the preheated oven, bake for about 25 minutes until cheese on top is toasted and until sauce is bubbly.

Nutrition Information

- Calories: 604 calories;
- Cholesterol: 113
- Protein: 38.9
- Total Fat: 26.4
- Sodium: 914
- Total Carbohydrate: 52.1

---

340.   Turkey A La Matt

Serving: 6 | Prep: 15mins | Ready in:

Ingredients

- 1 1/2 pounds turkey breast, cooked and cubed
- 2 carrots, diced
- 2 potatoes, peeled and cubed
- 1 cup frozen green peas
- 1 (4.5 ounce) can mushrooms, drained
- 1/2 cup pearl onions
- 1 (10.75 ounce) can condensed cream of chicken soup
- 1 (10.75 ounce) can condensed cream of mushroom soup

- 1 cup crushed saltine crackers

Direction

- Set the oven to 350°F (175°C) and start preheating.
- In a medium pot of boiling water over high heat, place turkey breasts. After about 5 minutes, add cubed potatoes and diced carrots to the pot; boil all for about 5 minutes more. Drain water; place vegetables in a medium bowl.
- Add mushroom soup, chicken soup, onions, mushrooms and peas to the bowl. Cube cooked turkey breasts; stir into the mixture. Combine well; transfer mixture to a 2-quart casserole dish and spread. Place coarsely crushed saltine crackers on top.
- Bake with a cover for 30-40 minutes at 350°F (175°C).

Nutrition Information

- Calories: 390 calories;
- Sodium: 984
- Total Carbohydrate: 36.6
- Cholesterol: 98
- Protein: 40.8
- Total Fat: 8.4

---

341.   Twenty Minute Chicken

Serving: 6 | Prep: 5mins | Ready in:

Ingredients

- 3 boneless, skinless chicken breast halves
- 1/2 large onion, chopped
- 2 (10 ounce) packages sliced fresh button mushrooms
- 1/4 cup olive oil
- salt and freshly ground black pepper to taste
- 1 clove garlic, chopped (optional)
- 1 cup shredded mozzarella cheese

Direction

- Turn the oven to 400°F (200°C) to preheat. Rinse the chicken breasts, use paper towels to pat dry, and halve each breast.
- In a big frying pan, heat 2 tablespoons oil over medium-high heat. Quickly sear the chicken, turn, for 5 minutes, or until no sign of pink remains.
- In the meantime, heat 2 tablespoons oil in a separate big frying pan over medium-high heat. Mix in garlic (if using), onions, and mushrooms; cook for 5 minutes, or until they are tender and nice.
- Add the contents of the 2 frying pans to a baking dish, sprinkle over the top with cheese, and bake for approximately 5 minutes.

Nutrition Information

- Calories: 219 calories;
- Total Fat: 13.1
- Sodium: 160
- Total Carbohydrate: 4.9
- Cholesterol: 46
- Protein: 21.2

---

342.   Veal Forestiere

Serving: 6 | Prep: 15mins | Ready in:

Ingredients

- 1 1/2 pounds thin veal cutlets
- 1/4 cup all-purpose flour for coating
- 3 tablespoons butter
- 1 tablespoon minced garlic
- 1 tablespoon minced shallot
- 1/2 pound crimini mushrooms, sliced
- 1/2 cup Marsala wine
- 1/2 cup veal stock
- 1 (10 ounce) can artichoke hearts, drained and sliced
- salt and pepper to taste

Direction

- Slightly flour veal cutlets and shake the excess off. Warm butter over medium-high heat on a big skillet until melted. Cook cutlets in pan for 1-2 minutes on each side until browned and almost cooked through. Take out veal from the pan and reserve.
- Sauté shallots and garlic in skillet until shallots become soft. Add in mushrooms, continue cooking until mushrooms start to moist. Add in the wine; cook 2-3 minutes longer, stirring with a spoon to scrape the bottom of the pan. Add in stock and letting it simmer for 5-10 minutes or until liquid starts to reduce.
- Put back the veal into the pan with artichokes, cooking until heated thoroughly. Sprinkle with pepper and salt. Serve on plates and scoop sauce all over the veal.

Nutrition Information

- Calories: 261 calories;
- Cholesterol: 71
- Protein: 18
- Total Fat: 10.5
- Sodium: 578
- Total Carbohydrate: 19

---

343.   Veal Meat Loaf

Serving: 8 | Prep: 15mins | Ready in:

Ingredients

- 2 pounds ground veal
- 2 eggs, lightly beaten
- 1 cup dry bread crumbs
- 1/2 cup warm water
- 1 (1 ounce) envelope dry onion soup mix
- 2 large carrots, grated
- 1 pint shiitake mushrooms, sliced

Direction

- Preheat an oven to 175°C/350°F.
- Mix shiitake mushrooms, carrots, soup mix, water, dry breadcrumbs, eggs and ground vela in bowl; put in 9x5-inch loaf pan.
- In preheated oven, bake for 1 hour till internal temperature is 70°C/160°F.

Nutrition Information

- Calories: 237 calories;
- Total Fat: 8
- Sodium: 512
- Total Carbohydrate: 15.8
- Cholesterol: 127
- Protein: 23.7

---

344.   Vegan 'Meat' Sauce On Polenta

Serving: 6 | Prep: 15mins | Ready in:

Ingredients

- cooking spray
- 1 large onion, cubed
- 1 (12 ounce) package vegetarian soy meat crumbles
- 1 (8 ounce) package sliced mushrooms
- 1 cup tomato sauce
- 2 teaspoons dried oregano
- 1 teaspoon garlic powder
- salt and ground black pepper to taste
- 1 (16 ounce) tube prepared polenta, sliced into 12 pieces

Direction

- Heat a big skillet on moderate heat and use cooking spray to coat. Add onions; cook and mix for 5 to 7 minutes until golden. Add mushrooms and soy crumbles; cook for about 5 minutes until browned and softened. Stir in oregano, tomato sauce, pepper, garlic powder, and salt. Lower to low heat; cook for about 2 minutes until sauce is heated through.

- Use a cooking spray to coat a skillet. Cook each side of polenta over medium heat for around 4 minutes each side until golden.
- On each serving plate, place 2 pieces of polenta; top with sauce.

Nutrition Information

- Calories: 165 calories;
- Total Fat: 2.8
- Sodium: 689
- Total Carbohydrate: 21.7
- Cholesterol: 0
- Protein: 13.8

| 345. | Vegan Lettuce Wraps |

Serving: 4 | Prep: 40mins | Ready in:

Ingredients

- Dipping Sauce:
- 1/3 cup vegetarian hoisin sauce
- 1 teaspoon water, or more to taste
- 1/2 teaspoon sambal oelek (chile paste), or more to taste
- Seasoning Sauce:
- 1 tablespoon vegetarian oyster sauce
- 1 tablespoon water
- 1/2 teaspoon sambal oelek (chile paste) (optional)
- 1/2 teaspoon mushroom seasoning
- 1/4 teaspoon sesame oil
- 1/4 teaspoon white sugar
- 1/4 teaspoon salt
- Wraps:
- 1 tablespoon vegetable oil
- 2 slices ginger
- 5 ounces fried tofu, diced
- 4 ounces jicama, peeled and diced
- 3 fresh shiitake mushrooms, diced
- 1/4 teaspoon salt

- ground black pepper to taste
- 1/2 red bell pepper, diced
- 8 large butterhead lettuce leaves
- 1 tablespoon toasted sesame seeds, or to taste

Direction

- To prepare dipping sauce, combine 1/2 teaspoon sambal oelek, 1 teaspoon water and hoisin sauce together.
- In a bowl, combine 1/4 teaspoon salt, sugar, sesame oil, mushroom seasoning, 1/2 teaspoon sambal oelek, 1 tablespoon water and oyster sauce together to prepare seasoning sauce.
- In a big skillet, heat the oil over medium heat. Cook and mix the ginger for 30 seconds till aromatic. Put the pepper, 1/4 teaspoon salt, shiitake mushrooms, jicama and tofu; cook and mix for 5 minutes till mushrooms turn golden brown. Put seasoning sauce and red bell pepper; cook and mix for a minute till heated completely. Take off heat.
- In the middle of every lettuce leaf, put 1 or 2 tablespoons tofu mixture. Scatter sesame seeds over. Put a teaspoon of dipping sauce; roll up the lettuce to seal tofu mixture. Redo with the rest of lettuce leaves and tofu mixture. Serve with the rest of dipping sauce on the side.

Nutrition Information

- Calories: 225 calories;
- Protein: 8.4
- Total Fat: 13
- Sodium: 730
- Total Carbohydrate: 20.9
- Cholesterol: 1

| 346. | Vegan Pasta With Spinach, Mushrooms, And Garlic |

Serving: 2 | Prep: 15mins | Ready in:

Ingredients

- 1/2 (16 ounce) box penne pasta
- 3 tablespoons olive oil, divided
- 1 (8 ounce) package sliced fresh mushrooms
- 1 bunch spinach, roughly chopped
- 2 cloves garlic, chopped
- 2 tablespoons balsamic vinegar
- salt and ground black pepper to taste

Direction

- Boil a big pot of lightly salted water, then add penne and cook for about 11 minutes, stirring from time to time, until it becomes tender yet firm to the bite; drain.
- In a skillet, heat 1 tbsp. of olive oil on medium heat and cook the mushrooms for 3-5 minutes, until light brown. Mix in garlic and spinach. Cook for about 3 minutes until the spinach becomes wilted. Add the drained pasta and mix to blend. Stir in balsamic vinegar and leftover 2 tbsp. of olive oil, then add pepper and salt to season.

Nutrition Information

- Calories: 658 calories;
- Total Carbohydrate: 94.7
- Cholesterol: 0
- Protein: 23.5
- Total Fat: 23.9
- Sodium: 228

347.   Vegan Stuffing

Serving: 10 | Prep: 30mins | Ready in:

Ingredients

- 1 loaf vegan, gluten-free, brown rice bread (such as Food for Life®), cubed
- 2 tablespoons vegan margarine (such as Earth Balance®)
- 1 1/2 cups mixed forest mushrooms, diced
- 1 1/4 cups sweet onion, chopped
- 2 1/2 teaspoons dried sage
- 1 1/2 teaspoons dried rosemary
- 1/2 teaspoon dried thyme
- sea salt and freshly ground black pepper to taste
- 6 tablespoons vegan margarine (such as Earth Balance®), melted
- 1 1/2 cups low-sodium vegan broth
- 8 ounces fresh cranberries
- 1 cup Granny Smith apple, peeled and chopped
- 1/3 cup minced fresh parsley

Direction

- Preheat the oven to 175°C or 175°Fahrenheit. Use aluminum foil to line a baking sheet.
- Transfer the bread cubes onto the foil-lined baking sheet. Toast for 10mins in the preheated oven until aromatic and pale golden. Take it out of the oven but keep the oven on. Cool the bread cubes then move to a big bowl.
- While toasting the bread, melt 2tbsp margarine on medium heat in a big pot. Put the onions and mushrooms in melted margarine and cook for 5mins until the onions are a bit translucent. If needed more moisture, add a bit of vegetable broth. Cook and stir in black pepper, sage, salt, thyme, and rosemary for another 2mins using a wooden spoon until well incorporated.
- Move the mushroom mixture with the toasted bread in a bowl then toss to distribute the mixture evenly. Add 6tbsp melted margarine and vegan broth onto the mixture. Gently but thoroughly mix in parsley, apple, and cranberries. In a casserole dish, spread the stuffing then use aluminum foil to cover.
- Bake for 45mins in the preheated oven; checking at the 25mins mark to avoid burning. Remove the cover then gently mix. Bake for another 15mins until brown on top. Slightly cool to serve.

Nutrition Information

- Calories: 337 calories;
- Total Fat: 19.8
- Sodium: 154
- Total Carbohydrate: 37.9
- Cholesterol: 0
- Protein: 2.4

348. Vegetable And Tofu Stir Fry

Serving: 4 | Prep: 30mins | Ready in:

Ingredients

- 1 tablespoon vegetable oil
- 1/2 medium onion, sliced
- 2 cloves garlic, finely chopped
- 1 tablespoon fresh ginger root, finely chopped
- 1 (16 ounce) package tofu, drained and cut into cubes
- 1/2 cup water
- 4 tablespoons rice wine vinegar
- 2 tablespoons honey
- 2 tablespoons soy sauce
- 2 teaspoons cornstarch dissolved in
- 2 tablespoons water
- 1 carrot, peeled and sliced
- 1 green bell pepper, seeded and cut into strips
- 1 cup baby corn, drained and cut into pieces
- 1 small head bok choy, chopped
- 2 cups fresh mushrooms, chopped
- 1 1/4 cups bean sprouts
- 1 cup bamboo shoots, drained and chopped
- 1/2 teaspoon crushed red pepper
- 2 medium green onions, thinly sliced diagonally

Direction

- Place a large skillet with oil on medium-high heat. Stir in onions; cook for 1 minute. Mix in ginger and garlic; cook for 30 seconds. Mix in tofu; cook till golden brown.

- Mix in baby corn, bell pepper and carrots; cook for 2 minutes. Mix in crushed red pepper, bamboo shoots, bean sprouts, mushrooms and bok choy; heat through. Take away from the heat.
- Mix soy sauce, honey, rice wine vinegar and water in a small saucepan; simmer the mixture. Cook for 2 minutes, then mix in the water and cornstarch mixture. Simmer till the sauce is thickened. Transfer the sauce over the tofu and vegetables. Garnish with scallions.

Nutrition Information

- Calories: 215 calories;
- Cholesterol: 0
- Protein: 13.6
- Total Fat: 9.4
- Sodium: 507
- Total Carbohydrate: 24

349. Vegetarian Balsamic Mushroom And Spinach Stuffed Shells

Serving: 24 | Prep: 45mins | Ready in:

Ingredients

- 24 jumbo pasta shells
- Mushrooms:
- 1 tablespoon butter
- 1/2 tablespoon olive oil
- 5 cloves garlic, sliced
- 1 (8 ounce) package sliced fresh mushrooms
- 1 tablespoon balsamic vinegar
- Spinach:
- 1 tablespoon olive oil
- 2 cloves garlic, minced
- 4 cups fresh baby spinach
- Filling:
- 1 (12 ounce) container whole-milk ricotta cheese

- 1 1/4 cups shredded Italian cheese blend
- 1/2 cup grated Parmesan cheese
- 1 large egg
- 3 tablespoons chopped fresh basil
- 1 teaspoon kosher salt
- 1/2 teaspoon ground black pepper
- Sauce:
- 1 (28 ounce) can crushed tomatoes
- 2 tablespoons chopped fresh basil
- 1/2 teaspoon salt
- 1/2 teaspoon dried oregano
- 1/4 teaspoon red pepper flakes
- Topping:
- 2 tablespoons grated Parmesan cheese

Direction

- Pour slightly salted water in a big pot and bring to a rolling boil. Mix in the shells and bring back to a boil. Cook the pasta without a cover for 8 minutes, mixing from time to time, till soft but firm to the bite. Drain cautiously.
- In a big skillet, heat olive oil and butter over moderately-low heat. Put in the garlic; cook and mix for 5 minutes till slightly browned. Put in vinegar and mushrooms. Let cook for 5 minutes longer, mixing from time to time, till mushrooms are tender. Drain off any excess liquid and turn garlic and mushrooms into big mixing bowl to let cool.
- Wash and dry the skillet. Put olive oil into the dry skillet over moderate heat. Put in the garlic and cook for 2 minutes till slightly browned. Put in the spinach and cook for 3 to 4 minutes till wilted. Put the spinach into mushroom mixture in mixing bowl.
- Put pepper, salt, basil, egg, Parmesan cheese, Italian cheese blend and ricotta into spinach and mushroom mixture. Stir well to incorporate.
- Preheat an oven to 190 °C or 375 °F.
- Open the canned tomatoes and put red pepper flakes, oregano, salt and basil right away into the can. In a 9x13-inch baking pan, put a quarter of the sauce.
- Fill a big spoonful of filling into each pasta shell and arrange in baking pan filling-side

facing up. Cover with leftover sauce and securely cover using aluminum foil.
- In the prepped oven, bake for 30 minutes till heated through.
- Scatter 2 tablespoons of Parmesan cheese over. Put pan back to oven, raise the temperature to 200 °C or 400 °F, and cook for 15 to 20 minutes longer till bubbling.

Nutrition Information

- Calories: 115 calories;
- Sodium: 284
- Total Carbohydrate: 11.5
- Cholesterol: 20
- Protein: 6.4
- Total Fat: 5.2

---

350. Vegetarian Garden Stir Fry

Serving: 3 | Prep: 15mins | Ready in:

Ingredients

- 1 serving cooking spray
- 1/2 cup sugar snap peas
- 1/4 cup cherry tomatoes, halved
- 1/2 cup dried fruit and nut mix, such as cranberries, almonds, and cashews
- 1/4 cup chopped mushrooms
- 1/4 cup bell pepper, thinly sliced
- 2 tablespoons chia seeds
- 2 teaspoons cayenne pepper, or to taste
- 1 tablespoon garlic, minced
- salt to taste
- 3 tablespoons egg whites
- 2 tablespoons shredded Cheddar cheese, or as desired

Direction

- Use cooking spray to grease a large skillet and heat over medium-low heat. Add in chia seeds, bell pepper, mushrooms, nut and fruit mix, cherry tomatoes, and sugar snap peas. Stir-fry for approximately 2 minutes. Use salt, garlic, and cayenne for seasoning. Keep cooking and stirring for approximately 2 more minutes.

- Slowly stir in egg whites, mix till they are thoroughly cooked, yet not crusty, for 3-5 minutes. Remove stir-fry to a large bowl and use Cheddar cheese to dredge on. Allow cheese to melt and it is ready to serve.

Nutrition Information

- Calories: 158 calories;
- Total Fat: 4.5
- Sodium: 120
- Total Carbohydrate: 25.6
- Cholesterol: 6
- Protein: 6.3

351. Vegetarian Sloppy Joe

Serving: 4 | Prep: 15mins | Ready in:

Ingredients

- 1 tablespoon olive oil
- 1 small onion, chopped
- 1 (15 ounce) can brown lentils
- 1 (15 ounce) can stewed tomatoes, cut small
- 1/4 cup barbeque sauce
- 1/4 cup ketchup
- 2 tablespoons mild miso paste
- 1 ounce dried shiitake mushrooms, cut small
- 2 tablespoons ground allspice
- 2 cloves garlic, minced, or more to taste

Direction

- In a big frying pan, heat oil over medium heat. Add onion, stir and cook for 10 minutes the onion is brown and soft. Add garlic, allspice, shiitake mushrooms, miso paste, ketchup,

barbeque sauce, tomatoes, and lentils; stir and cook for 20-25 minutes until the mixture is thick and the flavors blend.

Nutrition Information

- Calories: 232 calories;
- Cholesterol: 0
- Protein: 9.9
- Total Fat: 4.5
- Sodium: 1024
- Total Carbohydrate: 41.7

352. Veggie Ranch Pizza

Serving: 10 | Prep: 15mins | Ready in:

Ingredients

- 1 unbaked pizza crust
- 1 1/2 cups Ranch-style salad dressing
- 2 cups shredded Cheddar cheese
- 1/2 cup shredded carrots
- 1/2 cup chopped cauliflower
- 1/2 cup chopped fresh broccoli
- 1/2 cup chopped onion
- 1/2 cup chopped red bell pepper
- 1/2 cup sliced fresh mushrooms
- 1 pound mozzarella cheese, shredded

Direction

- Start preheating the oven to 350°F (175°C).
- On a baking sheet or pizza pan, put pizza crust, and evenly spread the top with the dressing. Sprinkle Cheddar cheese over, and then mushrooms, red pepper, onion, broccoli, cauliflower, and carrots. Put mozzarella cheese on top.
- Put in the preheated oven and bake until the cheese melts and turns light brown and the vegetables are soft, about 15-20 minutes.

Nutrition Information

- Calories: 490 calories;
- Total Fat: 36.1
- Sodium: 992
- Total Carbohydrate: 19.2
- Cholesterol: 68
- Protein: 21.4

353.   Veggie Tacos

Serving: 6 | Prep: 15mins | Ready in:

Ingredients

- 1 tablespoon olive oil
- 1 1/2 pounds cremini mushrooms, coarsely chopped
- 1 red bell pepper, diced
- 1 (15 ounce) can pinto beans, rinsed and drained
- 1 (1 ounce) packet taco seasoning mix
- 2 green onions, sliced thinly
- 1/4 cup water
- 6 (8 inch) whole wheat tortillas

Direction

- In a skillet, heat the olive oil on moderately-high heat. Put in the red bell peppers and mushrooms; sauté for 20 minutes till mushrooms are meaty and soft. Put in the water, green onions, taco seasoning mix and pinto beans. Mix thoroughly; keep cooking for 5 minutes longer till the entire liquid is evaporated.
- Distribute mushroom filling equally among tortillas. Top with your desire taco toppings.

Nutrition Information

- Calories: 220 calories;
- Cholesterol: 0
- Protein: 11.6
- Total Fat: 3.3

- Sodium: 761
- Total Carbohydrate: 42.4

354.   Vietnamese Kabocha Squash Soup

Serving: 8 | Prep: 30mins | Ready in:

Ingredients

- 12 dried shiitake mushrooms
- 1 (10.5 ounce) package bean-thread noodles, or to taste
- 1 kabocha squash, quartered and seeded
- 1 pound ground turkey
- 1 1/2 teaspoons fish sauce, or more to taste
- 1 pinch ground white pepper
- 3 quarts water
- 1 quart chicken stock
- 1 pound shrimp
- 2 scallions, chopped
- 3 tablespoons chopped cilantro, or to taste
- cracked black pepper to taste

Direction

- Set the oven for preheating to 425°F (220°C).
- Slice 4 of the shiitakes into smaller cubes and 8 of them into halves. Submerge in hot water and soak for half an hour to rehydrate. Meanwhile, soak noodles in cold water for 15 minutes.
- Place the kabocha squash on a baking pan and add some water to the pan.
- Roast the squash inside the preheated oven for about 15 minutes until softened.
- Drain the noodles and cut into small pieces. Stir together diced shiitakes, noodles, turkey, white pepper and fish sauce well with a fork. Mixing the mixture well makes a delicious and chewy meatballs.
- Bring the chicken stock and water to a boil in a big stockpot. Form the turkey mixture into a quenelles or shape of an egg balls with 2, wet and hot spoons. Put the meatballs and cook for

- 10 to 30 seconds into the boiling broth until they floats.
- Peel the squash if preferred and cut into cubes measuring 1 1/2-inch per each. Put into the soup with shrimp and the halved shiitakes. Cook for 5 minutes more until shrimp is opaque.
- Taste and add more fish sauce if preferred. Place cilantro, black pepper and scallions on top.

Nutrition Information

- Calories: 411 calories;
- Total Fat: 5.5
- Sodium: 561
- Total Carbohydrate: 69.7
- Cholesterol: 128
- Protein: 25.7

---

355.   White Pizza With Porcinis

Serving: 12 | Prep: 20mins | Ready in:

Ingredients

- 2 1/2 pounds bread flour
- 1 ounce salt
- 1/2 ounce honey
- 2 1/2 cups warm water
- 1 (.25 ounce) package active dry yeast
- 3 tablespoons olive oil
- 1 clove garlic, minced
- 8 ounces rehydrated porcini mushrooms
- salt and pepper to taste
- 1/8 cup cornmeal
- 1 cup shredded fontina cheese
- 1/2 cup grated Parmesan cheese
- 2 tablespoons chopped fresh parsley

Direction

- In an electric mixer with a dough hook, mix together warm water, honey, salt and flour. Process for 2 minutes over low heat. Add in yeast; mix over medium speed for 6 minutes more. Drizzle with oil and combine for an additional 2 minutes. The dough will be a little firm. Form into 6-ounce balls. The pizza will be rounder if the balls are rolled rounder. Settle in a warm area covered with a moist towel until doubled in volume.
- Set oven to 230°C (or 450°F) and start preheating, then place the pizza stone in prepared oven. Make sure to bring in pizza stone prior to preheating to make it warm in advance.
- In a large skillet, heat olive oil to medium heat. Mix in garlic and sauté for 30 seconds. Add in mushrooms; sauté for another 2 minutes. Season with pepper and salt to taste.
- Unroll or pat pizza dough out to 1/4" thick on a surface dusted with a little flour. Place on a cornmeal-coated wooden plank; brush a little olive oil onto the crust. Sprinkle Parmesan and Fontina cheeses onto the crust, then add sautéed mushrooms. Gently place pizza onto pizza stone.
- Bake at 450°F (230°C) for about 10-15 minutes until crust turn golden brown and cheese has bubbled and melted. Add parsley to decorate.

Nutrition Information

- Calories: 498 calories;
- Protein: 21.1
- Total Fat: 9.5
- Sodium: 1038
- Total Carbohydrate: 80.5
- Cholesterol: 13

---

356.   White Wine And Mushroom Sauce

Serving: 4 | Prep: 15mins | Ready in:

Ingredients

- 2 tablespoons unsalted butter
- 5 cloves garlic
- 1 green bell pepper, diced
- 1 small onion, chopped
- 1 (8 ounce) package sliced fresh mushrooms
- 1 cup white wine
- 1 cup chicken broth
- 2 tablespoons cornstarch
- 1/4 cup cold water
- 1/4 cup heavy cream
- 1/4 cup grated Romano cheese
- 1/4 cup grated Parmesan cheese

Direction

- In a heavy skillet over medium heat, melt butter. Put in garlic and cook for about 5 minutes in hot butter until it is browned.
- In the skillet, mash the garlic and add to butter, stir well. Put in onion and green bell pepper; cook for 5-7 minutes for the onion to turn translucent.
- Add mushrooms into the onion and pepper mixture, stir; cook for about 5 minutes with stirs until the mushrooms are browned slightly. While stirring, stream in heavy cream. Put in Parmesan cheese and Romano cheese. Keep on cooking for another 5-10 minutes until the cheese is melted and the mixture is hot.
- In the skillet, add wine and let it cook for 5-10 minutes for the liquid to reduce by half. Put in chicken broth; cook until it simmers. Let it cook for about 5 minutes until it is reduced slightly.
- In a small bowl, combine cornstarch and water to dissolve the cornstarch completely. Stir the mixture into the liquid in skillet and cook for 5-10 minutes with regular stirs to thicken the liquid.

Nutrition Information

- Calories: 254 calories;
- Sodium: 421

- Total Carbohydrate: 12.5
- Cholesterol: 49
- Protein: 7.4
- Total Fat: 15.1

357.   Wild Mushroom Sauce

Serving: 4 | Prep: 5mins | Ready in:

Ingredients

- 4 tablespoons butter
- 1/4 cup finely chopped shallots
- 2 ounces portobello mushrooms, sliced
- 2 ounces crimini mushrooms, sliced
- 2 ounces shiitake mushrooms, sliced
- 2 ounces morel mushrooms, sliced
- 2 ounces chanterelle mushrooms, sliced
- 1/2 cup red wine
- 6 fluid ounces beef demi glace
- salt and freshly ground black pepper to taste

Direction

- Melt the butter on medium heat in a saucepan. Sauté the shallots briefly, then whisk in all mushrooms. Sauté for roughly 3 minutes till becoming soft and translucent. Add the red wine, and let it simmer for 3 minutes. Whisk in the demi-glace, and let it simmer till the sauce becomes thick or for 6 minutes.

Nutrition Information

- Calories: 389 calories;
- Protein: 4.5
- Total Fat: 30.4
- Sodium: 1923
- Total Carbohydrate: 21.1
- Cholesterol: 32

358.   Wild Mushroom Stuffing

Serving: 5 | Prep: | Ready in:

Ingredients

- 2 cups hot water
- 1 ounce dried porcini mushrooms
- 1 3/4 pounds egg bread, crust trimmed
- 6 tablespoons unsalted butter
- 4 cups coarsely chopped leeks
- 1 cup shallots, chopped
- 1 1/4 pounds crimini mushrooms, sliced
- 1/2 pound fresh sliced shiitake mushrooms
- 2 cups chopped celery
- 1 cup chopped fresh parsley
- 1 cup chopped toasted hazelnuts
- 3 tablespoons chopped fresh thyme
- 2 tablespoons chopped fresh sage
- 2 eggs
- 3/4 cup chicken stock
- salt to taste
- ground black pepper to taste
- 1 cup dried porcini mushrooms

Direction

- Mix porcini mushrooms and 2 cups of hot water, let sit till mushrooms are tender. Approximately half an hour. Allow to drain, setting aside soaking water. Press porcini to dry and roughly chop.
- Preheat the oven to 165°C or 325°F. Among 2 baking sheets, distribute cubed bread. Bake till starting to brown. Approximately 15 minutes. Let cool then put to a huge bowl.
- In a heavy Dutch oven, liquify butter over medium-high heat. Put shiitake mushrooms, crimini or button, shallots and leeks. Sauté for 15 minutes till soft and golden. Add in porcini mushrooms and celery and sauté for 5 minutes more. To the bowl with the bread crumbs, put the mixture. Add in sage, thyme, hazelnuts and parsley. Put pepper and salt to season and mix in the beaten eggs.
- To bake stuffing in a turkey: with the stuffing, stuff the primary cavity. In a big glass measuring cup, mix half cup of the saved porcini soaking liquid and broth. To the leftover stuffing, put sufficient broth mixture to moisten. Into a buttered baking dish, scoop the leftover stuffing. Cover using a buttered foil. Let stuffing bake in a dish together with turkey for half an hour till heated through. Remove the cover and let bake for 15 minutes till top is crisp.
- To bake every stuffing in pan: preheat an oven to 325°F. Grease a baking dish, 15x10x2-inch in size with butter. Add 3/4 cup of broth and 3/4 cup of saved porcini soaking liquid into the stuffing. Put into the prepped dish. Cover using a buttered foil and let bake for an hour till heated through. Remove the cover and bake for 15 minutes till top is crisp.

Nutrition Information

- Calories: 969 calories;
- Sodium: 938
- Total Carbohydrate: 116.5
- Cholesterol: 192
- Protein: 37.5
- Total Fat: 40.8

359.   Winter Vegetable Hash

Serving: 6 | Prep: 15mins | Ready in:

Ingredients

- 3 tablespoons olive oil
- 2 tablespoons butter
- 1 pound Yukon Gold potatoes, diced
- 1/2 pound fresh shiitake mushrooms, diced
- 1 red bell pepper, diced
- 1 small acorn squash, diced
- 1 shallot, finely chopped
- 2 teaspoons garlic powder
- 1 pinch salt
- 1 pinch ground black pepper
- 1 cup chopped kale

- 4 sprigs fresh sage

Direction

- Put butter and oil in big skillet on medium heat; melt butter. Mix shallot, squash, pepper, mushrooms and potatoes in; season with pepper, salt and garlic powder. Cook for 25 minutes, occasionally mixing, till potatoes are tender.
- Mix sage and kale into skillet; cook till kale wilts for 5 minutes. Serve.

Nutrition Information

- Calories: 223 calories;
- Sodium: 76
- Total Carbohydrate: 28.9
- Cholesterol: 10
- Protein: 4.1
- Total Fat: 10.9

360.   Zesty Lemon Carrot Salad

Serving: 3 | Prep: 5mins | Ready in:

Ingredients

- 1 (8 ounce) package baby carrots
- 10 mushrooms
- 1 teaspoon ground cumin
- 1 teaspoon ground coriander
- 1 teaspoon minced garlic
- 1/4 cup lemon juice

Direction

- In a pot, mix together coriander, cumin, mushrooms and baby carrots, then put in sufficient water to just cover the mixture. Bring to a boil and cook for 15-20 minutes, until carrots are softened. Drain the mixture and turn to a big bowl.

- In a small bowl, stir together lemon juice and garlic then pour over carrot mixture. Stir to coat evenly.

Nutrition Information

- Calories: 51 calories;
- Sodium: 63
- Total Carbohydrate: 10.9
- Cholesterol: 0
- Protein: 2.7
- Total Fat: 0.6

361.   Zesty Tilapia With Mushrooms

Serving: 4 | Prep: 15mins | Ready in:

Ingredients

- 1 ounce dried porcini mushrooms
- 2 tablespoons butter
- 2 (4 ounce) fillets tilapia, halved
- kosher salt to taste
- ground black pepper to taste
- 1 tablespoon lemon zest
- 2 limes, juiced
- 2 green onions, chopped

Direction

- Add dried porcini mushrooms in a small bowl and pour in enough amount of water to cover the mushrooms. Let soak until they are rehydrated, for about 20 minutes then chop.
- In a frying pan, melt 1 tablespoon of butter over medium heat. Put tilapia in the pan, and use pepper and kosher salt for seasoning. Dredge 1/2 of the lemon zest on top. Pour half of the lime juice in the pan and keep on cooking for 5 minutes.
- Flip the fish and use pepper and kosher salt to taste. Dredge the rest of the lemon zest on top and pour in the rest of the lime juice. Add

porcini mushrooms, green onions and the remaining butter into the pan and stir. Keep on cooking until the fish can be easily shredded with a fork, for 5 minutes.

Nutrition Information

- Calories: 146 calories;
- Cholesterol: 36
- Protein: 14.2
- Total Fat: 6.9
- Sodium: 322
- Total Carbohydrate: 8

---

362. Ziti With Italian Sausage

Serving: 8 | Prep: 15mins | Ready in:

Ingredients

- 1 pound Italian sausage, casings removed
- 1/2 cup diced celery
- 1/2 cup diced onion
- 1 (14.5 ounce) can peeled and diced tomatoes
- 1 (15 ounce) can tomato sauce
- 1/4 teaspoon garlic powder
- 1 1/2 teaspoons salt
- 1 teaspoon dried oregano
- 1 pound dry ziti pasta
- 2 (4.5 ounce) cans sliced mushrooms, drained
- 8 ounces shredded mozzarella cheese
- 1/4 cup grated Parmesan cheese

Direction

- In a skillet, cook the sausage with onion and celery over medium heat for 5-10 minutes or until the sausage is brown evenly. Drain the excess grease. Put aside.
- In another skillet, combine oregano, salt, garlic powder, tomato sauce and tomatoes over medium-low heat. Simmer while you prep the pasta.

- Boil the lightly salted water in a large pot. Cook pasta until al dente, about 8-10 minutes; then drain.
- Start preheating the oven to 350°F (175°C). Layer the ziti, the mushrooms and the sausage, followed by the mozzarella cheese, then the sauce in a 3-quart baking dish. Repeat these layers, and place grated Parmesan on top.
- Bake in prepared oven for 45 minutes or until bubbly and brown.

Nutrition Information

- Calories: 465 calories;
- Total Fat: 17
- Sodium: 1620
- Total Carbohydrate: 52.3
- Cholesterol: 43
- Protein: 24.6

---

363. Zucchini Boats With Ground Turkey

Serving: 8 | Prep: 35mins | Ready in:

Ingredients

- 4 zucchini
- 1 pound ground turkey
- 1/2 cup chopped green bell pepper
- 1/2 cup chopped sweet red pepper
- 1 small onion, chopped
- 1/2 cup chopped fresh mushrooms
- 1/2 cup chopped fresh spinach leaves
- 1 cup shredded Cheddar cheese
- 1 (6 ounce) can tomato paste
- 1 pinch garlic powder, or to taste
- salt and ground black pepper to taste

Direction

- Trim zucchini ends; cut in 1/2 lengthwise. Spoon out and set pulp aside, leaving a half inch shell.
- Set the oven to 350°F (175°C) and start preheating. Grease a 9x13-inch baking dish.
- Over medium heat, in a skillet, mix spinach, mushrooms, onion, sweet red pepper, green bell pepper, turkey and reserved zucchini pulp. Cook for 8-10 minutes until the turkey is no longer pink. Drain. Take out of the heat; add pepper, salt, garlic powder, tomato paste and half cup Cheddar cheese; combine well. Scoop mixture into zucchini shells; put in the greased baking dish. Top with the rest of Cheddar cheese.
- Bake in the prepared oven for 25-30 minutes, uncovered, until zucchini becomes tender.

Nutrition Information

- Calories: 184 calories;
- Total Fat: 9.3
- Sodium: 320
- Total Carbohydrate: 9.6
- Cholesterol: 57
- Protein: 17.4

---

364.   Zucchini Linguine Alfredo

Serving: 8 | Prep: 20mins | Ready in:

Ingredients

- 6 zucchini, trimmed
- 1/2 teaspoon salt
- 2 tablespoons extra-virgin olive oil
- 2 tablespoons minced garlic
- 1/2 teaspoon salt
- 1 tablespoon freshly ground black pepper, or to taste
- 1 (6 ounce) package portobello mushrooms, chopped
- 1 (16 ounce) package linguine pasta

- 3/4 cup shredded Parmesan cheese
- 1 (15 ounce) jar mushroom Alfredo sauce (such as Bertolli®)

Direction

- Shred zucchini with food processor's shredding blade; toss in a colander with 1/2 tsp. of salt. Drain zucchini for 2-3 hours if possible. Put zucchini on several paper towel layers; squeeze as much liquid out as you can.
- Heat olive oil in a big skillet on medium high heat; mix and cook 1/2 tsp. of salt, black pepper and garlic for 1 minute till garlic is fragrant. Mix in portobello mushrooms; cook for 15 minutes till mushrooms turn brown, juice evaporates and mushrooms release their liquid. Mix shredded zucchini into mushrooms; cook for 5 minutes till zucchini are tender yet not mushy, mixing often.
- Boil a big pot of lightly salted water; cook linguine at a boil for 11 minutes till tender yet firm to chew. Drain; put linguine in a big serving bowl.
- Toss mushroom Alfredo sauce, Parmesan cheese, zucchini-mushroom mixture and pasta till combined thoroughly.

Nutrition Information

- Calories: 438 calories;
- Total Fat: 22.1
- Sodium: 945
- Total Carbohydrate: 47.7
- Cholesterol: 27
- Protein: 13.9

---

365.   Zucchini Saute

Serving: 6 | Prep: 20mins | Ready in:

Ingredients

- 1 tablespoon vegetable oil
- 1 onion, sliced

- 2 tomatoes, chopped
- 2 pounds zucchini, peeled and cut into 1 inch thick slices
- 1 green bell pepper, chopped
- salt to taste
- ground black pepper to taste
- 1/4 cup uncooked white rice
- 1/2 cup water

Direction

- In a sauté pan, heat oil over medium heat. Put in onion then cook and stir for 3mins. Put in green pepper, zucchini and tomatoes then mix. Use black pepper and salt to season. Decrease heat then cover. Allow it to simmer for 5 minutes.
- Mix in water and rice then cover. Cook for 20 minutes over low heat.

Nutrition Information

- Calories: 94 calories;
- Protein: 3.2
- Total Fat: 2.8
- Sodium: 19
- Total Carbohydrate: 16.1
- Cholesterol: 0

Index

Conclusion

Thank you again for downloading this book!

I hope you enjoyed reading about my book!

If you enjoyed this book, please take the time to share your thoughts and post a review on Amazon. It'd be greatly appreciated!

Write me an honest review about the book – I truly value your opinion and thoughts and I will incorporate them into my next book, which is already underway.

Thank you!

If you have any questions, **feel free to contact at:** *author@bizarrerecipes.com*

Mavis Olsen

bizarrerecipes.com

Made in the USA
Monee, IL
05 February 2023

26954334R00118